INTERPRETING OFFICIAL STATISTICS

Interpreting Official Statistics examines the official statistics produced about the current state of British society. It documents some of the ways in which information has been suppressed, manipulated and misinterpreted since 1979. And it looks at what can actually be learned from available data about poverty, unemployment, crime and health, and the social divisions of class, gender, ethnicity and disability. This invaluable guide is designed to help students know what figures are available, and to discover when and how politicians are misusing statistics.

The book provides a detailed analysis of key data sets such as Households Below Average Income, administrative and survey measures of unemployment and crime, Population Census data on ethnicity, different sources of data on women and work, the relationship between class and health, safety at work, and new data sources on disability. The importance of the Labour Force Survey is reflected in discussions of its different uses. Also included is a critique of official definitions of social class, and a chapter on the effects of the 1980 Rayner review on the statistical base, and current debates about appropriate institutional and legal guarantees of statistical integrity.

This essential guide will help students of social science understand how important the way statistics are collected and compiled is to the proper interpretation of figures.

This book contains contributions from Paul Abberley, Steve Fenton, Theo Nichols, Robert Reiner, Peter Townsend and Jackie West.

Ruth Levitas is Senior Lecturer in Sociology and **Will Guy** is Lecturer in Sociology, both at the University of Bristol.

INTERPRETING OFFICIAL STATISTICS

Edited by
Ruth Levitas and Will Guy

London and New York

First published 1996
by Routledge
11 New Fetter Lane, London EC4P 4EE

Simultaneously published in the USA and Canada
by Routledge
29 West 35th Street, New York, NY 10001

Routledge is an International Thomson Publishing company

Typeset in Baskerville by LaserScript, Mitcham, Surrey
Printed and bound in Great Britain by
TJ Press (Padstow) Ltd, Padstow, Cornwall

British Library Cataloguing in Publication Data
A catalogue record for this book is available from the British Library

Library of Congress Cataloging in Publication Data
Interpreting official statistics / edited by Ruth Levitas and Will Guy.
p.   c.m.
Includes bibliographical references and index.
1. Great Britain – Statistical services – Evaluation.
2. Great Britain – Statistics – Evaluation.   I. Levitas, Ruth, 1949–   .
II. Guy, Will, 1940–   .
HA37.G7158   1996
001.4'22–dc20   96-4895
CIP

ISBN 0–415–10835–7 (hbk)
ISBN 0–415–10836–5 (pbk)

CONTENTS

CONTENTS

ILLUSTRATIONS

FIGURES

TABLES

CONTRIBUTORS

Paul Abberley teaches a postgraduate course in disability studies at the University of Bristol. He is a member of the editorial board of *Disability and Society*, and sometime chairperson of the Avon Coalition of Disabled People.

Steve Fenton is Senior Lecturer in Sociology at the University of Bristol. He has published principally in the area of ethnic relations, and minorities and health, and also has research interests in nationalism.

Will Guy is Lecturer in Sociology at the University of Bristol and teaches quantitative and qualitative research methods. He has been teaching courses on official statistics with Ruth Levitas for fifteen years, with contributions from other colleagues. His research interests are wide-ranging and include health, education, ethnicity – especially Gypsies Roma – and Eastern Europe.

Ruth Levitas is Senior Lecturer in Sociology at the University of Bristol, where she teaches research methods, including official statistics, and political sociology. Her publications include *The Ideology of the New Right* (ed.) (Polity Press, 1986), *The Concept of Utopia* (Philip Allen, 1990), and she is currently working on concepts of social exclusion.

Theo Nichols is Professor of Sociology at the University of Bristol. He has written extensively in the field of economic sociology and amongst other things is currently writing a book on the sociology of industrial injury.

Robert Reiner is Professor of Criminology in the Law Department, London School of Economics, and has written numerous books and articles on policing and criminal justice topics. He was formerly Reader in Criminology at the University of Bristol, and is currently President of the British Society of Criminology.

Peter Townsend is Emeritus Professor of Social Policy at the University of Bristol and teaches a graduate programme on statistical indicators. His best-known books on poverty are *Poverty in the UK* (1979) and *The*

International Analysis of Poverty (1993). He served as consultant to the UN for the World Summit for Social Development (1993 and 1995) and conducted research on poverty for the UNDP and ILO. He is President of the Child Poverty Action Group.

Jackie West is Lecturer in Sociology at the University of Bristol. She has published on gender and the labour process, women in the labour market and equal opportunities. Her recent research has been on South Asian women and work, health service restructuring and sexual health provision for young people.

ACKNOWLEDGEMENTS

In a collection such as this with several authors the list of those to whom we are individually and collectively indebted is too long to include in full. Ruth Levitas and Will Guy would like to thank their co-authors for their commitment to the project, and for producing their contributions under sometimes difficult circumstances. Particular thanks are due to Paul Convery and the staff of the Unemployment Unit for advice and help with Chapter 3 – and to Paul, and Ian Farnden, for comments on a draft of this chapter. We are also grateful to Nigel Tibbs, Information Research Officer at the County of Avon Planning Department, and to his colleagues, for sharing their expertise in interpretation of Census data, especially in relation to ethnicity.

We are grateful to Pluto Press for permission to reprint Theo Nichols' 'Social class: official, sociological and Marxist' from John Irvine *et al.*, *Demystifying Official Statistics*; to *Sociological Review* and Blackwells for permission to reprint, with minor revisions, 'Problems in monitoring the safety performance in British manufacturing at the end of the twentieth century'; and to OPCS for permission to reproduce from the General Household Survey the diagram which appears here as Figure 4.3.

As always, thanks are due to our partners and children who have tolerated with (usually) good humour our obsession with obscure tables, piles of newspaper clippings, and general inattention to normal life. And we are deeply indebted to all those academics and journalists who have monitored the fate of official statistics over the last sixteen years and who have kept this issue on the political agenda. We are committed to the belief that the wide dissemination and careful interpretation of information is essential to an informed democracy. We have written this book with that end in view.

INTRODUCTION

Ruth Levitas and Will Guy

SOCIAL SCIENCE AND SOCIAL STATISTICS

At the beginning of the film *Annie Hall*, Woody Allen tells a joke: 'Two elderly women are at a Catskill Mountain resort, and one of them says, "Boy, the food at this place is really terrible." The other one says, "Yeah, I know, and such small portions."' Woody adds: 'That's essentially how I feel about life.' This ambivalence is also reflected in how sociologists feel about official statistics.

Sociologists have always made use of official statistics because the government has the financial and legislative power to collect data on a scale much greater than any other body can do. In the 1950s, sociologists were also attracted to survey data and quantitative measurement because it seemed to support the discipline's claims to scientific status. But in the late 1960s and throughout the 1970s, many sociologists became sceptical to the point of hostility about statistical data. There are two main reasons for this, one philosophical and one political.

The philosophical objection is that quantitative measurement can be seen as treating facts as unproblematically given in the world. While this might be appropriate for the natural sciences (although this is questioned too), it is quite inappropriate where human behaviour is concerned. Rather than treating people, and aspects of their behaviour, as objects to be counted, sociologists, it is argued, should be concerned with understanding the myriad complex meanings which inform human activity and constitute social life. They should also be aware of how the processes of conducting research are implicated in the results obtained, rather than presenting a false distance between the researcher and the results. Sociology should therefore concentrate on qualitative, not quantitative research. Moreover, so-called 'facts' are not unproblematic; the very categories that are used are the outcome of implicit theories about social life and social relationships – theories that are obscured by claims to neutrality and objectivity.

The political objection supports the last point, but not necessarily the

1

first. Rather than rejecting all quantitative work, it is particularly critical of claims to objectivity and neutrality. Since concepts used in measurement do not arise naturally from the world itself, but are the consequences of the questions we ask about the world, these claims act to disguise the value-laden character of all research. The objections may be particularly strong in relation to official statistics, since it is argued that these necessarily reflect in their definitions the interests of the state. Because they are produced by government for government, they are unlikely to use categories and definitions which generate the kind of understanding of social life which sociologists themselves seek. In an excellent collection on the conceptual and empirical weaknesses of official statistics, it was argued that

> [O]fficial statistics are in fact a selection of data offering far less of use to the radical critic than the reactionary. . . . [T]he concepts employed serve to reinforce the arguments advanced by political and intellectual representatives of the ruling class.
>
> Miles and Irvine (1979: 126–7)

These views were by no means universal among sociologists, who, despite popular mythology, have never been predominantly either theoretically or politically radical. In November 1980, an article appeared in *Sociology* asking why sociologists did not make more use of official statistics (Bulmer 1980). Bulmer argued that the wholesale rejection of official statistics on either theoretical or political grounds is misplaced. There are of course problems both about conceptual definitions and about measurement, and in some cases – notably crime and suicide, on which many of the general critiques focused – quite severe problems. But not everything is equally problematic. As far as technical questions of error are concerned, the professional statisticians compiling official data are well aware of the limitations of the data with which they work. Moreover, Bulmer claimed that in many areas there is a conceptual convergence between social statisticians and sociologists. In rejecting official statistics, sociologists cut themselves off from huge sources of important data which demonstrate important regularities and relationships in the society they are studying (Bulmer 1980).

Bulmer's article marked a turning point in attitudes to official statistics among sociologists, not so much because of the strength of the argument itself, but because of the context in which it appeared. The particular impact of Bulmer's case rested on two factors, neither of which is explicit in the article. First, there were considerable changes and developments in social statistics between 1967 and 1978 while Claus Moser was director of the Central Statistical Office, and Wilson, Heath and Callaghan Prime Ministers. Secondly, the Thatcher government was elected in May 1979. In January 1980, Thatcher asked Derek Rayner to oversee a review of the

2

Government Statistical Services. Rayner's report was published in December 1980, and followed by a White Paper in 1981, *Government Statistical Services*, requiring extensive cuts, especially in the area of social statistics. Once sources of data were under threat, their potential value was more visible.

We set out to compile this book for two reasons. We wanted to document some of the changes which had taken place since Rayner. It appeared to us that although there have been serious consequences both of those cuts and of apparent political interference in statistics during the 1980s, there are also counter-tendencies. Some data sets, notably the Labour Force Survey (LFS), have been significantly extended in scope and frequency. There has also been an explosion of secondary analysis by academics of the data which is available. One reason for this has been dissatisfaction with the analyses officially produced. It has been made possible by the widespread availability of computing facilities, and a greater willingness of sociologists to acquire and use the necessary skills. An increasing amount of data is available on-line, through the ESRC (Economic and Social Research Council) data archive and elsewhere, and this trend is likely to continue.

A side-effect of the Rayner cuts also appears to have been the development of something of a rift between professional statisticians and government ministers, and at least the potential for greater collaboration between government statisticians and academics. The setting up of user groups for the major social surveys such as the LFS, the General Household Survey (GHS) and the Family Expenditure Survey (FES) has been a further step in this direction. Facilities such as the LFS helpline have also made it much easier to use the data sets which are available, and indeed to compile this book.

But these counter-tendencies should not be overstated. They are developments which may make official data more easily accessible to academic experts. They do not make data more easily available to the public in the interests of informed political debate. Moreover, the (relative) ease of conducting secondary analysis carries the danger of forgetting that the concepts used in any research derive from the questions and interests of its original intentions. The extent to which secondary analysis can bend data sets to the service of sometimes quite different agendas is necessarily limited.

We therefore set out to explore first the availability, and secondly the interpretation, of official data in some of the areas of enquiry of most central interest to us as social scientists. We were not able to undertake a comprehensive assessment of the whole range of social statistics: such a task would occupy several volumes rather than one. We wanted to look at key areas which had provoked public concern over the 1980s, especially unemployment and poverty, or which, like crime, are constantly in the public domain. And we wanted to examine the areas which relate particularly to our concerns as sociologists trying to understand the key social divisions of gender, ethnicity, class and (dis)ability, as well as their impact on the health and well-being of individuals. We have tried to do this in a way which will be useful both to social science students approaching official data, and to lay readers who may simply want to know what figures are available and how they can best be understood.

The questions that run through the different contributions are these. Is the available data better or worse than it was in 1979? Has there been evidence of suppression or manipulation of data? Has this been offset or outweighed by new data sets and the possibilities of secondary analysis? How are the divisions of class, gender and ethnicity revealed or repressed in the figures? What *is* revealed about increasing or decreasing inequality and its concomitant risks? What conclusions may legitimately be drawn from the data, and what does the data *not* tell us?

The first chapter deals with the content and consequences of the Rayner review, the loss of public confidence in the statistical pronouncements of politicians in the 1980s, the responses of the Royal Statistical Society, and a consideration of the current state of play. The second and third chapters deal with two issues which have been very much in the public eye: the measurement of poverty, and the measurement of unemployment. The first two chapters are perhaps the bleakest in the book. They present a grisly story of partially successful attempts to undermine the statistical base itself, and of blatant attempts to suppress and distort information derived from that base. Although Chapter 3 reveals a similar depressing mixture of bone-headedness and duplicity in the production and use of official data, because of the expansion of the LFS there is an alternative to the well-known and widely derided claimant count measure of unemployment.

Chapter 4 reprints an earlier article by Theo Nichols criticising the theoretical basis of official definitions of class. Written in 1979, it predates the Rayner review. It is also clearly located in debates current in the 1970s about the relative merits of neo-Marxist, neo-Weberian and official conceptualisations of class. We decided to include it in its entirety because it takes as its central theme not just how society may be described, but how modern capitalist society may be adequately understood. In the mid-1990s, this question of understanding capitalism is again coming to the fore, illustrated by the enormous popularity of Will Hutton's *The State We're In*; but there is resistance to understanding the centrality of class to such analysis, particularly in official circles. The theoretical issues raised in 1979 remain relevant. They are brought up to date by a postscript, written for this collection, which outlines both changes in official measures, and other developments in conceptualising class, except for those relating to class and gender, which are dealt with in the following chapter. Chapter 5

4

focuses on the relationship between class and health. This is one area where, despite the increasing unwillingness of government in the 1980s to produce analyses on the basis of class, the data has again improved in some respects, even if it has deteriorated in others. The reason for this is the continuation of the Longitudinal Study, based on a 1 per cent sample of the 1971 Census; although this study was threatened by the Rayner review, it escaped termination. It is the basis of the strongest evidence for widening inequalities in health resulting from widening inequalities in income. Chapter 6 is a brief overview of how work, rather than poverty or unemployment, may adversely affect health, as indicated by measures of industrial injuries, and the limitations of these measures.

Chapter 7 looks at the data on gender segregation in the labour force. Much of this derives, again, from the LFS. It is clear that while there is an increasing volume of information, and of secondary analysis, interpretation of the data is extremely difficult. Chapter 8 deals mainly with Census data on ethnicity. Again, in some ways the data has improved. The development of a question on ethnicity for the 1991 Census (considered for 1981, but not included) produces a better measure than classifying household by place of birth of the head of household. However, questions are raised over the undifferentiated category 'white', which both makes the Census distinction fundamentally one of colour rather than ethnicity, and obscures the position of Britain's largest ethnic minority, the Irish. Again, the coincidence of sociological concerns with ethnicity with official ones is far from absolute, and this shows in the official definitions used. This is equally true of the again largely new data on disability discussed in Chapter 9. The final chapter deals with the crime figures. The long-standing problems of interpreting an administrative measure have, as for unemployment, not diminished. But here again, new survey measures have been introduced which supplement that generated as a by-product of police procedures. There are still enormous problems in making sense of the figures, but there is more, rather than less, data available.

In some ways, then, the situation in many areas is less gloomy than we might have anticipated given the intentions of the Rayner review. A major reason for this has been the development of the LFS, from a biennial survey in 1979 to a quarterly survey with an enlarged sample in 1992. The survey became annual, in fact, following a recommendation in the Rayner review – one of the few recommendations for expansion. But this appears to have happened mainly because of obligations to supply comparable data to the European Union – an obligation of which Rayner was deeply suspicious. However, the definitions used in the LFS are problematic – not least the definition of unemployment, a fact frequently overlooked by those who would base the headline figures on measures derived from this survey.

But if the picture is less bleak than we had anticipated in terms of the amount of data available in many areas, in other ways things are no better, or are worse. The debates outlined in Chapter 1 show that the insistence on the neutrality and objectivity of facts still dominates discussion of official statistics and their production. The presentation of statistics in particular ways for political ends, and the abolition of inconvenient measures, continue. It is understandable that professional statisticians should try to counter this by appeals to objectivity. But it is also abundantly clear that the definitions used in official statistics still produce measures which embody the interests of the state rather than of citizens. It is therefore only with the utmost care that such data can be interpreted for democratic purposes.

And in another way, the picture is bleak indeed. What the statistics reveal when close attention is given to their real meaning is a stark worsening of inequalities since 1979 – a picture successive Conservative governments have sought to obscure. Much of the work which reveals this has been done outside the Government Statistical Services, such as the Rowntree report into income and wealth (Rowntree 1995), but much of it does rely upon the continued collection of official statistics, however conceptually flawed. To the extent that secondary analysis is necessary, the easy availability to the general public of properly presented and interpreted statistical information is diminished. This is exacerbated by new charging policies which mean that although analyses can be requested from government departments, this is not a real possibility either for individuals or for most non-governmental organisations. We can only conclude that extreme and continued vigilance is necessary in both the defence, and the interpretation, of official statistics.

REFERENCES

Bulmer, M. (1980) 'Why don't sociologists make more use of official statistics?', *Sociology* 14, 4: 505–23. Reprinted in M. Bulmer (ed.) (1984) *Sociological Research Methods: An Introduction,* London: Macmillan.

Government Statistical Services (1981) White Paper, Cmnd 8236, London: HMSO.

Miles, C. and Irvine, J. (1979) 'The critique of official statistics', in J. Irvine, I. Miles and J. Evans, *Demystifying Official Statistics,* London: Pluto Press.

Hutton, W. (1995) *The State We're In,* London: Jonathan Cape.

Rowntree (1995) *The Joseph Rowntree Foundation Inquiry into Income and Wealth,* 2 vols, York: Rowntree Foundation.

1

THE LEGACY OF RAYNER

Ruth Levitas

This chapter charts the effects on official statistics, particularly social statistics, of the Rayner review in 1980, which led to cuts throughout the Government Statistical Service (GSS). These cuts, and the presentation of statistics by government ministers, led both to problems in the reliability of the figures themselves, and to a loss of public confidence in official data. Throughout this period, the Royal Statistical Society, an eminently respectable body which includes senior members of the GSS, has repeatedly expressed concern about government policy, and has called for legislation to protect statistics and statisticians from political manipulation and interference.

THE GROWTH OF OFFICIAL STATISTICS

Until 1941, the collection of official statistics in Britain was a matter for individual government departments. Calls were made for the setting up of a Central Statistical Office (CSO) from 1871, including repeated proposals from the Royal Statistical Society. But the CSO was finally set up at the request of Winston Churchill, to undertake 'the collection from government Departments of a regular series of figures on a coherent and well-ordered basis which cover the development of our war effort' (Ward and Doggett 1991: 30). Its remit included responsibility for all statistics prepared for cabinet committees. Importantly, however, the CSO, whose director was responsible to the Prime Minister, operated alongside the statisticians in individual departments: the organisation of the Government Statistical Services was decentralised from the outset.

Expansion of official statistics followed in the post-war years, mainly in order to develop a system of national accounting to facilitate management of the economy. Belief in the need for better statistical information was not confined to those committed to national planning or to Keynesian economic strategies. *The Economist* argued that '[g]ood statistics are far more important to a country whose economic policy proceeds by guiding and assisting industries and firms whose decisions are free, than to one that operates through an imposed plan' (Ward and Doggett 1991: 51). Proposals for further expansion were contained in a report to the House of Commons Estimates Committee in 1966 – by which time there were 150 professionally trained statisticians in the Civil Service, of whom twenty–six were within the CSO. One of the new roles for the CSO was the development of publications for the whole of the GSS.

In 1967, Claus Moser was appointed director of the CSO, a post he retained until 1978. During these years, there were dramatic improvements in the quality and scope of data collected and, more importantly, disseminated to the public; and the number of statisticians rose to 550. Meetings between Moser and Harold Wilson (who had been head of the Manpower Statistics Branch of the Ministry of Labour before the war) led to proposals from Moser which Wilson described as 'the Great Charter of statistical reform' (Wilson 1973: 4–5) – proposals which were more wide-ranging than those of the Estimates Committee. Wilson described the consequent expansion of social statistics 'with their vast potential both for public administration and social conscience' as 'a revolution' (Wilson 1973: 9). Although Wilson also notes the role of individual ministers, including Barbara Castle as Minister of Transport, in initiating and developing new statistical series, it is plain that Moser was the driving force. Moreover, it is also clear that Wilson's main interest in the development of statistics was a managerial interest: the new General Household Survey, for example, was commended for its utility in estimating potential calls on the social services. His major fear was that international currency pressures would scupper rational decision-making based on statistical information (Wilson 1973: 11, 16). Moser, however, was committed both to the use of statistics to improve social well-being, and to the dissemination of statistical information in a comprehensible manner as the basis for informed public discussion (Moser 1980, Ward and Doggett 1991: 77).

The CSO was given a strengthened role in 1968, when the remit of the director was widened to that of head of the Government Statistical Services. Reorganisation produced the Business Statistics Office in 1969 and the Office of Population Censuses and Surveys (OPCS) in 1970. Staff expansions were considerable, and so too was the expansion of the base of social statistics. The sample size for the Family Expenditure Survey (FES) was doubled. The General Household Survey was launched in 1971. *Social Trends* was first published in 1970, edited by Muriel Nissel. It contained no mission statement, but the editorial referred to the 'aim of presenting a clear and incisive picture of social conditions in the United Kingdom' and to the need to identify gaps in coverage; while Moser's own lead article explained the developments in and shortcomings of social statistics (Moser 1970).

Moser resigned from the GSS in 1978. His advice to his successor was to collect a bit less and analyse a lot more, and above all 'never give in upon an issue that you feel deep down is an integrity issue' (Ward and Doggett 1991: 77). There has been a tendency, among academics at least, to regard the attitude of the Conservative governments of 1979–95, reflected in the Rayner review, as peculiar in their insistence that the sole function of the GSS is to provide information to government for government. What may actually be more peculiar is the eleven years of Moser's headship of GSS. The expansion of social statistics in those years resulted partly from a wider view of the information government needed in order to govern. The use of this expansion to provide a broader base of social data, and to encourage democratic access to this data, seems to have been Moser's particular contribution.

Ironically, then, the period during which sociologists were most sceptical of official statistics may have coincided with a period when statistics were least firmly bound to the interests of the state and when constructive views about their improvement might have met with the most sympathetic hearing. Even in the 1970s there were political pressures, however. Muriel Nissel recalls being told that the poverty trap was hypothetical. She was also prevented from publishing the first information (produced at her instigation) on the distribution of wealth between men and women; the grounds given were that women enjoyed the wealth owned by their husbands. Pressure came mainly from the Treasury, and could sometimes be circumvented 'by publishing in a chart what you couldn't say in words' (Phillips 1989). In the 1980s, after the Rayner review, the pressures were to become significantly worse.

THE RAYNER REVIEW

The Rayner review of the GSS took place during 1980, and reported at the end of the year. The new director of the CSO, John Boreham, said that the review had his strong personal backing (Ward and Doggett 1991: 82). Because of the decentralised structure of the statistical services, the review team co-ordinated nineteen separate scrutinies of statistical services in individual government departments, assessed some specific blocks of work 'of interdepartmental significance' and prepared a report on the CSO. In many cases, departmental reviews had been put in place by individual ministers before the overall review was set up, and in its first year (that is, six months before Rayner's report was published) the government had 'reduced the numbers involved in statistical work from about 8,850, including 540 statisticians to 8,500, including 520 statisticians' (Rayner 1980: 2). The purpose of the review (as summarised in the initial study of OPCS) was:

> to examine critically the statistical services available to each Minister and the use made of them by (a) assessing each statistical activity to

9

see whether the costs to government and to those outside are justified by the benefits obtained and whether the work could be undertaken more efficiently; (b) recommending the best means for the continuing scrutiny of the cost of, and the need for, individual statistical services.

(OPCS 1980: 1)

The terms of reference included the statement that:

Ministers wish to reduce the burden imposed by Government on the private sector and to create a smaller and more efficient public sector, and to these ends statistical services, as well as all other aspects of Governmental activities, must be reviewed.

(OPCS 1980: 2.1)

Given the brief of the Rayner review and the general ethos of the Conservative government, the recommendation of cuts and 'greater efficiency' was hardly surprising. But there were three linked elements in the report which were of specific concern to social scientists. One was that the proposed cuts fell with particular severity on social statistics. Not only did the report make reference to work done by OPCS and the Departments of Transport and the Environment on 'the annual Census of construction, consumer attitude surveys and [European] Community work on social indicators', all of which were deemed 'of doubtful value' (Rayner 1980: 19). It recommended abandoning plans for a 1986 Census. It proposed cuts in the major social surveys (including a substantial cut in the sample size of the General Household Survey), the merger of the Family Expenditure Survey and the National Food Survey, and cuts in the International Passenger Survey. It also proposed contracting-out of some *ad hoc* surveys currently undertaken by the Social Survey Division (SSD) of OPCS, and introducing an internal market whereby such surveys as were undertaken by the SSD were paid for by the commissioning departments out of existing budgets.

Secondly, there was an explicit statement that only those statistics required by government for government could justifiably be collected: 'Information should not be collected primarily for publication. It should be collected primarily because government needs it for its own business' (Rayner 1980: 17). Expecting the collection of data for general use was seen as another version of expecting the government to be a 'universal provider' (Rayner 1980: 9). The CSO was regarded as 'too heavily committed to serving the public at large' (Ward and Doggett 1991: 84). Moreover, the information regarded as necessary for government purposes was narrowly defined, in terms that reflected Thatcher's view that there was no such thing as society. The OPCS review said of the GHS that 'although the Survey is popular with the Department it is not self

10

evident to us that social phenomena really necessitate this continuous monitoring' (OPCS 1980: 10.10). It is clear that the GHS had been in danger of abolition, but was defended by the CSO's director. Rayner's final report commented that 'It is also true that to axe the survey would be likely to create an outcry that the government does not want to know about the well-being of its citizens' (1980: 33). He therefore limited himself to recommendations to cut the sample, and to require the director of the CSO to justify the survey's continued existence annually on the basis of a log of its uses by other departments (ibid.).

More generally, questions were raised about the utility of social surveys: 'It is our view that the social surveys undertaken by SSD are sophisticated and expensive operations to be utilised only where major complex studies are essential for the intelligence processes of government departments' (OPCS 1980: 10.12). Suspicion was voiced about the statistical demands of the European Community. In 1984, Boreham wrote to the Royal Statistical Society in support of the narrowing of the remit of official statistics generally, arguing that those statistics not needed by government should be provided by the free market:

> I cannot see why the market mechanism cannot provide for collecting and processing statistics not needed by Government. It already does so quite satisfactorily for market research and for a moderate range of social and economic research by universities and other institutions. The area of dispute . . . comes down to those statistical surveys which some people . . . believe that the Government ought to need.
>
> (Boreham 1984: 185)

Doubts were cast not only on the work of the SSD, but on the Population Statistics Division. It was again suggested that data was unnecessarily collected for publication rather than for clear policy purposes, and that the interpretative work done was excessively wide-ranging, partly due to the increased influence of social science interests:

> We do not think it wise to have individuals spending a lot of their time on university-level research in the Civil Service. . . . If an outsider does not consider a topic of sufficient interest, or cannot get a research grant to pursue the topic, it is likely that it is not worth OPCS' resource either.
>
> (OPCS 1980: 11.6)

Rayner himself concluded that 'British universities have so far shown little interest in demographic research about the United Kingdom but that is not sufficient reason for OPCS to continue with it' (1980: 31). Areas of work in which cuts were suggested were fertility, ethnic statistics and regional demography, with the frequency of population projections reduced to two-yearly. Questions were raised over the future of the Longitudinal Study, based on a 1 per cent sample drawn from the 1971 Census.

Some of the detailed cuts represented a cavalier attitude to the reliability of data collected. Among the general questions to be considered in all surveys were improvements in 'value for money' including issues of 'timing, frequency, coverage, less statistical refinement such as chasing non-respondents' (Rayner 1980: 69). Cuts were recommended in the coverage and quality checks of the 1981 Census. The cuts to the GHS sample resulted in an increase of sampling error of 8 per cent (Mayes 1984: 15). It was recognised that the merging of the Family Expenditure Survey and the National Food Survey (which did not, in fact, take place) would reduce the reliability of the FES. Despite the fact that this survey is, among other things, the major source for the weights used in compiling the Retail Price Index, the cost saving – of £155,000 a year to OPCS and £66,000 to the Ministry of Agriculture, Fisheries and Food which was responsible for the NFS – was seen as overwhelming: 'Savings of this order should not be allowed to escape' (Rayner 1980: 32). Moreover, OPCS staff were criticised for 'a fulsome and perfectionist attention to technical details'; their performance in future should be 'judged on the basis that meeting their deadlines is more important than great refinement' (Rayner 1980: 35). Boreham (1984: 178) was later to comment that 'our reaction to the cuts over the past few years has been to take risks with quality while maintaining the existing framework of statistics'.

The third strand in the Rayner Report was the recommendation that subsidies to the cost of publication of statistics should cease – implying substantial rises in the cost of government publications. Subsidy was defined as 'not covering costs incurred in checking, tabulating, editing, printing and distributing figures for publication, i.e. any costs which the government would not incur for its own purposes'; and '[s]ubsidy of statistical publications should be quickly curtailed'. In addition, more of the published data made available was to be in the cheaper form of computer printout or microfiche (Rayner 1980: 17).

The recommendation was also made and accepted that the remit of the director of the CSO be altered. The new remit included the following instructions:

> For the future, the Prime Minister would like the Director to take a particular responsibility with regard to securing value for money. For example, as professional head of the GSS, he should keep before the Directors of Statistics in Departments the scope for economies in their operations and the opportunities provided by statistical methods for reducing costs and improving value for money in Government more generally. . . . Subsequently, the Prime Minister

would like to be kept informed by means of an annual report – about the cost of Government Statistics and the contribution they are making to economies and improvement in the public sector.

(Rayner 1980: 65–6)

These recommendations were a clear repudiation of Moser's often-expressed view that statistics were essential to public information and the conduct of an informed democracy – a view echoed by others, and enshrined in the institutional briefs of government statistical services in other countries. But most of the Rayner recommendations were followed through in the White Paper, *Government Statistical Services* (1981). The overall savings, excluding Northern Ireland Departments, involved a 28 per cent cut in staff (a total of 2,550 jobs) and a 25 per cent cut in expenditure between April 1979 and April 1984; Rayner (1980: 22) described this as an 8 per cent cut in the Statistician Group and a 40 per cent cut in the Social Survey Officer Group. The CSO was to suffer cuts of 25 per cent in staff and 33 per cent in funding, and OPCS 28 per cent and 26 per cent respectively; but the cuts for the OPCS excluded running down staffing following the 1981 Census, and included a cut of £1.5 million in the budget for analysing Census data. Some departments, notably the Inland Revenue, the Department of Employment and the Department of Health and Social Security, were to have even greater cuts imposed upon their statistical operations.

In the face of this onslaught on key data sets in social statistics, it is hardly surprising that social scientists sprang to their defence. The Social Statistics Section of the Royal Statistical Society held a special meeting on 10 June 1981, shortly after the publication of the White Paper. Hoinville and Smith (1982: 195) report that 'the discussion was sometimes very forceful and the atmosphere was described by one member as being electric'. The three central themes (besides the overall reduction in staffing and funding) identified by Boreham in his opening statement were: the elimination of inessential work; a reduction in checking and validation, and an increased use of sampling which would lead to greater risks of error; and continual scrutiny of efficiency in providing support to government. Amazingly, he also suggested that the review 'fell within the spirit of the closing remarks made by Sir Claus Moser in his Presidential Address to the Society'; the issues Moser had identified had included 'how to achieve a truly outward-looking role of the GSS towards the rest of the community as well as government' and 'how to ensure that statistical integrity always wins the day' (Hoinville and Smith 1982: 196, Moser 1980).

Peter Townsend, however, spoke for most of the social scientific community when he argued that the curtailment of the statistical services amounted to 'a restriction of democracy'. The government had a responsibility not only to produce information for its own purposes, but to produce – and disseminate at reasonable cost – information which enabled the public to test the government's claims against reality, and to participate in informed debate on issues of social concern and public policy. Moser described the proposals to cut data-checking as 'short-sighted', and plans to cut the Social Survey Division as 'sheer madness'. There was concerted opposition to the principle that the GSS should be concerned solely with the needs of government, and to the new pricing policy which would make data less accessible. The review was condemned as poorly conducted and narrow in its objectives. There were calls for a National Statistical Council, and for a Government Commission to undertake a proper review of the GSS (Hoinville and Smith 1982: 197–9).

SOCIAL TRENDS

Despite protests, most of the Rayner recommendations were implemented, and by April 1984 staff numbers in the GSS had fallen by nearly 30 per cent (Mayes 1984: 1). One area where the changes in policy were apparent was in that flagship of social statistics, *Social Trends*. Muriel Nissel remained editor until 1974. During this period, the length went up from 181 to 260 pages, while the price remained constant at £2.90. From 1975 to 1980 the lead editor was Eric Thompson, and it is during this period that pressures on the publication are first apparent: the price rose steadily from £4.90 in 1975 to £7.90 in 1979 while the length remained unchanged; in 1980, however, although the length rose to 313 pages, the price shot up to £12.90. Increasing frustration shows in the editorials. In 1976, the purpose of *Social Trends* is described as 'to present a wide range of information which all sides in the political arena can accept as setting the factual context within which divergent political forces and pressure groups can argue about policy' (*Social Trends* 1976: 6). Although even the 1980 issue reiterated the aim of providing 'a background to public discussion of social changes and policies' (*Social Trends* 1980: 10), there had been a clear change in climate. In 1979, Thompson noted that 'it has not been possible to find the staff resources to include a Social Commentary in this issue' (*Social Trends* 1979: 9). In 1980, although 'this year we have again been able to include a Social Commentary' it is 'an overview of changes in material living standards since the early 1950s' and 'is, however, basically a view of material things' excluding consideration of 'changes in family and other personal relationships and other aspects of the quality of life' (*Social Trends* 1980: 10).

From 1981, the lead editor was Deo Ramprakash. There was no immediate change to the stated aim: 'to provide a rounded picture of significant social changes . . . to serve a broad spectrum of interests' (*Social Trends* 1981: 11) although the length was shorter than any issue since 1973 and there was a massive price-hike to £16.50. Attempts were made to treble the price to £45 (Dean 1995). But in 1982 – the first issue after the White Paper – while the cost rose 'only' to £19.95, the stated aim is radically different:

> Social Trends is a descriptive brief for government about broad changes in society. . . . To enhance the value of this kind of information to government, the material in Social Trends is arranged in chapters which correspond broadly to the administrative functions of government.
>
> (Social Trends 1982: 11)

Although Social Trends still 'serves a wide variety of customers', 'wider accessibility also maximizes the total value of the money which government spends to collect the information it needs for its own business'; and '[f]or the taxpayer, the Social Trends team makes every effort to contain costs and to reassess priorities whenever relative costs and benefits change' (ibid.). As in previous years, however, the editorial still stated that updated versions of discontinued tables would normally be available on request, without mention of charge for these, an offer that was not to disappear until the late 1980s. Under various editors from 1983 to 1993, the description of the aims of Social Trends remained unchanged, with only minor changes in wording:

> This new edition of Social Trends again includes thirteen chapters, most of which correspond broadly to the administrative functions of Government. . . . As the primary user of Social Trends remains Government, each chapter is oriented as far as possible towards current policy concerns.
>
> (Social Trends 1983: 10)

It was not until 1994, under the editorship of Jenny Church, that the opening statement of the purpose of Social Trends changed. The volume now bears on its front cover the mission statement of the CSO: 'Our mission is to improve decision making, stimulate research and inform debate within government and the wider community by providing a quality statistical service', while the editorial introduction says that 'Social Trends is aimed at a very wide audience: policy-makers in the public and private sectors; market researchers; journalists and commentators; academics and students; and the general public' (Social Trends 1994: 3). However, price remains a barrier to accessibility. The cost rose only marginally from 1982 to 1991 and then began to climb again; but between 1994 and 1995, it shot up from £27 to £34.95. Moreover, it would be too sanguine to suppose that the new mission statement represents a real commitment to openness, a point to which we shall return.

The changes that took place in Social Trends during the 1980s were not merely changes in presentation. In line with the Rayner view that

15

interpretation was an inappropriate activity for government statisticians, the social commentaries which originally prefaced the volume were dropped, and from 1981 to 1984 there was no introductory article at all. The space for commentary as a whole was reduced, and the balance of data altered. The proportion of tables dealing with 'law enforcement' rose to 11 per cent in 1982, 1983 and 1984; in 1975 this category, then headed 'public safety', constituted 7 per cent of the total. Tables on income and wealth had totalled forty, or 12 per cent, in 1975; by 1983 they had dwindled to nineteen, less than 7 per cent. Among the casualties was the series on families and persons normally with low net resources. Notably, one of the first statistical casualties of the Thatcher years had been the abolition in 1979 of the Royal Commission on Income and Wealth. Moreover, both in *Social Trends* and elsewhere, there was an increasing reluctance to provide analyses of data by social class: on 30 October 1987, *The Times* reported plans within the OPCS to abolish class categories altogether.

COOKING THE BOOKS?

As the decade progressed, however, questions about access to data escalated, as did more fundamental questions about the integrity of the data that was available. The government was repeatedly accused of delaying, suppressing, abolishing and manipulating data for its own political ends. Whereas Rayner had declared that 'Ministers in the UK are rarely accused of cooking the books' (Rayner 1980: 22), this had become patently untrue. One issue which remained of political salience throughout the 1980s was the treatment of the unemployment statistics. As described in Chapter 3, following the White Paper on *Government Statistical Services* and an additional report by Rayner (1981) on *The Payment of Benefits to Unemployed People*, there was in 1982 a change from a registrant-based count to a claimant-based count. There were however many other changes to this administrative measure of unemployment, all of which had the effect of reducing the total. The government was repeatedly accused of fiddling the figures. Even Boreham was reported in 1989 as saying that the unemployment figures were 'a dirty business'. He did indeed say to camera that:

> The unemployment figures are always difficult because they are highly political and there is always a temptation to make them look smaller. And denying people unemployment benefit so that the level of unemployment counted by unemployment benefit goes down is always attractive, and that is a sort of cheating.

> (*Dispatches* 1989)

In the same programme, Moser said that there had been too many changes in the figures, a view echoed by Ian Gilmour, a minister in the first

Thatcher government. Christopher Huhne, economics editor of the
Guardian, said:

> I have absolutely no doubt that successive Ministers, starting with
> Norman Tebbit when he was Secretary of State for Employment, have
> deliberately set about making changes in the way that unemployment
> is counted, which have had the effect of reducing the total, and that
> has been extremely politically convenient for them.
>
> (*Dispatches* 1989)

Ward and Doggett identify the unemployment figures as one of two
major issues about the integrity of statistics and their use between 1978
and 1985 – although Boreham said that they were 'not integrity issues' but
'matters of statistical management' (Ward and Doggett 1991: 93). The
second issue was the Tax and Price Index (TPI), a new index requested by
the government in 1979. Whereas the Retail Price Index, used as a
headline figure for inflation, takes into account indirect taxation, it does
not take into account direct taxation, and thus gives no indication of the
relationship between changes in gross and net incomes. The TPI was
contentious for several reasons. Some of these were questions about what
was and was not included in it, and the complete lack of consultation on
this matter with interested parties such as the trade unions. The Royal
Statistical Society held a meeting to discuss the new index in November
1979 (Bartholomew 1981: 12).

Moser himself expressed qualms about a second monthly index, on the
grounds that it 'might undermine confidence in the RPI', especially if the
two indices were used in a competitive manner (Moser 1980: 7). The
interpretation placed on the invention of the TPI by lay observers was that
its purpose was to give a lower figure for inflation to depress wage
settlements; unfortunately for the government, the TPI was actually higher
than the RPI from mid-1980 until 1983. Although the index is still
published monthly in *The Retail Price Index*, it is not widely quoted in public
debate. Moser's argument in favour of a single index, while a reasonable
argument against the TPI given its obvious purpose, is undermined by
some of the weaknesses of the RPI itself, which aggregates the expenditure
of all households except those of pensioners mainly dependent on state
benefits and those with very high incomes. The effect of this aggregation is
to obscure the differential rates of inflation for different groups, which
reveal that the poorest 10 per cent had a rate of inflation higher than the
general index for the whole of the ten years from 1982 to 1992 (Hills 1995:
35). While a Pensioner Price Index is derived by government statisticians
from the same data as the RPI, the construction of a Low Paid Price Index
has been left to the Low Pay Unit.

There were in fact many other issues on which the statistics and their
manipulation by politicians caused concern during the 1980s. The

decentralised structure of the GSS meant that most statisticians were located in individual departments, not in the CSO, which arguably made them more vulnerable to pressures from ministers to alter the basis on which statistics were produced. In any case, they had no control over changes in administrative measures like the claimant count, or over the interpretation ministers chose to put upon available data. In 1989, Channel 4 broadcast a *Dispatches* investigation into the integrity of official statistics, in which they reported on ten examples of overt interference with data. One, of course, was unemployment; the others were far less well known.

First, the programme raised the question of the timing of the release of figures. In fact, while Moser was at the CSO, he had introduced fixed release dates for major indicators like the unemployment figures and the RPI, with an embargo on ministers releasing them in advance, although he noted that by 1989 there were cases where ministers were complying only with the letter and not the spirit of this (Phillips 1989). But not all figures were governed by this, and sometimes there were delays. On 23 July 1986, the date of a royal wedding, delayed figures on the Health Service relating to 1979–84 were published. They showed a loss of 196 hospitals, 17,025 beds, 3,051 doctors, 20,000 other staff and 35 hospital schools. On the same day, figures were published that showed that the radiation emissions from Sellafield were fifty times the level previously disclosed. On 25 July, one hour before the House of Commons broke for the summer recess, a written answer included figures showing a huge rise in the numbers living in poverty.

Secondly, *Dispatches* raised the issue of the manipulation of figures themselves. It was revealed that the calculations of the fall in public spending were inflated by the extraordinary device of treating the income from asset sales (particularly the privatisations of nationalised industries and utilities) not as income, but as reductions in expenditure. Asset sales of former hospital sites were treated as capital spending on the health service. Efficiency savings of 1 per cent a year imposed upon the health service were treated as increased government spending; the income from prescription charges was treated as spending on the health service. Norman Fowler was able to announce a huge increase in the number of 'hospital schemes' under way partly by including those planned as well as those actually started, but primarily by including every scheme over £1 million; previously the definition would have been over £5 million. One hospital appeared five times. Figures were published for the number of new beds in the Health Service, showing an increase of 17,000, but ignoring the number of old beds that had disappeared (over 20,000). It had been claimed that hospital waiting lists had decreased – an impression fostered by excluding 'self-deferrals' from the lists; this meant that anyone unable to have an awaited operation at the very short notice given to patients, who therefore 'self-deferred', was not included in the figures of those awaiting treatment. If such people were included, the waiting lists had gone up, not down.

Thirdly, the evidence could be buried or abolished. One example illustrates the effect of the Rayner recommendation that a larger proportion of data should be produced in mechanically readable form (as well, perhaps, as deriving from the cuts in the budget for analysing the 1981 Census). Not only were the results of the Census delayed. Having been due on the date of the royal wedding, they were actually released during the parliamentary recess. Townsend reported that the published analysis did not include the customary analysis of death by social class. The figures for this had to be extracted from twenty-two microfiche tables. Although technically 'published', they were hardly disseminated in a form to which many people would have access. On investigation, they turned out to show that there had been widening inequalities in mortality rates (an issue dealt with in detail in Chapter 5 below), as well as sharpening social class gradients in a number of diseases. The treatment of the poverty figures (Chapter 2) was even more alarming. Data which used to be published annually was reduced to biennially, then seriously delayed, and then replaced altogether by another, non-comparable, series (*Dispatches* 1989).

The conclusions drawn in the programme were unequivocal. Huhne said:

> There is no doubt in my mind that the standards both of the collection of government statistics and the standards with which they are used by Ministers when they have been collected are lower today than they were under the last government or under its predecessor.
>
> (*Dispatches* 1989)

Clive Ponting accused the government of a concerted policy to get the figures they wanted, while Ian Gilmour said that

> The persistent and consistent manipulation of figures . . . to serve the government's cause is something which is wrong and is worrying because the integrity of government statistics is something that should be above party politics.
>
> (*Dispatches* 1989)

Boreham, who had retired from the CSO in 1985, but was still bound by the Official Secrets Act not to reveal the substance of conflicts between statisticians and ministers, nevertheless did make abundantly clear that such conflict existed:

> There is a frontier zone in which the government's desire to show that it is doing well, and the statistical service's desire to be objective and neutral, leads to constant skirmishing. Usually, Ministers had an

interest in making sure that what was published did not do them a great deal of harm.

(*Dispatches* 1989)

Why else would he have written in his note on integrity:

Where necessary we should try, by logic and diplomacy, to persuade colleagues and Ministers of the risks of losing public confidence they would run if they suppressed, delayed or misused our statistics, or selected figures to satisfy their particular social, economic or political viewpoint. We should recognise that even though Ministers are personally responsible for the content and accuracy of their replies to Parliamentary Questions, we also have an important responsibility to try to make sure that our Ministers are supplied with figures that are accurate and relevant and are not intended to mislead the questioner.

(Boreham 1985: 20)

Townsend, however, suggested that perhaps the statisticians themselves were implicated, if only for failing to challenge what had been going on:

It's difficult from the evidence to conclude that the government isn't cooking the books. One can only argue that there has been much more political interference and possibly tacit agreement on the part of many of those in senior ranks of administration.

(*Dispatches* 1989)

The programme might also have referred to the infamous case of the Black Report, commissioned in 1977 by David Ennals, the then Health Minister, and completed in 1980. As Chapter 5 below shows, this was a crucial documentation of the effects of inequality and deprivation upon health. It was not formally published by the government, although 260 duplicated copies were made available on August bank holiday. Its recommendations, which included restricting the advertising and sale of tobacco, were said by the government to be 'quite unrealistic in present or any future economic circumstances' (*Guardian* 17 December 1993). When *The Health Divide* (Whitehead 1987) was published, it too was produced in very limited numbers so that access to the data was restricted. Yet another instance was the delay of two and a half years in the publication of the NACNE (National Advisory Committee on Nutrition Education) Report on diet and health which drew attention to the excessive amounts of fat, sugar and salt in the British diet. This delay was caused by the interests of the food industry, especially the sugar lobby, which was represented on the NACNE committee. The final report refers to 'intense commercial pressures to maintain sucrose intakes', and the effect of these in delaying acceptance of the report's findings (Walker and Cannon 1984: xiii).

THE PICKFORD REPORT

Both the *Dispatches* programme and a series of articles in the *Guardian* (15 March 1989) occurred at a time when the Royal Statistical Society was expressing considerable concern about the lack of public confidence in the integrity of official statistics. Boreham had been replaced at the CSO in 1985 by Jack Hibbert. In his inaugural address, Hibbert stressed the importance of good working relationships with the users of statistics. But his early years as head of the GSS were clouded by problems with the economic statistics. In 1986 and 1987 the quality of the national accounts visibly deteriorated, with large discrepancies appearing between three different measures of Gross Domestic Product (GDP). An inquiry was set up, which led to the publication of the Pickford Report in 1989 (Pickford *et al.* 1989).

The Pickford Report was concerned with macro-economic statistics, not with the full range of government statistics as Rayner had been; but it was also concerned with the effects of the institutional structure of the GSS. The review team were not convinced by the argument that the Rayner cuts were to blame for the particular problems with macro-economic indicators, although there was no disagreement that the quality of these had deteriorated through the 1980s. They argued that the problems (largely unspecified) were 'deep-seated and pervasive, have multiple causes, and have existed for a long time' (Pickford *et al.* 1989: 3). However, they did report that a number of those interviewed argued that the implementation of the Rayner Report had had adverse consequences on the quality of data, and drew particular attention to the problems caused by the introduction of sampling into the Census of Employment. Although they found 'individual statisticians concerned about the quality of their own statistics', they argued that the main difficulty was a lack of central initiative to resolve the problem; the influence of the CSO had declined, especially its ability to persuade individual departments to compile their statistics in specific and compatible ways (Pickford *et al.* 1989: 32–3). The three main CSO committees concerned with economic statistics, which had met a total of eleven times in 1978 and seven times in 1979, had met on average 2.4 times a year between 1980 and 1988, with the number gradually declining throughout that period. The most important of these, CSO(E), whose brief was 'to consider and decide questions relating to statistics for economic policy', had not met at all since 1984. There were counter-accusations about the reasons for this decline. Some attributed it to a failure of will on the part of the CSO. Others blamed departments for prioritising their own policy interests above collective ones (Pickford *et al.* 1989: 156–7).

The attempt to exonerate Rayner was thoroughly unconvincing. But the report's recommendations were largely structural: to strengthen the position of the CSO, enlarging it by transferring groups of statisticians from elsewhere in the GSS, and enhancing its status, either by making it a

21

separate Chancellor's Department, or an agency of the Treasury. Despite the fact that the original location of the CSO in the Cabinet Office reporting directly to the Prime Minister had been intended precisely to avoid pressure from the Treasury, this proposal was implemented, with the director of the CSO reporting to the Chancellor. Responsibility for the Family Expenditure Survey and the RPI was transferred from the Department of Employment to the enlarged CSO.

COUNTING WITH CONFIDENCE

By the end of the 1980s, public confidence in the reliability of official statistics was at an all-time low. A report by Bernard Benjamin which argued that the quality of official statistics had declined was itself suppressed (Phillips 1995). An article appeared in the *Guardian* which said that 'the charges being levelled against the service amount to the politicisation of knowledge, a form of intellectual corruption and a scandalous abuse of power' (Hibbert 1990: 149). In November 1989, the Royal Statistical Society (RSS) set up a working party to 'provide an independent review of the criteria and mechanisms for monitoring the integrity and adequacy of, and public confidence in, official statistics' (ibid.: 126). Moser himself had described the reorganisation of the CSO as 'a serious error' (ibid.: 142). In a discussion with Hibbert at the RSS in December 1989, participants placed considerable blame on the consequences of the Rayner review, which was described as 'a major step backwards' and 'a triumph of expediency over professional integrity' (ibid.: 130, 138). As well as concern about the new reporting structure, there was a further call for a statistical service oriented to the whole community; more methodological work involving academics outside the GSS; and a National Statistical Council, an independent watchdog to oversee or advise the GSS (ibid.: 141).

The RSS Working Party reported in July 1990. The report, *Counting with Confidence*, was unequivocal that 'the indirect results of the post-Rayner reforms have been harmful to quality' (RSS 1991: 26). It included figures showing the continued decline in staffing of the GSS from 1984 to 1989. Its central conclusion was that:

> [T]he Government Statistical Service lacks appropriate constitutional support for the proper exercise of its function. It currently lacks autonomy, control over operational decisions and publications, managerial responsibility for its staff, a proper basis of methodological research from which to make operational decisions, and the resources to resolve problems of accuracy, internal consistency and external validity.
>
> (RSS 1991: 33)

It recommended the centralisation of the GSS, the setting up of a research unit on methodology, a National Statistical Commission, and an Official Statistics Act safeguarding the autonomy and constitutional position of official statistics, which, it noted, exists in most Western countries. Moser, who had been a member of the working party, made yet another plea for a National Statistical Commission in his presidential address to the British Association for the Advancement of Science in the summer of 1990 (Moser 1990: 13).

A NEW DEAL?

In a further discussion in June 1991, Peter Stibbard of the Department of Employment complained that perceptions were 'stuck in an early 1980s timewarp' (Moore 1992: 22). The implication was that the problems had, if not gone away, radically diminished. After all, the GSS had issued a new code of practice in 1984 (GSS 1984), and Boreham (1985) had stressed the importance of integrity. The impression that the government had cleaned up its act might be borne out by the new mission statement of the CSO, claiming to serve the community. But in reality, in 1995 the situation is not so very different.

This is in spite of the fact that the 1993 White Paper on *Open Government* commended open access to official statistics. A BBC investigation into the reality of open government described the code of practice as 'in practical terms . . . a guide for the civil service of how to keep that door shut'. All sorts of reasons may be given for withholding information, including commercial sensitivity. But even where access to information is permitted, government departments and subcontracting agencies may charge for the cost of preparing and supplying it. The costs can be prohibitive, running into thousands of pounds, for information which should be in the public domain. One participant pointed out that 'barriers of this kind are really as effective as an Official Secrets Act in stopping the public getting information' (*Face the Facts* 1995).

And not only do the arguments over the measurement of unemployment rumble on, with the RSS producing a special report on them at the beginning of 1995. The coverage of the 1991 Census has been shown to be seriously deficient: some estimates put the shortfall at 2 million people. The poll tax is blamed for at least part of the undercounting, and the shortfall is particularly noticeable among young men in inner city wards (OPCS 1994, *Guardian* 6 January 1995: 9, 23). The consequences for social statistics are considerable (Simpson and Dorling 1994).

What is at issue with the Census coverage is the quality of data, not that any one is deliberately cooking the books. Other illustrations will serve to show that political interference has not ceased, and public confidence not improved. In December 1993, Jean Corston, MP for Bristol East, complained that DSS ministers were deliberately obstructing the provision of information about the poorest groups in the population, citing specific delays, withholding and manipulation of the data. The then director of the CSO, Bill McLennan, spoke in December 1994 of the need to restore public confidence in official statistics; he supported calls for a UK Statistics Act, as well as calls for dropping the use of the claimant count as the headline measure of unemployment. McLennan had also authorised the consultation of a number of bodies, including the Radical Statistics Group, on gaps and deficiencies in the coverage of social statistics (Church 1993). But in January 1995, the twenty-fifth anniversary issue of *Social Trends* appeared without the planned lead article by its first editor, Muriel Nissel. It had been censored by McLennan, who defended his action in a letter to the *Guardian* (25 January 1995) on the grounds that it was 'strong on opinions' which 'are not statistical facts'. Nissel had made reference to the pressures on the GSS in the 1980s, and on *Social Trends* in particular. She also confirmed that there had been ministerial interference: 'From time to time, there has been great pressure on directors of statistics in departments to withhold or modify statistics, particularly in relation to employment and health, and professional integrity has forced some to threaten resignation' (Nissel 1995: 24). Phillips (1995) suggested that the pressure to censor the article may have come from elsewhere: not only was it inconsistent with McLennan's general conduct as director of the CSO, but he was about to leave for Australia, and had little interest in defending the indefensible record of successive Conservative governments (Phillips 1995).

On 20 February 1995 the *Guardian* reported on the continued delays to the publication of a number of reports produced by the Home Office. In April, John Major publicly pledged to maintain the integrity of official statistics (*Guardian*, 6 April 1995). Less than two months later, it was announced that the CSO was planning to scrap its 'longer leading indicator', which predicted a rapid slowdown in the economy in late 1995 and early 1996 (*Guardian*, 30 May 1995). It is an open question how the GSS will fare under its new director, Tim Holt, who took over in July 1995, just as the statisticians from the dissolved Employment Department are transferred to the CSO.[1] But the need for a National Statistics Council and an Official Statistics Act seems as great as ever.

NOTE

1 In April 1996 the CSO and the OPCS were merged to form the Office for National Statistics (ONS). Tim Holt became Director of the ONS, Registrar General for England and Wales as well as Director of the CSO and Head of the GSS.

REFERENCES

Bartholomew, D. J. (1981) 'The Tax and Price Index', *Journal of the Royal Statistical Society* Series A, 143: 12.

Boreham, J. (1984) 'Present position and potential developments: some personal views: official statistics', *Journal of the Royal Statistical Society* Series A, 147: 174–85.
—— (1985) 'Integrity in the Government Statistical Services', *Statistical News*, February.
Church, J. (1993) 'User views on data collection by the Government Statistical Service', *Radical Statistics* 55: 10–11.
Dean, M. (1995) '*Social Trends* chief censors its history', The *Guardian*, 21 January.
Dispatches (1989) 'Is the government cooking the books?' London: Channel 4.
Face the Facts (1995) 19 January, BBC Radio 4.
GSS (Government Statistical Service) (1984) *The GSS Code of Practice* (Cmnd 9270), London: HMSO.
Government Statistical Services (1981), White Paper (Cmnd 8236), London: HMSO.
Hibbert, J. (1990) 'Public confidence in the integrity and validity of official statistics', *Journal of the Royal Statistical Society* Series A, 153, Part 2: 123–50.
Hills, J. (1995) *Joseph Rowntree Foundation Inquiry into Income and Wealth: Volume 2: A Summary of the Evidence*, York: Joseph Rowntree Foundation.
Hoinville, G. and Smith, T. M. F. (1982) 'The Rayner Review of Government Statistical Services', *Journal of the Royal Statistical Society* Series A, 145: 195–207.
Mayes, D. G. (1984) *Statistics by or for Government?: Recent Changes in Official Statistics*, Discussion Paper 9, London: National Economic Development Office.
Moore, P. G. (1992) 'A National Statistical Commission', *Journal of the Royal Statistical Society* Series A, 155: 5–28.
Moser, C. (1970) 'Some general developments in social statistics', *Social Trends*, pp. 7–11.
—— (1980) 'Statistics and public policy', *Journal of the Royal Statistical Society* Series A, 143: 1–31.
—— (1990) *Our Need for an Informed Society*, London: British Association for the Advancement of Science.
Nissel, M. (1995) 'Vital statistics', *New Statesman* 27 January.
OPCS (1980) *The Review of the Government Statistical Services: Initial Study of the Office of Population Censuses and Surveys*, London: HMSO.
—— (1994) *1991 Census Validation Survey: Coverage Report*, London: HMSO.
Open Government (1993) White Paper (Cm 2290), London: HMSO.
Phillips, M. (1989) 'How the cards are stacked', The *Guardian* 15 March.
—— (1995) 'We've figured the fiddles, thank you', *The Observer* 29 January.
Pickford, S., Cunningham, J., Lynch, R., Radice, J. and White, G. (1989) *Government Economic Statistics: A Scrutiny Report*, London: HMSO.
Rayner, D. (1980) *Review of Government Statistical Services: Report to the Prime Minister*, London: HMSO.
—— (1981) *The Payment of Benefits to Unemployed People*, London: HMSO.
RSS (Royal Statistical Society) (1991) 'Official statistics: counting with confidence', *Journal of the Royal Statistical Society* Series A, 154 Part 1: 23–44.
Simpson, S. and Dorling, D. (1994) 'Those missing millions: implications for social statistics of non-response to the 1991 Census', *Journal of Social Policy* 23, 4: 543–67.
Social Trends (annual) London: HMSO.
Walker, C. and Cannon, G. (1984) *The Food Scandal: What's Wrong with the British Diet and How to Put it Right*, London: Century.
Ward, R. and Doggett, T. (1991) *Keeping Score: The First Fifty Years of the Central Statistical Office*, London: HMSO.
Whitehead, M. (1987) *The Health Divide: Inequalities in Health in the 1980s*, London: Health Education Council.
Wilson, H. (1973) 'Statistics and decision-making in government – Bradshaw revisited', *Journal of the Royal Statistical Society* Series A, 136: 1–19.

2

THE STRUGGLE FOR INDEPENDENT STATISTICS ON POVERTY

Peter Townsend

For more than a hundred years official statistics of low income and poverty have been a matter of heated debate and controversy. This was especially true of the 1960s but is also true of the 1990s. Their role at the end of the 1990s will be the theme of this chapter.

Statistics don't fall out of the skies. Like words – of which they are of course an extension – they are constructed by human beings influenced by culture and the predispositions and governing ideas of the organisations and groups within which people work. Statistical methodologies are not timeless creations. They are the current expression of society's attempts to interpret, represent and analyse information about economic and social (and other) conditions. As the years pass they change – not just because there may be technical *advances*, but because professional, cultural, political *and* technical conventions change in terms of *retreat* as well as advance. This is what lends them particular fascination.

How, then, do any of us know whether the statistics we use, including those about poverty, provide a partial, distorted or completely false representation of 'reality'? One way of obtaining confidence in our results is by using the methodology of comparison (especially comparison with statistics collected elsewhere) and techniques like statistical testing and the randomised control trial – which can readily be understood and accepted, even if sometimes complex to absorb. Another is to distinguish between statistics which are strictly limited *indicators* of conditions and statistics which are general *descriptors* of conditions. Such methods can be applied to any example of social conditions – including low income and poverty. But we can also obtain confidence in our results by insisting on evidence of the origin or source of statistics and how they come to be selected, assembled and disseminated. We must adopt reasoned *theory* about their construction, development and conventional interpretation.

Every student of social science in general and poverty in particular needs to be grounded in how information about social conditions is acquired. Statistics form a substantial part of such information. Acquiring information is much more than looking up handbooks of statistics. We have to become self-conscious about the process of selection. Everyone understands that there is a choice between qualitative and quantitative data and that the two are – or should be – interdependent. But that marks only the beginning. *Alternative* definitions have to be formulated, so that reasons can be given for the one that is selected. The same principle applies to measurement, theory and policy – which form a necessary part of the investigative process. Pursuit of this framework of principle of course leads us into its subdivisions. We have to examine the *components* of different conditions and show how they are connected. We have to measure *trends* in the conditions in which we are interested. We have to show what are the necessary steps in building justifiable explanations of those conditions and trends, and prioritise elements of those explanations. And we have to frame the multiple prospective policies which will therefore modify or change the conditions observed, and distinguish them from existing policies.

The key idea is to strive to stand outside statistical convention to consider *alternative* perspectives, methodologies, theories and policies, which might oblige conclusions that are over-confidently reached to be modified and, at the very least, put into better proportion.

AN ILLUSTRATION FROM THE STATISTICS OF POVERTY

I will give an illustration from the recent interpretation and treatment of poverty and then go on to discuss the various issues about the organisation of statistics which arise from such illustrations.

First, successive governments in the United Kingdom have chosen to avoid using the term 'poverty'. Thus, in 1989, the Secretary of State for Social Services, John Moore, accepted that there had been poverty in the nineteenth century but denied it existed in the latter part of the twentieth century (Moore 1989). Relative definitions were 'bizarre'. Estimates of the number of people said to be living in 'poverty' were 'arbitrary and exaggerated' (Moore 1989: 12) and represented 'an attempt to discredit our real economic achievement in protecting and improving the living standards of our people' (Moore 1989: 14). 'Their purpose in calling poverty what is in reality simply inequality is so that they can call western material capitalism a failure.' It would be strange indeed if statisticians in the government service did not take heed of such pronouncements and if their publications took no account of them.

Mr Moore is not an isolated example. Many UK ministers resist giving certain kinds of social information which in many other countries is routinely available. When invited in 1995 to give an estimate of the number of people in Scotland living in poverty a junior minister, Lord James Douglas-Hamilton, stated in the House of Commons, 'Statistics on patterns of household disposable income are provided in *Households below*

Average Income reports. . . . The best response to low household income is to sustain economic recovery and to assist those in greatest need' (Douglas-Hamilton 1995).

What has to be emphasised is that 'poverty' is a long-accepted concept, with operational definitions in nearly all countries of the world. There are elaborate studies of its measured extent. Examples are the United Nations (UN 1995b); the World Bank (1990, 1993); the United Nations Development Programme (1995); the International Labour Office (Rodgers 1995); the European Union (Eurostat 1994) and many national governments, including Sweden and the United States (Committee on Ways and Means 1995).

What such contemporary studies reveal is different criteria of selection for either a scientific, or a social, threshold of 'poverty' when examining the ranking of income (or expenditure) for different countries. There are three examples from recent history of this threshold approach which crop up many times, with minor variations, in the extensive historical literature. (1) Sometimes the threshold has been set as the income sufficient to buy bare 'subsistence', that is, the food, clothing, fuel and shelter to maintain life from day to day. (2) Sometimes the threshold has been set to provide 'basic needs' in the local community, meaning the subsistence needs of each individual, as in the example above, *plus* specified collective facilities for drinking water, sanitation, and basic health care and education. (3) And sometimes the threshold has been set as families having the minimum resources to escape 'relative deprivation', and to perform their necessary roles as citizens or workers, fulfil family and community obligations and participate at the barest level in long-established social customs.

These three can be seen as successively wider definitions of scientific criteria which have to be met in deciding how much is the minimum income required to meet individual and social needs, and therefore determine a poverty 'line' (see Townsend 1993, 1994). But there are also measures of 'relative poverty' which do not pretend to use criteria or indicators of social conditions or behaviour *outside* income (or alternatively *outside* the budgetary pattern of expenditure) to determine what the minimally acceptable amount should be. These measures are arbitrary or expert choices of appropriate cut-off points in the distribution of income. The European Union currently uses a cut-off point of half average disposable income; by measuring the distribution of income in different countries it is possible to show how many in each population fall below this arbitrary measure of low income. As any study of examples will show, the results vary for different countries, depending on the 'shape' of their distribution of household income.

An even more restricted version of this approach has been to collect information about the poorest tenth (decile) or fifth (quintile) and about higher tenths or fifths. Like a tall cake the population is ranked according to income, and then cut into equal horizontal slices. The United Kingdom government has now adopted this course without conceding that any particular cut-off point represents 'poverty' – and without the advantage, like the European Union example quoted above, of showing how the extent of low income in the population compares with other populations or varies from year to year.

LOW INCOME

Each of the people holding the position of Prime Minister in the early 1990s stated repeatedly that all sections of the British population had experienced a real improvement in their disposable income since 1979. In her final speech as Prime Minister in the House of Commons in 1989 Margaret Thatcher insisted on this point twice. From 1992 John Major adopted similar practice. In reply to a question from Jean Corston, MP on 22 February 1994, he affirmed that 'the net disposable income of people at all ranges of income has increased'. Two days afterwards the late John Smith, then Leader of the Opposition, pursued the point and invited the Prime Minister to withdraw his remark on the previous Tuesday. John Smith referred specifically to the fall in the real income of the poorest 10 per cent. John Major retorted by repeating what he had already said about the rise in the 'real median income of the bottom fifth' before housing costs, and went on to state that the real incomes of vulnerable groups like the pensioners, the unemployed and the low-paid had all increased (see Appendix, p. 40). He did not refer only to those in the poorest tenth or fifth but included people from such categories at all levels of income.

These public exchanges cannot be understood except in context. Jean Corston wrote to the Prime Minister on 23 February 1994 saying that the statement that the net disposable income of people at all ranges of income had increased was 'not true'. The Department of Social Security had shown in its latest report on households below average income that the 10 per cent of the population (6 million) with least income had smaller disposable income, in real terms, than in 1979 (DSS 1993: 61). This also applied to some in the next tranche of income. 'Indeed, written parliamentary answers given to me last year showed that "as many as 5.7 million of the people with lower real income than in 1979 were in families with children."' On 11 April 1994 the Prime Minister replied: 'Your question [addressed in person to him in February] referred to *Social Trends 1994* and to the income growth of the poorest 20 per cent of the population. *Social Trends* show that the income of this group increased by 3 per cent before housing costs [he did not concede that the same table (Table 5.21) showed a *decrease* in that income by 3 per cent *after* housing costs]. My reply was therefore entirely accurate.'

The Prime Minister went on to say that the DSS report on *Households*

Below Average Income used 'different reference groups for which different income growth results apply. I have to dispute the interpretation which you place on the figures, which is not sustainable.' He argued that the report did not track individuals over time, and it was therefore impossible to conclude that the real incomes of 'anyone in the bottom decile actually declined over time'. He pointed out that the ownership of certain consumer durables among the poorest tenth had increased and that the richest groups in the population were paying large amounts in taxation.

During the subsequent summer and autumn the exchange about the statistics of the distribution of income deepened. Jean Corston also sought and was granted a formal meeting with the head of the Government Statistical Service about the defects of official statistics on low incomes. In a letter to the Prime Minister of 25 May 1994 Jean Corston presented a wide array of official statistics, drawn from the government's publications but also from written answers to parliamentary questions. She fastened in particular on the evidence about families with children. She quoted figures from the Treasury showing that the poorest 10 per cent and the second poorest 10 per cent of families with children, including more than 3 million children, had lower average household income in 1992 than in 1979. In a reply of 8 August John Major maintained his previous position and Jean Corston then took advantage of new data published late in the year to write at length on 27 October 1994 saying that 'the evidence cannot be shrugged off. Either the Prime Minister doesn't understand the information provided by his own Department, or he is deliberately misleading the House of Commons and the nation.' In a letter to him she pointed out that 'the calculations made by the DSS show an income loss between 1979 and 1991/1992 among the poorest 20 per cent of households with children. When income is measured before housing costs the average household is 2 per cent, or £156 per year, worse off at April 1994 prices. When income is measured after housing costs the average household is 12 per cent, or £520 per year worse off.'

The statistics given in the replies are reproduced in Tables 2.1, 2.2 and 2.3. Table 2.1 shows the percentage loss or gain of each fifth of households with children (covering in total 35 million in a population of 57 million), in 'real' terms. In 'real' terms means standardising information for different years by adjusting for inflation, or rise in prices. The normal procedure is to increase or diminish incomes in each year to conform with what the income would be in relation to the prices applying to the latest convenient date for which there is information, say, April 1994.

In examining income data for different years the selection of the median (the mid-point in the distribution) is different from the selection of the mean (averaging the incomes of each household or individual in the whole group). If, below the mid-point of the incomes of the poorest tenth (representing nearly 6 million) incomes *fall* dramatically, and if, above

Table 2.1 Percentage change in real incomes of quintile medians and the mean of families with children, 1979–1991/92

	Quintile 1 bottom 20%	*Quintile 2* 20–40%	*Quintile 3* 40–60%	*Quintile 4* 60–80%	*Quintile 5* top 20%	*Mean*
Before housing costs	(–2)	(7)	22	33	51	32
After housing costs	(–12)	(1)	20	32	49	29

Source: Written answer to Parliamentary Question put by Jean Corston, MP for Bristol East, *Hansard*, 26 October 1994, cols 691–2

Note: Estimates in brackets are stated by the DSS to be uncertain; see Appendix 5 of *Households Below Average Income* (DSS 1990a) for details of the tests applied to estimates of changes in real income.

the mid–point of the richest tenth, incomes *rise* dramatically, then the choice of medians instead of means to structure information about trends will greatly understate the growth of inequality in the distribution of incomes. Among other trends, this appears to have occurred in the UK in the 1980s and 1990s. When the DSS substituted the former series of statistics about low incomes with the new series entitled *Households Below Average Income* the Social Security all-party Committee of the House argued unsuccessfully for the former series to be published as well (DSS 1988, 1990a, 1990b, 1991; Social Services Committee 1988, 1989, 1990). The DSS also chose first to give little or no information about the top half of the income distribution, and second to refrain from giving statistics of mean income in parallel with statistics of median income (see Townsend and Gordon 1992 for a full discussion of the problems of the conventions selected).

Table 2.2 helps to illustrate another of the conventions adopted by the DSS. The table supplies statistics of 'equivalised' income, not actual cash income or even income standardised according to the prices prevailing in relation to income at a particular time, say, April 1994. To 'equivalise' income is to adjust it in relation to what it would be in a 'standard' household, in this case a household consisting of a man and woman only. The income of single person households is therefore increased to represent the income equivalent to what it would be for a couple, and the income of couples with different numbers of children, and of different combinations of adults, is reduced to indicate what would be equivalent to a household consisting only of a couple. Two problems arise. One is that in the process of equivalisation far more incomes are reduced than are increased and the figures in Table 2.2, especially for richer households, are a considerable understatement of the size of actual cash incomes in contemporary purchasing terms. This can lead to confusion and misunderstanding – and incidentally suggests that wherever possible

Table 2.2 Equivalised incomes of families with children: quintile medians and the mean for 1979 and 1991/92 in April 1994 prices

	Quintile 1 bottom 20% (£)	Quintile 2 20–40% (£)	Quintile 3 40–60% (£)	Quintile 4 60–80% (£)	Quintile 5 top 20% (£)	Mean (£)
Before housing costs						
1979	103	138	165	198	261	180
1991/92	100	148	202	263	394	238
After housing costs						
1979	86	117	141	172	227	155
1991/92	76	118	169	226	399	200

Source: Written answer to parliamentary question put by Jean Corston, MP for Bristol East, Hansard, 26 October 1994, cols 691–2

Note: All estimates are subject to sampling error.

'equivalisation' should be avoided. Thus trends in the distribution of income can be expressed separately for each major type of family.

The second problem is more serious. What allowance is to be made for children in households? What fraction of the income *needs* of a two-adult household should children of different ages additionally represent? How do we decide what income for a family of man and woman and two young children is 'equivalent' to the income of a man and a woman? There are many different answers to this question from scientists around the world (Bradbury 1989, Buhmann *et al.* 1989, Saunders and Whiteford 1989, Whiteford 1985, Townsend and Gordon 1992, Gordon and Pantazis 1994) and the DSS does not offer two, or three, alternative methods (as is common practice, for example, in population projections). They have adopted a method of weighting taken from expenditure data applying to the late 1970s. But the extra amount *spent* by a family of man and woman and two young children cannot be said to represent the extra amount they *need* to spend to be assured of being 'equivalent'. It is possible to argue that children's income needs are undervalued by the DSS and that, like the definition of poverty, scientific criteria of need *outside* conventional distributions of income or expenditure have to be sought. Otherwise judgements become circular, and the incomes available to families with children are used as the basis for statements about the incomes they need. If DSS assumptions about the income needs of children were more generous then the trend of increasing poverty among families with children would be sharper than it has been made out to be. However, even on the basis of existing DSS conventions Table 2.2 shows that the equivalised income per week of families with children has diverged very sharply between different ranks of the population.

Table 2.3 brings out the general trend more specifically for particular definitions of family circumstances. This table avoids the problem of equivalisation, and it is unfortunate, to say the least, that the official DSS report on *Households Below Average Income* contains no illustrative figures of this kind.

Table 2.3 Change in annual income 1979–1991/92, at April 1994 prices

Household composition		Poorest tenth (£)	Richest tenth (£)
Single adult		– 364	+ 5,616
Couple with no children		– 676	+ 10,616
Couple with child aged 3		– 780	+ 12,012
Couple with child aged 16		– 884	+ 14,040
Couple with children	aged 3, 8	– 996	+ 14,300
	aged 3, 8, 11	– 1,092	+ 16,592
	aged 11, 16, 17	– 1,300	+ 20,488

Source: Written answer to parliamentary question put by Jean Corston, MP for Bristol East, *Hansard*, 26 October 1994, cols 699–700

Note: *Hansard* substituted the following for the typewritten answer: £936 for £996; £10,140 for £10,616; £16,952 for £16,592.

CURRENT EXCHANGES ABOUT LOW INCOME STATISTICS

With the emergence of new evidence, in official reports and separately, in reworking and extending official data – in answers to parliamentary questions, and in 'secondary analysis' carried out by different bodies (for example by the Bristol Statistical Monitoring Unit, in Townsend 1991a and 1991b, Townsend and Gordon 1992, or the Institute for Fiscal Studies: Johnson and Webb 1990a, 1990b, 1992), the exchanges inside and outside Parliament have continued. Jean Corston wrote to the Prime Minister on 17 February 1995, and her letter was answered by the Secretary of State for Social Security, Peter Lilley, on 4 April 1995. He was 'not clear' why she suggested that the government 'is withholding information', and he directed attention both to the range of published statistical reports and to the policies of his department which 'will help the least well-off'. In a speech on 10 July 1995 he seized on a report examining the movement of households into and out of the poorest tenth of households from one year to the next. Clearly the rise and fall of living standards is important. But the question is whether the degree and extent of such movement is greater than it has been in the past; whether the movement is cyclical, generational, developmental, terminal, serious in the sense that it crosses a major threshold, or minimal and short term.

What has happened is that departmental statisticians appear to have been colluding with ministers to circumvent questions addressed strictly to trends in the disposable incomes of particular ranks of the population. One diversion has been, as in this example, to claim that many poor families do not stay poor, that incomes often fluctuate and, somehow, this excuses the phenomenon. Another is to call attention to changes in the composition of the poor (more self-employed, more one-parent families, and more unemployed, and fewer pensioners, for example) as if this is a sufficient explanation of their low income. A third has been to claim that the poor spend more than the amounts that have been registered as representing their income, but this neglects expenditure from savings and loans and neglects too those people who spend less than their designated income. And yet a fourth diversion has been to claim that more of the poor than in the past have consumer goods like telephones and videos, when no attention is called to any corresponding deterioration in, say, access to free or subsidised public services and utilities, deterioration in conditions at work or of work, and risk of homelessness.

These examples help to convey the nature of the controversy about the statistics of poverty. They attract more (diversionary) attention than they did in the past, but none of them is new (Townsend 1972; 1979: esp. 262–7). Each of them is important in any overall analysis of the statistics of poverty. But all of them deserve dignified rebuttal if they are put forward as governing statements of structural trends. Important they may be, but they are subsidiary factors. Investigation of the statistics of poverty leads to an insistence on the question of proportionate importance and priority.

THE PROBLEMS OF PERCEPTION AND SELECTION

Differences of opinion about the reading of statistics which have been illustrated above apply widely both in the sciences and the social sciences. How can an observer deal with them and attempt to sort out truth from falsehood? In this instance it is clear that representatives of the two principal political parties have different interests. A Prime Minister will not easily accept trends which appear to throw doubt on the effects of the policies which his or her government has adopted. Similarly, an opposition spokesperson will be looking for evidence of the failings in those selfsame policies. Both expect different results from their own principles and policies. And this calls attention to the different perceptions which are held, although those are themselves entrenched in a complex structure of organisation and belief.

It would be wrong to dismiss the exchange as a simple example of political bias. Political representatives need repeated confirmation of the courses of action which they have chosen, and therefore of the grounds for choosing that action in the first place. They require support of a statistical and scientific kind as well as personal political and public support. In short, perceptions of social conditions are 'structured', and the corresponding measurements and explanations of those conditions and the action taken to treat those conditions are also 'structured'. In disentangling the structural context of the production, presentation and selection of statistics a student has to examine each of the principal connecting links, remembering that each group and organisation has its own role to play and a perspective which itself has to be explained.

THE STATISTICAL ROLE OF A GOVERNMENT DEPARTMENT

How does a government department uphold a minister's, including a Prime Minister's, position? There is of course a duty to the government's statistical service in general, and to the edicts of the statistical profession (Moser 1980, Royal Statistical Society 1991, Nissel 1995b). There are the cumulative traditions and practices of the statistics branch of a particular department of state. New recruits to the staff quickly learn what these are. There are also technical developments of expertise which all such branches or units are eager to display. This is partly a question of pride in keeping up with advances in computers and software, for example, but also in gaining ascendancy by adopting new or newly fashionable statistical methods.

To say these are temptations is not to reject them, or to reject the strength of their appeal in particular places. But they need to be placed in proportion. In a correct, but perhaps muted form, the problem has been set out by the former head of the Government Statistical Service (Moser 1980) and by Muriel Nissel, in her review marking the 25th edition of the publication of *Social Trends*, the government's annual statistical report. In an unprecedented step her review was withdrawn from intended publication by the government's chief statistician, Bill McLennan, because it was over-political in interpretation, and has since been published elsewhere (Nissel 1995a, 1995b). This censorship was reported widely in the press. The review illustrates the growth of concern about official statistics but, like the strictures from the Royal Statistical Society (1991), this might be said to be gently expressed. Thus, the 1995 edition of *Social Trends* omitted a table given in the previous year (Table 5.21) about trends in the distribution of income, and, despite growing concern about mortality by occupational or social class in the UK and many other countries, failed to represent the trends in its pages. The same is true of

35

alternative measures of trends in unemployment, homelessness and other forms of deprivation.

REVIEWING A KEY OFFICIAL STATISTICAL PUBLICATION

Here one major source of official statistics about low income will be illustrated. The series of reports on *Households Below Average Income* (*HBAI*) produced by the DSS (see DSS 1990a, 1993, 1994, 1995a) provides examples of both selection in narrow ministerial interests and lack of proportion generally in the presentation of information about the distribution of income.

1 *There is no acceptance in official publications of a meaningful concept of 'poverty'*, despite protracted discussion and operational measurement by the United Nations, the World Bank, the European Union and nearly all of the nation states of the world, including the United States.

2 *The measurement of low income is unnecessarily restricted and the statistical output therefore of limited value.* The practice of measuring low income in relation to minimum rates of benefit in social security, which was sustained under successive governments during the 1970s and early 1980s, was abandoned in favour of a more aseptic relative measure (DHSS 1988). The Select Committee for Social Services (for example Social Services Committee 1988, 1990) and then the Select Committee on Social Security (for example Social Security Committee 1991, 1995, DSS 1993, 1995b) questioned this practice and urged the government to think again. It was felt to be useful as well revealing to show how many income units in the population had more or less than the minimum levels decided for benefit. These select committees (which, as in the case of all parliamentary committees, consist of a majority of members from the government side of the House) went so far as to commission parallel sets of statistical data. But the government resisted the continuation of the old series and has continued to provide obstacles to any restoration of that practice. There are of course objections to any particular methodology. The government makes little concession to the criticisms of its present methodology, and despite reasoned arguments for a continuation in some form of the old series reiterates the old objections: that supplementary benefit and income support need to be standardised in relation to a price index; that there is under-reporting of receipt of income support; that actual family income of recipients of income support is not calculated; and that 'the analysis sheds no light on how low income families fare relative to the rest of society' (DSS 1995b: 5). The Select Committee and organisations like the Child Poverty Action Group and the Institute for Fiscal Studies

have put forward various ways by which the criticisms could be met or accommodated. The last point quoted is especially surprising, published as it was in 1995. With the exception of a few tables in appendices, the annual *HBAI* reports do not compare the poorest with the richest income groups.

3 *The HBAI reports do not examine the growing divide between rich and poor.* This undermines their usefulness. During the 1980s and 1990s perhaps the greatest structural change in world society has been the growing inequality, or polarisation, between richest and poorest countries but also between rich and poor within both rich and poor countries (Townsend 1993). One principal value in examining low income within any country must be to examine relativity to high income, with all the consequential knowledge which arises from comparisons by economic and family status, and the distribution of earnings and taxation. During a period when the incomes of the richest groups in society have increased more substantially than in any comparable period of twentieth-century history it is not easy to condone a government methodology which excludes the richest half of the population. That is also theoretically barren, because the incomes of the poor are not only the responsibility of the poor. They are members of institutions for earnings, pensions, taxes, building society mortgages and the rest which deal with all, or cross-sections, of the population. And it is equally injudicious in relation to policy, because without information about the effects of different systems of the distribution and redistribution of income there is small scope either for necessary new policies or for fine-tuning.

4 *Significant features of trends in the distributions of income have been distorted.* The problem of distortion can arise from dense presentation of complex issues without prioritisation, through omission, and through selected emphasis. Thus one of the latest *HBAI* reports covers 185 pages, including five pages of summary, fifty-three of text, fifty-six of tables and seventy-one of appendices. The summary does not make the relative losses on the part of the lower half of the population the central feature of its analysis. The diminishing gains of each successive income group on page 62, for example, is not highlighted in the summary as it deserves to be highlighted, and there are no reasoned explanations of the different contributory elements (for example see Rowntree 1995, the report of the Joseph Rowntree Foundation on incomes and wealth). After sixteen years it is surely exceptional in post-war history that the poorest third of the population have gained so little from economic growth and that large sections among them have gained nothing at all and even incurred losses. If there is such as thing as statistical news, then this must be news.

The ramifications in official statistics of 'distortion' must also be noted.

The side headings are distorting. The first side heading in the summary in the report published in 1995 is 'Income Growth' – under which a reference to the *loss* of the poorest tenth (decile) is placed down page. Under the side heading 'Income Growth in Economic Status Groups' we discover that two of the groups singled out, the poorest 20 per cent of unemployed, and the poorest 20 per cent of self-employed, experienced a *fall* in disposable income in the fourteen years covered by the report. Moreover the summary glosses over a highly important finding tucked away in Appendix 11.

We find in the Appendix that statisticians in the DSS had developed two rock-bottom definitions of low income: (1) below the 1979 average income of the poorest tenth; and (2) below half average 1979 household income for the whole population. Note that the baseline in both cases is 1979 income. In the 1995 report the number of people in households with less than the 1979 income of the poorest tenth had grown from 990,000 in 1979 to 1.68 million in 1992–93. And the problem for families in work who have children can also be shown. The number of children in households with full-time workers and incomes below half the 1979 average is up from 426,000 in 1979 to 1.25 million in 1992–93. Perhaps such illustrations help to show that different structural trends have to be ranked in terms of their importance, but also have to be theorised so that the connections can be properly made in developing an exposition to do with the composition of low income groups by economic and family status as well as quantities of income from different sources.

There are other important criticisms: the poorest households are under-represented – corresponding in some ways with large-scale non-response to the 1991 Census (see Simpson and Dorling 1994). Homeless people are not represented at all. The DSS has failed so far to help meet the need to develop a more inclusive measure of income (especially to cover forms of wealth – see Good 1990) and it is not yet known whether the long-awaited results of the Family Resources Survey will fill the gap. Compared with, say, the practice of the equivalent US administration there is unnecessary delay in publishing results, and the DSS resists publishing general distributional data for single years. As a review of the *HBAI* methodology concluded:

> There is an insufficient sense of urgency in publishing results; the basic information is overlaid and reformulated in ways which are not scientifically or statistically justified; and too little attempt has been made to improve and supplement the collection of basic information about income.
>
> (Townsend and Gordon 1992: 27)

CONCLUSION

Detailed examination of the recent history of official statistics of poverty and low income, and especially the DSS reports of *Households Below Average Income*, demonstrates the need for a transformation in their production, treatment and publication. From the time of the publication of the Rayner review onwards (Rayner 1980) strong dissatisfaction has been expressed professionally (Royal Statistical Society 1991, Taylor 1990) and publicly (for example Phillips 1990, 1991, Oppenheim 1990) about official statistics. One journalist who has devoted much of his career to reporting social trends has concluded that 'the integrity of the service – and even more departments which produce reports of their own – fall way below the independence and impartiality that was achieved in the 1970s' (Dean 1995: 2).

The criticisms have also arisen from within the Conservative government's own ranks. In a lengthy analysis of increases in the extent of poverty a member of the Cabinet in the early 1980s, Sir Ian Gilmour, has said:

> Measuring poverty in the Thatcher era is difficult because of the inadequacy, and sometimes deliberate obfuscation, of government statistics. That in itself is revealing. Just as a government will only find it necessary to fiddle the unemployment figures when unemployment is rising fast, it will only fudge and conceal the figures on poverty when it knows that poverty is spreading; when a government is reducing poverty it will make the statistics as transparent as possible and loudly proclaim them.
>
> (Gilmour 1992: 112–13, and generally Chapter 6)

There are defensive statements in official reports (for example Government Statistical Service 1995, Eurostat 1993: 115–29). On behalf of Eurostat the need for greater scientific *independence* of statistics has been acknowledged as also *national* instead of *government* control of them (Eurostat 1993: 220).

Suitable action to remedy the problems in British official statistics of poverty and low income could flow, perhaps unexpectedly, from the agreement reached at the Copenhagen World Summit on Social Development, March 1995 (attended by 117 heads of state) to 'elaborate at the national level, the measurements, criteria and indicators for determining the extent and distribution of absolute poverty. Each country should develop a precise definition and assessment of absolute poverty'. And 'national poverty eradication plans' should be drawn up to 'address the structural causes of poverty, encompassing action on the local, national, subregional, regional and international levels. These plans should establish, within each national context, strategies and affordable time-bound goals and targets for the substantial reduction of overall poverty and the eradication of absolute poverty' (UN 1995a: paras 26b and 26d). A range of policy measures, but also statistical measures to monitor different trends, is set out (see UN 1995a: paras 26–30 in particular).

Organisationally, this would mean, following the recommendations of the Royal Statistical Society, establishing a statistical service more independent of government, including the appointment of a National Statistical Commission. The Labour Party has put forward a similar proposal for an independent National Statistical Service (Straw 1995). Perhaps this might be achieved, with an eye on international developments, in conjunction with the introduction of a Freedom of Information Act.

There would be implications not just for government statisticians, but for statisticians elsewhere. New work would have to be done on the scientific criteria of alternative definitions and measures of poverty for international and national use (Townsend 1994). Perceived meanings and effects of poverty would have to be distinguished better from independently validated meanings and effects. The possibilities of creative statistical work of practical value nationally and internationally on poverty have never been greater. But work independent of government and which is adequately resourced within public service needs to be guaranteed.

APPENDIX: EXCHANGE IN PRIME MINISTER'S QUESTIONS, 1994

22 February 1994

Ms Corston: Is the Prime Minister aware that *Social Trends 1994*, a Government publication, reveals that as a direct consequence of Tory Government policy since 1979 the average disposable income of the richest 20 per cent of households has increased by £6,000 a year while the 20 per cent of households at the bottom of the income scale have had their average disposable income cut by £3,000 a year? Does that reveal the hypocrisy of the Prime Minister's professed commitment to creating a nation at ease with itself?

The Prime Minister: The hon. Lady was being selective in what she said – [*Interruption*]. She was selective from the report. The net disposable income of people at all ranges of income has increased and the proportion of total tax take paid by those on top incomes has increased, not been reduced.

24 February 1994

Mr John Smith: On Tuesday this week the Prime Minister, in answering a question from my hon. Friend the Member for Bristol, East [Ms Corston] told the House that the net disposable income of people of all ranges of income had increased since 1979. The Prime Minister must know that that was not correct. Will he now withdraw that remark?

The Prime Minister: No, I shall not withdraw it . . . . In fact, I was about to quote, as it might be helpful to the House if I do. The latest edition of *Social Trends* found that 'before housing costs, the real median income of the bottom fifth increased . . . between 1979 and 1990–1991'.

Those figures, of course were taken at the bottom of the recession before there was a distinct improvement in the economy and in the position of most people.

Mr John Smith: Did the Prime Minister look at the publication issued by the Department of Social Security – by his own Government – which made it clear on page 1 that the real income of the bottom 10 per cent decreased both before and after housing costs were taken into account? Which is correct – the Prime Minister's assertions or what his own Department has published?

The Prime Minister: I responded earlier by quoting what was actually said in *Social Trends*. I will say this to the right hon. and learned Gentleman. Since 1979 real incomes have gone up sharply for vulnerable groups; more than 40 per cent for pensioners; up for the unemployed and up for those in work but on relatively low pay. There is an improvement in living standards at all levels, even among those who are the least well off.

Mr John Smith: Can I take the Prime Minister to the precise point on which we are in dispute? Does he maintain that the real income of the bottom 10 per cent of the population increased between 1979 and now?

The Prime Minister: I quoted to the right hon. and learned Gentleman – [Hon. Members: 'Answer'.] I will answer the question. The right hon. and learned Gentleman put the question in his own way. I will answer the question in my own way. I refer him to *Social Trends*, which relates to the original question. The figures for the poorest 20 per cent relate to a time when we were in recession and mortgage rates were high. I stick to the points I made a few moments ago.

REFERENCES

Bradbury, B. (1989) 'Family size equivalence scales and survey evaluations of income and well-being', *Journal of Social Policy* 18, 3: 383–408.

Buhmann, B., Rainwater, L., Schmaus, G. and Smeeding, T. (1989) 'Equivalence scales, well-being, inequality, and poverty: sensitivity estimates across ten countries using the Luxembourg Income Study (LIS) database', *Review of Income and Wealth*: 115–42.

Central Statistical Office (1995) *Social Trends* 25, London: HMSO.

Committee on Ways and Means, US House of Representatives (1995) *Overview of*

Entitlement Programs, 1995 Green Book, Washington DC: US Government Printing Office.

Corston, J. (1994) Written answers to parliamentary questions about low income (collected set), *Hansard*, 26 October, cols 689–703.

Dean, M. (1995) 'The taboo subject', *The Guardian* 1 February.

DHSS (1988) *Low Income Statistics, Report of a Technical Review*, London: Department of Health and Social Security.

Douglas-Hamilton, Lord J. (1995) Speech in House of Commons, *Hansard*, 28 June, cols 891–2.

DSS (1988) *The Measurement of Living Standards for Households Below Average Income*, Reply by the government to the fourth report from the Select Committee on Social Services (Cm 523), London: HMSO.

—— (1990a) *Households Below Average Income: A Statistical Analysis 1981–87*, London: Government Statistical Service, July.

—— (1990b) *The Measurement of Living Standards for Households Below Average Income* (Cm 1162), London: HMSO.

—— (1991) *Households Below Average Income: Stocktaking Report of a Working Group*, London: Department of Social Security.

—— (1993) *Households Below Average Income: A Statistical Analysis 1979–1990/91*, London: HMSO.

—— (1994) *Households Below Average Income: A Statistical Analysis 1979–1991/92*, London: HMSO.

—— (1995) *Households Below Average Income: A Statistical Analysis 1979–1992/93*, London: HMSO.

Eurostat (1993) *Organisation of Statistics in the Member Countries of the European Community* (report ed. Georges Als), Luxembourg: Office for Official Publications of the European Communities.

—— (1994) *Poverty Statistics in the Late 1980s: Research Based on Micro-Data*, Luxembourg: Office for Official Publications of the European Communities.

Gilmour, Sir I. (1992) *Dancing with Dogma: Britain under Thatcherism*, London: Simon and Schuster.

Good, F. J. (1990) 'Estimates of the distribution of personal wealth', *Economic Trends* October: 137–57.

Gordon, D. and Pantazis, C. (1994) *Breadline Britain in the 1990s: a Report to the Joseph Rowntree Foundation*, York: Joseph Rowntree Foundation.

Government Statistical Service (1995) *Official Statistics Code of Practice*, London: HMSO.

Johnson, P. and Webb, S. (1990a) *Low Income Families, 1979–87*, London: Institute for Fiscal Studies.

—— (1990b) *Poverty in Official Statistics: Two Reports* (IFS Commentary 24), London: Institute for Fiscal Studies, October.

—— (1992) 'The treatment of housing in official low income statistics', *Journal of the Royal Statistical Society* Series A 155, 2: 273–90.

Moore, J. (1989) *The End of the Line for Poverty*, London: Conservative Political Centre.

Moser, C. (1980) 'Statistics and public policy', *Journal of the Royal Statistical Society* Series A 143: 1–31.

Nissel, M. (1995a) 'Vital statistics', *New Statesman and Society* 27 January: 24.

—— (1995b) 'Social trends and social change', *Journal of the Royal Statistical Society* Series A 158, 3: 491–504.

Oppenheim, C. (1990) 'Count me out: losing the poor in the numbers game', *Poverty* 76, Summer: 11–14.

Phillips, M. (1990) 'Statistics in the poverty of integrity', *Guardian* 27 July.
—— (1991) 'Private lies and public servants', *Guardian* 9 January.
Rayner, D. (1980) *Review of Government Statistical Services*, London: HMSO.
Rodgers, G. (ed.) (1995) *New Approaches to Poverty Analysis – The Poverty Agenda and the ILO*, Geneva: International Institute for Labour Studies.
Rowntree (1995) *The Joseph Rowntree Foundation Inquiry into Income and Wealth*, 2 vols, York: Joseph Rowntree Foundation.
Royal Statistical Society (1991) 'Official statistics: counting with confidence', Report of a working party on official statistics in the UK, chaired by Professor P. G. Moore, *Journal of the Royal Statistical Society* Series A, 154, 1: 23–44.
Saunders, P. and Whiteford, P. (1989) *Measuring Poverty: A Review of the Issues*, Report prepared for the Economic Planning Advisory Council, Discussion paper 89/11, Canberra: Australian Government Publishing Service.
Simpson, S. and Dorling, D. (1994) 'Those missing millions: implications for social statistics of non-response to the 1991 Census', *Journal of Social Policy* 23: 543–67.
Social Security Committee (1991) *Low Income Statistics: Households Below Average Income Tables 1988*, First report, Session 1990–1, House of Commons 401, London: HMSO.
Social Security Committee (1995) *Low Income Statistics: Low Income Families 1989– 1992* (Cm 2871), London: HMSO.
Social Services Committee (1988) *Families on Low Income: Low Income Statistics*, Fourth report, Session 1987–8, House of Commons 565, London: HMSO.
—— (1989) *Minimum Income*, Memoranda laid before the Committee, Session 1988–9, House of Commons 579, London: HMSO.
—— (1990) *Low Income Statistics*, Fourth report, Session 1989–90, London: HMSO.
Straw, J. (1995) 'Labour to establish unified National Statistical Service independent of government', Speech to the Royal Statistical Society, 27 April.
Taylor, D. (1990) 'Statistics in crisis', *Unemployment Bulletin* 34, Autumn: 16–18.
Townsend, P. (1972) 'Politics and the statistics of poverty', *Political Quarterly* 43, 1 (January–March): 103–12.
—— (1979) *Poverty in the United Kingdom*, Harmondsworth: Allen Lane and Penguin.
—— (1991a) *The Poor are Poorer: A Statistical Report on Changes in the Living Standards of Rich and Poor in the United Kingdom, 1979–1989*, 1, Bristol Statistical Monitoring Unit, Bristol: University of Bristol, Department of Social Policy.
—— (1991b) *Meaningful Statistics on Poverty 1991*, 2, Bristol Statistical Monitoring Unit, Bristol: University of Bristol, Department of Social Policy.
—— (1993) *The International Analysis of Poverty*, Hemel Hempstead: Harvester Wheatsheaf.
—— (1994) 'The need for a new international poverty line,' in D. Gordon and C. Pantazis (eds) *Breadline Britain*, York: Joseph Rowntree Foundation.
Townsend, P. and Gordon, D. (1992) *Unfinished Statistical Business on Low Incomes? A Review of New Proposals by the Department of Social Security for the Production of Public Information on Poverty*, 3, Bristol Statistical Monitoring Unit, Bristol: University of Bristol, Department of Social Policy.
UN (1995a) *World Summit for Social Development: Declaration and Programme of Action*, 6–12 March 1995, New York: United Nations.
—— (1995b) *Economic and Social Conditions*, New York: United Nations.
UNDP (1995) *Human Development Report 1994*, New York and Oxford: Oxford University Press.
Whiteford, P. (1985) *A Family's Needs: Equivalence Scales, Poverty and Social Security*, Research Paper 27, Development Division, Department of Social Security, Canberra: DSS.

World Bank (1990) *World Development Report 1990: Poverty*, Washington DC: World Bank.

—— (1993) *Implementing the World Bank's Strategy to Reduce Poverty: Progress and Challenges*, Washington DC: World Bank.

3

FIDDLING WHILE
BRITAIN BURNS?
The 'measurement' of unemployment
Ruth Levitas

The unemployment figures have, since the mid-1970s, been the most politically sensitive of official statistics. In May 1979, when Thatcher took office, the official level of unemployment in the UK was 1,299,300. In January 1982, it was over 3 million. Having conducted an election campaign showing queues of unemployed people over the slogan 'Labour isn't working', presiding over such an unprecedented rise in unemployment was embarrassing. In the early 1980s, mass unemployment appeared to be a major political problem, as well as an expensive one. As unemployment soared, so did the social security budget. Arguments abounded about exactly how many unemployed people there really were: the level of unemployment was an indicator both of the government's economic (mis)management, and of its social and moral insensitivity. By 1994, very high levels of unemployment had become unremarkable, but rises and falls in the monthly figures were still headline news and the topic of political dispute. Tony Blair became leader of a Labour Party committed to achieving full employment. Conservative politicians variously celebrated falling unemployment figures as indicative of economic recovery, or claimed, like David Hunt, that full employment was a shared aim, while Michael Portillo, Hunt's successor as Employment Minister, insisted that government intervention in the labour market was inappropriate interference with market forces (*Newsnight*, 1 August 1994).

Central to these arguments have been questions about what the unemployment figures actually mean – and particularly questions about whether falls in the figures represent real drops in unemployment, or whether they are simply the product of changes in the way the count is compiled. That there have been repeated changes in the measurement of unemployment since 1979 is widely known, and many people believe that successive Conservative governments have simply fiddled the figures for political reasons. This view is substantially correct, but is incomplete. This chapter looks at the changes in the most familiar measure of unemployment. It shows that this seriously underestimates the number of people without work, and that the progressive changes make it virtually

45

useless as an indicator of whether or not unemployment is actually rising or falling. It also raises questions about recent calls to base the headline count of unemployment on the LFS rather than the claimant count.

However, the argument developed here also challenges the conclusion that official statistics on unemployment are worse than they were in 1979. First, the way unemployment was measured then was, although less restrictive than now, inaccurate and unsatisfactory. Secondly, official statistics based on the less well-known survey measures of unemployment derived from the Labour Force Survey since 1973 provide additional information. The increasing frequency of the LFS, the improved rapidity with which results are made available in printed form, and the availability of data in computerised form for secondary analysis, provide a supplementary body of information on unemployment of which the general public is almost totally unaware. This body of data provides the basis for our detailed knowledge of many of the inadequacies of the monthly count. There are therefore contradictory trends: increasing inadequacy and manipulation of the claimant count is counterbalanced by more information from the LFS made more easily and widely available to researchers, although not generally disseminated to a wider audience. Yet the volume of the LFS data presents a problem in itself. For the sheer quantity and complexity of this information, and the possibilities of re-analysing it, obscure the fact that the definition of unemployment and the way it is measured in the LFS again lead to serious underestimates of the extent of unemployment. Even if the problems with the LFS data are not the result of overt political interference, they are none the less political questions. This chapter examines the strengths and weaknesses of both sets of official statistics on unemployment, and looks at some alternative, unofficial estimates with which they can be compared.

THE CLAIMANT COUNT

Every month, radio and television newsreaders inform the nation of 'the number of people out of work and claiming benefits' in the previous month. Between May and June 1994, this figure fell by a little over 67,000 to 2,585,590, of whom 1,988,759 were men and 596,831 were women; in April 1994, 1,046,000 people had been unemployed for over a year (LRDFS, 21 June 1994). This measure of unemployment, referred to as the claimant count, is an administrative measure, a by-product of processes whereby the state provides limited material support for those unable to find work, and attempts to intervene in the labour market to match the supply and demand of labour, and/or to police the 'work-shy': the history of the definition and measurement of unemployment is bound up with these processes of state intervention (Burnett 1994, Morris 1994, Whiteside 1991).

The claimant count is normally carried out on the second Thursday of each month, and is based on computerised records of those successfully claiming unemployment benefit, successfully claiming income support on grounds of unemployment, or successfully claiming national insurance credits on the same grounds. The statistical tables in the monthly *Employment Gazette* give raw figures and figures broken down by age, gender, duration of unemployment, region, parliamentary constituency and travel-to-work area.[1] These figures are given both for the UK and for Great Britain (i.e. both including and excluding Northern Ireland), and when making comparisons between different sets of data it is important to ensure that the coverage is comparable. Unemployment figures are also available on-line.

The Department of Employment's own statisticians recognise that there are weaknesses in the claimant count as a measure of unemployment. Its positive aspects are those associated with any administrative source of statistics: they are relatively inexpensive; they are available quickly, on a frequent and regular basis; and, because they give a 100 per cent count, figures can be broken down for small areas. There are, however, a number of disadvantages. The figures cannot be used for international comparisons. Information about the characteristics of unemployed people is limited to that collected for administrative purposes (i.e. we know a little bit about a large number of people). The most serious disadvantage is that since the coverage depends on administrative rules, and changes whenever the administrative system changes, there are discontinuities in the statistics (Woolford *et al.* 1994).

This neutral term 'discontinuity' does not fully reveal what has happened in recent years. In times of rapidly rising unemployment, attempts to limit eligibility for benefits in order to control public expenditure mean that these 'discontinuities' result in reductions in the total count. This has been the case in the 1980s, as it was in the 1930s (Whiteside 1991: 72–85). The discontinuities in the count do not affect all groups of unemployed people equally. In recent years, they have affected women and young people disproportionately. Sometimes the goals of saving money and reducing the unemployment count come into conflict. This dilemma underlay the furore over invalidity benefits early in 1994: increasing numbers of people were being declared eligible for this benefit, which is slightly more generous than unemployment benefit and income support, simultaneously increasing public spending and reducing the numbers of claimant unemployed – revealing a conflict of interest between the Treasury and the Departments of Social Security and of Employment.

What, then, is the coverage of the claimant count, and how has this changed? In order to qualify for the benefits listed above, people must declare that for each day for which a claim is made they are unemployed, capable of work and available for work, and that they have been actively seeking work in the week for which they are claiming. Unemployed people who do not make a claim for benefits, or whose claim is disallowed for any reason, will not appear in the figures. Many people who are unemployed, however, will not be eligible for unemployment benefit, a contributory benefit with a current maximum duration of twelve months, or for income support, a benefit means-tested on household income; eligibility for national insurance credits, although more widespread, is less of an inducement to claim, since it affects future pension entitlement rather than immediate resources. Moreover, since married women may expect to derive pension rights from their husbands' national insurance contributions (although they lose these rights if they are divorced and the husband subsequently remarries), they are less likely to register. Many people who might reasonably appear eligible for unemployment benefit or income support on current criteria may have their claims disallowed, especially if they are deemed to be restricting their availability for work (Bryson and Jacobs 1992). Even assuming that the claimant count is reasonably accurate in relation to what it covers (which requires considerable faith in computers and their operators), there is no doubt that many unemployed people are excluded, especially women.

Prior to 1982, the unemployment count was not a claimant count; but a clerical, non-computerised, count of those registered at job centres or careers offices as seeking work, whether or not they were eligible for or claiming benefits. Registration was compulsory for those claiming benefits, but optional for others. The crucial change to a computerised count of claimants followed the publication in 1981 of a report by Derek Rayner, the *Report on the Payment of Benefits to Unemployed People*. The importance of this change was not simply that it removed an estimated 200,000 people from the count, but that it ensured that thereafter all changes in eligibility for benefits had an inevitable effect upon the count itself. A total of thirty changes were made to the employment count between 1979 and 1989, including the change from those registered for work to those in receipt of benefit; some further changes had been implemented or announced by the summer of 1994 (Taylor 1990, Gregg 1994). These changes have progressively limited entitlement to benefits. There are thus three consequences of the changes in the claimant count. First, there is the effect upon unemployed people of a benefit system using increasingly stringent criteria for the receipt of declining amounts of benefit. Secondly, the count cannot be treated as a continuous series, as its coverage becomes narrower over time. Thirdly, it cannot be regarded as a measure of unemployment. The examples below illustrate what some of the exclusionary changes mean and how the constant changes in the figures represent an increasingly punitive regime for unemployed people.

Young people have been particular victims of the changes. The 1988

48

Social Security Act removed benefit entitlement for almost all those under 18, and eliminated them from the count. Recent estimates suggest that in 1993, the average number of 16- and 17-year-olds unemployed on the still quite restrictive LFS definition (see p. 55) was 140,900, of whom 113,400 had no income at all. In the winter of 1993–94, of 122,500 unemployed young people, only 16,700 were included in the count (UUWB, July 1994). The rising incidence of destitution among young people, visible in our cities in recent years, is partly the result of this change.

Other changes have affected all age groups. The changes which have been most punitive for adult claimants, as well as having a significant effect on the figures, are those concerning the criteria for availability for or actively seeking work. From 1986, claimants were subjected to increasing scrutiny as to their availability. Women with children were particularly badly hit by the new test, because claimants were required to demonstrate that they were available within twenty-four hours, and mothers were required to show that they could immediately find full-time child-care for those below school age and part-time for older children, by someone other than a relative. If unable to do so, they were regarded as not available for work. In 1987, there were 107,000 disallowances of unemployment benefit claims for this reason alone (Whiteside 1991: 88).

The operation of the Restart programme, which was introduced in 1986 for those unemployed more than twelve months (later reduced to six months), has also led to withdrawal of benefit on grounds of non-availability. Claimants can be suspended from benefit for failure to attend Restart interviews: if they are not available for the interview, they are deemed not to be available for work, in some cases even if the reason for non-attendance is a hospital appointment which would be reasonable grounds for not being at work. The 1989 Social Security Act required that claimants must not only be available for work, but be able to prove that they were actively seeking it. (This Act also denies unemployed people the right to turn down any job of more than twenty-four hours per week, however poor the pay and conditions, after an initial period of unemployment of thirteen weeks.) In April 1990, the new Employment Service was launched, removing the separation between counselling about or policing of jobsearch activities by claimants, and benefit scrutiny; the Secretary of State announced 'a new advisory interview after 13 weeks of unemployment with a check on activity in looking for a job' (Bryson and Jacobs 1992: 16). Pressure has thus been put on claimants to justify their status at an increasingly early stage, partly in the hope that they can be excluded for not 'really' seeking work, or induced to stop claiming.

The process of closer policing of availability and jobsearch has continued, with new compulsory courses (Restart, Jobplan Workshops) for the long-term unemployed and for the young (Workwise). Pressure to pursue the issue of whether claimants are actively seeking work has

49

increased. The Employment Service has performance targets for identifying doubtful claims, irrespective of the number of such claims actually made (UUWB, July 1994: 3); in August 1994, Michael Portillo issued instructions which nearly doubled these targets (*Guardian* 18 August 1994). In May 1994, a memo suggested that hard-to-fill vacancies should be used to 'test' whether claimants are available for and actively seeking work (UUWB, July 1994). Between April 1994 and January 1995, 142,000 'doubtful' benefit claims had been referred, of which 80 per cent resulted in a benefit cut; this compares with about 110,000 referrals of which 50 per cent resulted in disqualification, in the corresponding period the previous year (LRDFS, 30 March 1995). Not only do these changes mean that an increasing number of unemployed people who attempt to claim will be denied benefit: the number of disallowances takes no account of those deterred by the increasingly stringent conditions from making a claim in the first instance. Those disqualified from benefit, or deterred from claiming, do not appear in the count.

In 1996, the introduction of the Jobseeker's Allowance (JSA) and Jobseeker's Agreement will lead to more changes of the same kind. Benefit rates will be brought in line with income support, and eligibility for contributory benefit will last only six months and include no allowances for dependants; those aged 18–25 will be paid at a reduced rate from the outset. After six months, the JSA will be means-tested for all (*Jobseeker's Allowance* 1994). The effect will be to reduce the income of the unemployed – and to reduce the figures yet again. The numbers of women counted as unemployed will fall disproportionately, since fewer women currently claiming unemployment benefit would be eligible for means-tested benefits. The Jobseeker's Agreement will increase yet again the difficulty of the hoops through which unemployed people have to jump to qualify for benefit, and deter still more unemployed people from claiming. The Unemployment Unit estimates that if applied to the July 1993 figures, the effect would be to remove 90,000 from the claimant count and save £210 million, as well as producing job losses in the Civil Service (UUWB, January 1994).

The statistical tables in the *Employment Gazette* also give 'seasonally adjusted' figures, which take account of the fact that unemployment is affected by seasonal factors such as the weather and holiday periods. The purpose of adjusting the figures to compensate for these seasonal variations is that it gives a clearer view of the overall trend. The adjustment is carried out using a statistical package called X11 (Lawlor 1990, White and Whitton 1993). Seasonal adjustment is in itself a perfectly reasonable procedure: however, the 'seasonally adjusted' figures at both national and regional level are also subjected to further adjustments known as 'current updating', which means that these series now systematically underestimate unemployment and rewrite history.

UNEMPLOYMENT

Current updating means that in order to produce a continuous series of figures, earlier figures are revised (downwards) to take account of changes which have subsequently taken place. 'Each time there is a change in coverage, the consistent series is recalculated for every month back to 1971 nationally and back to 1974 regionally' (Lawlor 1990: 602). This gives rise to a series known as SAUCCC – Seasonally Adjusted Unemployment Consistent with Current Coverage. In fact, not every change is incorporated into the backdated figures, but only those deemed changes in rules (such as no longer counting men over 60). Administrative changes like the new availability of work test in 1986, or 'purely statistical' changes such as delaying the compilation of statistics to 'reduce . . . over-recording' are not adjusted for (Lawlor 1990: 603). Only eight of the thirty changes between 1979 and 1990 were in fact incorporated in the production of a continuous series 'consistent with current coverage', but this was sufficient to constitute a thoroughly Orwellian rewriting of history. One version of this series tells us that the figures for the UK for May 1979 and January 1982 (given unadjusted in the first paragraph of this chapter as 1,299,300 and just over 3 million) were, on a seasonally adjusted basis consistent with coverage in December 1990 just 1,087,000 and 2,424,200.

THE UNEMPLOYMENT UNIT INDEX

The Unemployment Unit (an independent body) has dealt with the problem of discontinuity in a different way. Rather than subjecting the historical record to progressive amendment, for several years it calculated an index of unemployment based on the pre-1982 criteria. It revised the current figures upwards, rather than revising earlier figures downwards. Figures for the period 1982–93 can be obtained from the Unemployment Unit, and were routinely published monthly by *Labour Research*. The Unemployment Unit has stopped producing the index for two reasons. First, as time passes since changes were made to the basis of the claimant count, it becomes progressively more difficult to provide reliable estimates of what current levels of unemployment would have been if counted on earlier criteria. Secondly, the Unemployment Unit is supporting calls for measures of unemployment to be based principally upon the LFS, and thus now uses a measure derived from this.

The estimated continuous series given by the Unemployment Unit Index showed the dramatic effect on the unemployment count of the changes since 1979. It also suggested that the 'real' level of unemployment was much higher than that given by the claimant count. However, although there is no doubt that this index was a better indicator of unemployment than the claimant count, it was never an accurate estimate. To treat it in this way would be to assume that the pre-1982 definition of

51

unemployment and procedure for producing the count resulted in an accurate figure. But criticism of the figures is not new. Right-wing critics claimed that the pre-1982 figures overestimated the true level of unemployment by including school-leavers, job-changers, unemployable and voluntarily unemployed people as well as those fraudulently claiming benefits while working. The Institute of Economic Affairs, a right-wing think-tank, even argued that the proper way to compile an index of unemployment was to include only men between the ages of 25 and 55 who had been unemployed for more than six months (Wood 1972, 1975, Miller and Wood 1982). Left-wing critics argued that the official figures already underestimated unemployment principally by excluding those on government schemes, short-time workers, and the unregistered unemployed. There was clear evidence from other sources, including the General Household Survey and the Census, that even prior to 1982 there was a substantial amount of unregistered unemployment. And this evidence also showed that the figures systematically under-represented unemployment among women. The reliance on a measure of unemployment based on an administrative system within which women's entitlement to benefits was minimal was never satisfactory (Callender 1992).

The Unemployment Unit Index (UUI) therefore showed the extent to which repeated changes have reduced the count, not the real level of unemployment. However, a continuous series based on the pre-1982 definition has some merits compared with the SAUCCC series, despite Lawlor's claim that the technique of current updating 'has both conceptual and practical advantages over the alternative of attempting to assess what unemployment would now be on a basis of previous coverage' because this alternative 'would involve speculation about what the effect of demographic, economic and other changes on the figures might have been' (Lawlor 1990: 602). A recent Royal Statistical Society report agreed that the Employment Department was right to use SAUCCC as the best method for producing a consistent series (RSS 1995: 6). But if it is used to indicate changes in the actual level of unemployment, it is severely misleading. In fact, both approaches require estimates to be made. The trends shown over the ten-year period of the UUI do not differ markedly between the two series; but the UUI shows a consistently higher level. Since it is clear that the claimant count underestimates unemployment, it seems perverse to use figures which further understate it.

THE LABOUR FORCE SURVEY

In order to calculate the probable discrepancy between the claimant count and earlier definitions of unemployment, detailed information about specific groups of the population and their labour market activity, or lack of it, is necessary. Much of this information is drawn from the Labour Force Survey, which also provides a separate measure of unemployment based on an agreed definition permitting international comparisons (White and Leyland 1992). Other advantages of the survey measure of unemployment are that more information is collected about the individuals interviewed than is available from the claimant count, so that more detailed analysis is possible; and the same source provides parallel data on employment and 'economic inactivity'. But, like all surveys, the LFS is much more expensive to produce than the claimant count, and is subject to sampling and response errors. And because it is a sample survey rather than a count, the numbers in individual sub-groups may be too small to be relied on. The time needed to process survey data has in the past meant a delay of several months before the results became available; changes in the methodology and the use of up-to-date technology mean this now happens less often.

The LFS is a sample survey of private households conducted by OPCS, which has been carried out every two years from 1973 to 1983, then annually until 1991, and quarterly from 1992. The large national sample drawn from the Post Office Address File has a response rate of over 80 per cent, resulting in an effective sample of about 60,000 households or 150,000 individuals. Detailed information on economic activity and related topics is collected through a complex questionnaire administered by trained interviewers. The annual surveys were primarily carried out in the spring of each year, with most interviews conducted between March and May, on a total sample of about 60,000. Since 1992, this number of interviews has been conducted each quarter, on a rolling sample whereby 12,000 respondents are replaced each quarter, and information is sought from each participating household for five successive quarters, tracing changes over a full year. The results are grossed up to provide estimates for the population as a whole. With the move to the quarterly survey, there was some extension to the coverage of the sample, and changes were introduced into the method of conducting the interviews. Previously, all interviews were conducted face to face with conventional paper questionnaires, which were subsequently coded and analysed. Now computer assisted interviewing (CAI) has been introduced, and results are entered directly into portable computers, which route interviewers through the program. This diminishes error and non-response at the interviewing stage, and speeds up the whole process, making results available within three months of the end of each quarter, far more quickly than hitherto (Chamberlain and Purdie 1992). Repeat interviews may be conducted by telephone. Whether the use of computers and telephone interviews reduces the accuracy of the results is an open question.

Irrespective of the interview mode, a number of questions arise about the accuracy of the LFS. Like all survey research, the limits of the target population and the sampling frame, as well as response bias, may affect the results. Where unemployment is concerned, the exclusion of most of those living outside private households, for example in hostels or indeed without a fixed address, is likely to lead to an underestimate of the true numbers – especially given the rise in homelessness in recent years. Secondly, the results are subject to sampling error, the extent of which is rarely stated in conjunction with the results as they are used (although limited calculations now are included in the survey results themselves). Thirdly, the definitions used and the structure of the questionnaire exclude some groups who might reasonably be considered unemployed. One aspect of this is that those who are self-employed cannot be counted as unemployed, even if they have done no work, if their 'enterprise' continues (they are also ineligible for unemployment-related benefits). In industries as different as building and film and television, it is customary for people to be self-employed, but also to be contracted for specified periods, with potentially long gaps in between. The LFS does not recognise this as unemployment. With the general increase in self-employment and 'flexible working', this is likely to produce an under-estimate of unemployment. Fourthly, the information given about individuals may not be wholly accurate. The problem is not just that people may deliberately or otherwise misrepresent their own situation, but that about 30 per cent of the data is provided by proxy informants: if an individual is unavailable for interview, information may be sought from a related adult member of the same household. This applies not just to general information about employment status and occupation, but to detailed questions about hours of work, and, for the unemployed, jobsearch activities or reasons for not seeking work – matters on which accurate knowledge about another person may be quite unlikely. Students at boarding schools or living in halls of residence at colleges and universities are treated as part of their parents' household and information on them is collected by proxy.

Despite these limitations, the information provided by the LFS is invaluable for anyone seeking to explore labour market activity by different groups. Because the survey is so detailed, it is possible to look at the experiences of particular groups, by age, gender, ethnicity or levels of education (Woolford *et al.* 1994). It is LFS data which is used to estimate the numbers of young unemployed people excluded from the claimant count and from benefit. The LFS also provides information on ethnicity and unemployment, showing that unemployment is on average twice as high among ethnic minority groups, although it varies considerably between different ethnic minority groups as well as by age and gender (Sly 1994b). There is no doubt that the data is useful, but it must be used with care, and with close attention to the way in which it is collected.

The major problem about using the LFS as a measure of unemployment arises from the definition used. To be counted as unemployed in the LFS, respondents must have:

(a) done no paid work in the week in question (usually the week before the interview is held);
(b) wish to work;
(c) be available to work within the next fortnight;
(d) have made some effort to seek work in the past four weeks, or be waiting to start a job already obtained.

This, known as the ILO (International Labour Organisation) definition, is used because it is internationally agreed and therefore can be used for comparative purposes. Prior to 1987, the LFS calculated a different figure, based on those who had sought work in the previous week. This sometimes produced estimates for unemployment which were lower than the claimant count, and there were suggestions in the early 1980s that this should be taken as the 'official' figure. It is important to realise that this definition excludes from the ranks of the unemployed anyone who has done as little as one hour's paid work in the reference week.

The ILO definition generates figures for unemployment which are, in fact, not radically different overall from those given by the claimant count. This does not mean, however, that they suggest that the claimant count is approximately correct. The difference in definition means that we are dealing with two distinct, if overlapping, groups. The LFS routinely finds that about one-third of claimants are not unemployed on the ILO definition, while a similar number of non-claimants are unemployed (Woolford and Denman 1993). In the winter of 1993–94, of 2.74 million claimants, 0.99 million were not deemed unemployed by the LFS, and exactly the same number of unemployed non-claimants was identified.[2] Politicians and pundits are inclined to interpret this as showing that there are nearly a million claimants not 'really' unemployed. However, failure to meet the ILO criteria does not mean that people are not unemployed. They may have done some paid work in the survey week, but of course it is possible to have limited earnings from part-time (especially casual) work, and still be generally unemployed and a legitimate claimant, even if the extent to which this is possible has diminished. Those deemed 'employed' constitute just over a third of claimants not unemployed on the ILO definition. Others may be unavailable for work in the next fortnight – which could technically disqualify them from benefit. One must, however, question whether it is reasonable to expect people, especially those who have been out of work for a long time, to organise their lives so that they never have commitments which would prevent them taking up non-existent jobs immediately. Admitting such commitments to an LFS interviewer will, however, mean that respondents are deemed not available for work. Those who have not actively sought work in the last four weeks, are, like those unavailable, deemed to be economically inactive rather than unemployed. The 'inactive' make up nearly two-thirds of those claimants deemed not to be unemployed on the ILO definition.

The discrepancy between the LFS measure and the claimant count differs for men and women. Only about a fifth of unemployed claimants are women. They are less likely to meet the contributions criteria for unemployment benefit, have additional problems in establishing availability for work, and are less likely to qualify for income support than men. Even so, a higher proportion of women claimants than men are deemed by the LFS to be not unemployed. Most strikingly, however, the LFS finds that there are nearly as many women unemployed and not claiming as there are in receipt of benefit.

It would not be unreasonable to argue that anyone who meets the increasingly stringent conditions for unemployment-related benefits, *and* anyone who meets the ILO criteria, should be regarded as unemployed. Certainly some broader definition than either the ILO definition or the claimant count seems necessary. The Unemployment Unit now bases its estimates on a 'broad LFS definition', which drops the jobsearch criterion, and includes all those who have done no paid work, would like work, and are available for work. This is easily derived from LFS data, and includes some of those currently defined as economically inactive.

'ECONOMIC INACTIVITY'

Many of those defined as economically inactive could be regarded as unemployed. Besides the 2.74 million ILO-unemployed in the winter of 1993–94, an additional 2.4 million people (over 1.4 million women, over 0.9 million men) wanted work. A million people were available to start work within the next fortnight, although they failed to qualify as unemployed because they had not been looking for work in the last four weeks. Over a million said they wanted work, although they could not start within two weeks and had not actively sought a job in the qualifying period. In both groups, women outnumbered men.

But even this does not tell the whole story. The LFS also asks about people's reasons for non-availability or for not seeking work. The reasons given in response to these questions are strongly gendered. In each case, these are the 'main' reasons; this implies a recognition that there may be other reasons as well but these are not recorded. The most common reason given by (or for) men is that they believe there are no jobs available; the LFS does not include them as unemployed, but creates a sub-category of economic inactivity, the 'discouraged worker'. The most common reason given by/for women is that they are 'looking after home and family'; they are simply deemed to be 'economically inactive'.

Even leaving aside the issue of describing domestic labour as economic inactivity (Waring 1988), we might reasonably argue that neither of these groups should be treated as economically inactive, if they want paid work and do not have it. We might argue even more strongly that they should not be treated differently on the basis of responses to this particular question, which may simply indicate women's greater capacity to occupy themselves constructively when paid work is unavailable, or the pressures on the time of most women. Even if the specific answers can be taken as general reasons for not seeking work, it is very unclear whether the different responses of men and women actually indicate a real difference in orientation to the labour market, or whether they merely illustrate different discourses with which men and women come to terms with their exclusion from it. Yet further complications arise from the fact that a third of this information comes from proxy informants, so we do not know whether we are dealing with the discourses by which people understand, explain and structure their own behaviour, or those through which they understand, explain and try to control others. We do not know whether men or women are making the claims that women are not seriously seeking work because they are looking after their homes and families. Because women are more easily defined as economically inactive – by themselves, by their partners, by statisticians – the figures are likely to understate women's unemployment to a greater extent than men's.

The sequence of the pre-1992 LFS questions about reasons for not seeking work is rather odd, and seems to makes more sense in terms of the earlier versions of the LFS, when the main definition of unemployment was based on those who had looked for work in the past week, with the broader ILO definition (jobsearch in the last four weeks) added as a supplementary question. In the 1991 questionnaire, respondents were first asked a set of questions relating to the last complete week. If they did no paid work during this week, question 88 asked 'Were you looking for any kind of paid work last week?' It is with reference to this that questions 91 and 92 probed the reasons for those who said no. Respondents were asked (question 92) 'May I just check, what was the main reason you were not looking for work last week?', and the following pre-coded mutually exclusive categories were offered:

On YT/ET
Student
Long term sick or disabled
Looking after family/home
Retired from work
Doesn't want/need employment
Believes no jobs available
Not yet started looking
Any other reason

They were then asked if they would like work, and asked about their availability. Only later were they asked about jobsearch in the last four weeks, and here there was a series of questions put about specific methods of jobsearch. Those who were 'economically inactive' were defined on the basis of their responses to these later questions, and their answers to question 92 examined. When the survey results were published, however, these replies to a question specifically about why they were not seeking work *last week* were presented as reasons for economic inactivity (Naylor and Purdie 1992: 170). Using the answer to such a specific question as the basis for statements about people's general reasons for not seeking work seems highly dubious.

With the changes to the LFS in 1992, the questionnaire was revised. Respondents are now asked whether, despite not having looked for work in the last four weeks, they would like a regular paid job, either full-time or part-time. Depending on the response, they are then asked *either* why they did not want work *or* why they did not look for it in the last four weeks (questions 159–61). This sequence of questions makes more sense than the earlier version. However, it does not overcome the problems of collecting this sort of information from proxy informants. Moreover, it means that the data on this issue from 1992 is not strictly comparable with that from earlier surveys.

THE LFS AND THE CENSUS COMPARED

The issues of the sequence and wording of questions, and of who supplies information, have been noted as a problem by Employment Department statisticians, but in relation to the Census, not the LFS. LFS results for the spring of 1991 can be compared with the results of the 1991 Census, conducted in April. The Census gives a higher figure for unemployment, 2,485,000 rather than the 2,302,000 for the LFS. One reason for this is that the LFS records more people working very short hours than the Census, which permits people in this position to define themselves as unemployed, when the LFS would not do so (Sly 1994a). The gender composition of the discrepancy between the LFS and the Census reverses that between the LFS and the claimant count: the Census actually found 95,000 fewer women described as unemployed than did the LFS, and 277,000 more men. Sly suggests three reasons for this discrepancy. First, because the Census is a self-completion questionnaire, the questions had to be kept simple, permitting more flexibility in the requirements about availability and jobsearch, and enabling 'discouraged workers' to classify themselves as unemployed. Secondly, the sequence of categories and questions may have led to more women being classified as 'looking after home/family' where this was their main actual activity, even if they were seeking work and unemployed on the LFS definition. Thirdly, Sly suggests that women *or their partners* might regard their part-time work or seeking work as less relevant than their domestic role, and raises the question of whether men are more likely to take responsibility for filling in Census forms. These problems are directly comparable to those noted above in relation to the LFS itself; the possibility that they have a larger effect in the Census does not contradict the probability that they affect the LFS data itself.

Other sources suggest that the Census may also underestimate the extent of unemployment among men, because there is a significant problem of missing data. This is a particular problem with the 1991 Census because of the effect of the poll tax; avoidance of registration for the poll tax affected electoral registration and willingness to respond to the Census. Official estimates suggested that about 1.2 million people are missing from the Census, with a predominance of young adult men in this undercount. In some urban areas, it is estimated that 25 per cent of men in their twenties are excluded from the count, and this is thought to lead to an underestimate of unemployment of about 4 per cent, or 90,000 for England and Wales (OPCS 1993, Dorling and Simpson 1993, Simpson and Dorling 1994). Later estimates suggested that the Census undercount may be as high as 2 million (see Chapter 1).

Consideration of the methods and results of the LFS therefore suggests that the level of unemployment, in the sense of the numbers of people who would like paid work but do not have it, is not only higher than the claimant count suggests, and higher than the figures contained in the LFS itself, but higher than the figure given by those qualifying on either count.

THE DISAPPEARING LABOUR FORCE

This gloomy conclusion is borne out when we look at the movement of the claimant count and the ILO measure over time. Statisticians at the Employment Department rightly observe that although the figures apply to two different constituencies, the broad movement over time of the two series is similar. They are, however, rather sanguine in apparently supposing that this suggests that changes in both measures reflect real rises and falls in unemployment. In mid-1994, even newspaper columnists noticed that, paradoxically, although unemployment (as measured both by the claimant count and by the LFS) was falling, this was accompanied by a fall, rather than a rise, in employment. If the numbers in work and the numbers out of work were dropping, the numbers in neither category, that is those 'economically inactive', must be rising. This happened in the early 1980s. Against a gradual rise in the workforce before 1980 and after 1984, there was a sudden dip in the combined total of employed and unemployed. As unemployment rose and work became more difficult to find, increasing numbers of people were either defining themselves, or being defined by official bodies, as economically inactive rather than unemployed.

The logic of this, in human terms, is not difficult to grasp. Unemployment carries a stigma of failure. And rather than aspire to the seemingly impossible, people will redefine their own situation. A redefinition as retired is culturally available at increasingly early ages, perhaps as low as 50 (and this is partly because of changes in the claimant count). A redefinition as full-time housewife and mother has always been culturally, though frequently not actually, available for women. Young people may stay at school longer and increasing numbers go into mass higher and further education; others may return to education as mature students. The group for whom such redefinitions are least available are adult men: and they make up the bulk of those the Department of Employment describes as 'discouraged workers' – that is, they want work but do not seek it because they believe none is available. This group, the 'discouraged workers', is officially regarded as economically inactive. The real difference between their situation and that of others so described may be marginal. And so too is the difference between their situation and the situation of those claimants who have very low expectations of finding work but are forced to engage in at least notional jobseeking in order to qualify for benefits. The line between 'unemployment' and 'non-employment' or 'economic inactivity' is imposed upon a reality that is far more complex and fluid. The process whereby when unemployment is high overall economic activity decreases explains the paradox of simultaneously falling unemployment and employment in 1994. As well as bringing into question the relationship between unemployment and economic inactivity, this phenomenon suggests an alternative way of looking at and estimating unemployment.

IMPLIED UNEMPLOYMENT

Both the claimant count and the LFS arrive at their figures for unemployment by attempting to identify and count the individuals concerned. In the case of the claimant count, of course, it is necessary to identify individuals, since it is they who will be eligible or ineligible for social security benefits. But in terms of the overall totals, we do not actually need to know which individuals are involved. It is possible to infer the number of unemployed by calculating the gap between the size of the total workforce and the numbers in employment. In other words, you can estimate the numbers you would expect to be working, and from the LFS and other sources (principally the Census of Employment), estimate the numbers actually in work. The difference between these gives you a figure for the level of unemployment, sometimes referred to as implied unemployment.

This technique was used by *Labour Research* in 1982, and suggested that at a time when the official total was 3 million, the real total was over 4.5

million. About 500,000 of these were people excluded from the count because they were students, were seeking part-time work, were temporarily stopped, were registered disabled, or were employed on a government training or job-creation scheme. The other million represent the gap between the total numbers employed or registered unemployed (which had dropped by 500,000 since 1979), and the potential working population, which was estimated to be 500,000 higher than the official 1979 level. The increased estimate was based partly on the estimates from the General Household Survey of the numbers of unregistered unemployed in 1979. But a major component was the calculation of how much the workforce should have grown, given the increase of 500,000 in the population of working age shown by official population statistics. Of course, not everyone of working age is part of the workforce. Economic activity rates, or labour force participation rates, vary by gender and age group, as well as over time. *Labour Research* assumed these rates constant at 1979 levels (92 per cent for men, 64 per cent for women), and showed the gap between the potential workforce and those actually in employment to be over 4.5 million. They went on to observe that this was a conservative estimate of unemployment, since the labour force participation rate of women had been rising at about 1 per cent a year throughout the 1970s. Had they assumed this trend to continue, a further 0.5 million would have been added to the figures. And 'an even more radical assumption would be that women should expect to work as much as men – this would add a further 25 per cent of women, or 4,000,000 more women kept out of work' (*Labour Research* December 1992).

At the time, this did seem a radical assumption, although it served to underline the extent to which caring responsibilities for both children and elderly or disabled relatives exclude women from paid work, and therefore the extent to which labour force participation rates are dependent upon other aspects of social policy, notably child-care provision. However, since the early 1980s, participation rates have become less unequal; women's participation in paid work has increased – albeit principally in low-paid, part-time work – while men's has declined.

Estimates of implied unemployment necessitate assumptions about participation rates, and these assumptions can always be contested. Nevertheless, it is a method which can reveal a picture of unemployment with startling discrepancies from the official picture. In 1989, MacInnes used a more sophisticated version of the same method to examine national and regional changes in unemployment between 1986 and 1988. Even the Labour Force Participation Rates assumed by MacInnes illustrate the changes taking place through the 1980s: his estimates were based on male activity rates rising from 85.9 to 86.9 per cent, and female activity rates rising from 67.0 to 69.1 per cent. On this basis, the drop in claimant unemployment of 880,000 between June 1986 and June 1988 could be shown to be almost entirely illusory, in that it represented a rise in economic inactivity, not a rise in employment. Implied unemployment in June 1988 stood at 3.5 million, compared to a claimant count of 2.2 million. MacInnes argued that those who in the past would have been able to register as unemployed were being forced off the register by cumulative changes to eligibility conditions, and further argued that the level of implied unemployment suggested that the amendments to the claimant count made for the Unemployment Unit Index were too small. (This may not be so, since not all of those shown by the implied unemployment technique to be unemployed would have been defined or accurately counted as such by the pre-1982 official count.) But MacInnes was also able to show something rather more startling, by using the method to examine regional changes in unemployment – and demonstrating that although unemployment had in fact fallen in the South (albeit not as fast as the claimant count suggested), it was continuing to rise in the north of Great Britain, especially in Scotland. The trend in the North was exactly the opposite of that suggested by the official figures.

UNDEREMPLOYMENT AND PART-TIME WORK

All of the methods for estimating unemployment are concerned with assessing the numbers of people without paid work who might be expected to be working. These figures are independent of analyses of the numbers of people in employment who are in full-time and those in part-time work. One of the striking phenomena of the 1980s was the decline in the numbers of men in full-time work, and the rise in part-time work. This rise in part-time work was most notable among women, but part-time work among men rose throughout the period as well. In the early 1990s, full-time jobs for women were also decreasing. And the definition of what constitutes full-time work was shifted downward to twenty-four hours per week by the Employment Department (although a ceiling of sixteen hours is imposed for income support purposes). Coupled with the fact that the LFS describes as 'employed' anyone undertaking any paid work, no matter how few the hours, the figures for those technically in employment (as well as those for self-employment) disguise a substantial amount of under-employment. The shortage of paid work is far worse than it looks.

AN ALTERNATIVE MEASURE?

Following the extension of the LFS, there have been a number of calls for the headline figure of unemployment to be based on this rather than on the claimant count (Gregg 1994). Bill McLennan, departing head of the Government Statistical Service, said 'nobody believes' the claimant count, and a new monthly measure should be derived from the LFS (LRDFS,

5 January 1995). In April 1995, a report from the Royal Statistical Society made the same point. It argued that measures should be derived from definitions and concepts, not administrative procedures – especially when those administrative procedures were open to abuse:

> Evidence for . . . manipulation is necessarily hard to come by . . . . The anecdotal evidence that we received about pressures to meet targets reinforced our belief that statistics derived as outputs from administrative procedures should not be used to monitor those procedures. . . . [T]he CC [claimant count] is much more susceptible to this kind of interference than survey figures based on internationally agreed definitions.
>
> (RSS 1995: 11)

The RSS did, however, draw attention to the problem of the definition of unemployment in the LFS, particularly the practice of counting people as employed on the basis of one hour's paid work. However, in June 1995, the Employment Department said that a change to an LFS-based measure would be too expensive (*Guardian* 12 June 1995). In July 1995, the Employment Department was itself abolished, and its functions split between the Department of Trade and Industry and the Department for Education (now the Department for Education and Employment), with its statisticians transferred to the CSO.

CONCLUSION

While the official figures for unemployment, especially the claimant count, grossly underestimate the extent to which people are unable to find paid work, it would be a mistake to conclude from this that official statistics in general, or even those relating to economic activity, are useless. For all the information which has been mobilised here to criticise the official unemployment figures derives from official statistics, as do all unofficial estimates. Measures of unemployment illustrate perhaps more clearly than any other area of statistics the contradictory trends of the last fifteen years. Political, ideological and financial imperatives have made the claimant count one of the worst sets of official statistics there is, and one which is regarded with widespread cynicism. But the volume of alternative information available, particularly from the Labour Force Survey, is much greater than it was in 1979, and despite the shortcomings of the data, there is considerable scope for secondary analysis. Users of this material should, however, be aware that the definitions used within it necessarily reflect the interests of the state in monitoring the labour market – and those interests may not be the same as the interests of citizens and workers.

NOTE

1 Following the creation of the new merged Department for Education and Employment, the *Employment Gazette* has been retitled *Labour Market Trends*.
2 LFS data has to be 'grossed up' from the sample to the whole. All LFS quarterly data from spring 1992 onwards have been revised to take account of new population estimates following from assessment of the 1991 Census results (Tonks 1995). The figures in this chapter have not been revised: the changes are small and the secondary analysis quoted is based on the unadjusted figures.

REFERENCES

Bryson, A. and Jacobs, J. (1992) *Policing the Workshy: Benefit Controls, the Labour Market and the Unemployed*, Aldershot: Avebury.
Burnett, J. (1994) *Idle Hands: The Experience of Unemployment 1790–1990*, London: Routledge.
Callender, C. (1992) 'Redundancy, unemployment and poverty', in C. Glendinning and J. Millar (eds) *Women and Poverty in Britain: the 1990s*, Hemel Hempstead: Harvester Wheatsheaf, pp. 129–48.
Chamberlain, E. and Purdie, E. (1992) 'The Quarterly Labour Force Survey – a new dimension in labour market statistics', *Employment Gazette* October: 483–8.
Dorling, D. and Simpson, S. (1993) 'Those missing millions: implications for social statistics of undercount in the 1991 Census', *Radical Statistics* 55: 14–35.
Gregg, P. (1994) 'Out for the count: a social scientist's analysis of unemployment statistics in the UK', *Journal of the Royal Statistical Society* Series A, 157: 253–70.
Jobseeker's Allowance (1994) White Paper (Cm 2687), London: HMSO.
Lawlor, J. (1990) 'Monthly unemployment statistics: maintaining a consistent series', *Employment Gazette* December: 601–8.
LRDFS (weekly) *Fact Service*, London: Labour Research Department.
MacInnes, J. (1989) *Regional Employment and Unemployment: Trends in Britain 1986–88*, Glasgow: Centre for Urban and Regional Research.
Miller, R. and Wood, J. (1982) *What Price Unemployment? An Alternative Approach*, London: Institute of Economic Affairs.
Morris, L. (1994) *Dangerous Classes*, London: Routledge.
Naylor, M. and Purdie, E. (1992) 'Results of the 1991 Labour Force Survey', *Employment Gazette* April: 153–72.
OPCS (1993) 'How complete was the 1991 Census?', *Population Trends* 71: 22–5.
Rayner, D. (1981) *Report on the Payment of Benefits to Unemployed People*, London: HMSO.
RSS (1995) *Report of the Working Party on the Measurement of Unemployment in the UK*, London: Royal Statistical Society.
Simpson, S., and Dorling, D. (1994) 'Those missing millions: implications for social statistics of non-response to the 1991 Census', *Journal of Social Policy* 23, 4: 543–67.
Sly, F. (1994a) 'Economic activity rates from the 1991 Labour Force Survey and Census of population', *Employment Gazette* March: 87–96.
—— (1994b) 'Ethnic groups and the labour market', *Employment Gazette* May: 147–59.
Taylor, D. (1990) *Creative Counting*, London: Unemployment Unit.
Tonks, E. (1995) 'Revisions to the Quarterly Labour Force Survey: re-weighting and seasonal adjustment review', *Employment Gazette* May: 223–32.
UUWB (monthly) *Working Brief*, London: Unemployment Unit.

Waring, M. (1988) *If Women Counted*, London: Macmillan.

White, A. and Leyland, J. (1992) 'How unemployment is measured in different countries', *Employment Gazette* September: 421–31.

White, A. and Whitton, J. (1993) 'A guide to "seasonal adjustment" and its application to labour market statistics', *Employment Gazette* April: 155–63.

Whiteside, N. (1991) *Bad Times*, London: Faber and Faber.

Wood, J. B. (1972) *How Much Unemployment?* London: Institute of Economic Affairs.

—— (1975) *How Little Unemployment?* London: Institute of Economic Affairs.

Woolford, C. and Denman, J. (1993) 'Measures of unemployment: the claimant count and the LFS compared', *Employment Gazette* October: 455–64.

Woolford, C., Patel, D. and Evans, A. (1994) 'Characteristics of the ILO unemployed', *Employment Gazette* July: 249–60.

4

SOCIAL CLASS: OFFICIAL, SOCIOLOGICAL AND MARXIST

Theo Nichols

This article was first published in 1979. It is reprinted here both because the theoretical issues remain relevant, and because it illustrates just how far debates have moved in the intervening period. It is followed by a postscript, written for this volume, which examines subsequent developments in the official treatment of class categories.

This chapter considers how official statistics relate to 'social class' – both in terms of what their content implies about our society, and in terms of the issues they raise about different concepts of 'class' itself.

It would be possible to simply outline and summarise here the various statistics which the state provides that are related to social class. However, some headway has been made already in detailing the statistics that are available (Reid 1977, *Social Trends* 1975) and a critique which merely pointed to the absence of data concerning certain distributions might easily give the impression that what was required was a simple matter of 'more facts'. Obviously, if we are to understand how societies work we do need facts. But we have to be careful not to put the cart before the horse. For there is a good case to be made that the 'coverage' of statistics relating to social class (whether, for example, state statistics tabulate 'social class' by this or that 'variable') is of secondary importance, and the same may be said of questions of a 'technical' kind (Hindess 1973: 12). Indeed, the present chapter has been constructed in the way it has in the hope that this will underline that the problems involved in the analysis of class cannot be reduced to purely technical statistical ones. It is in order that the primary importance of *theory* will become evident that it deals not only with social class in official statistics but also with different concepts of social class, in sociology and Marxism. And, since theory can have political implications, this is also why, by way of conclusion, some tentative remarks are made about the possible correlates for political practice of certain concepts of the working class; in particular about those which define it in a broad or narrow way.

The Registrar-General's 'social classes' are introduced in the first section. These are much used in social research, sometimes with only slight modification. But they are essentially descriptive categories that relate to *status*, and, as we see in the second section, they have something in common with some concepts of social class in sociology. These sociological concepts of class often stress the importance of different *dimensions* of social *stratification* (and the possible non-correspondence between different dimensions). But, like the Registrar-General's 'social class', they invite criticism from Marxists on the grounds that they do not *explain* the generation of inequalities in the structural dynamics of society, and only describe its results.

Yet in hard reality, this business about different concepts of social class in official statistics, sociology and Marxism is by no means as simple as it might seem so far. First – and this point has to be made as soon as one touches upon Marxist concepts of class relations (which are discussed in a third section) – some Marxism looks remarkably like some sociology. Second, even those Marxists who claim that their concepts are of explanatory value, still of course at some point take into account descriptive material, for example concerning what sociologists call 'work' and 'market situations'. This, it will be argued, raises a key issue in the analysis of class relations (restricted here to contemporary capitalist societies). The issue is not, to make this plain, whether reference to such matters should be included, but whether they should be included to the *exclusion* of a further, and different, level of analysis.

In this article, I introduce the term '*condition*' to refer to the level of analysis that tends to be the only level in official and sociological treatments (and in some Marxist ones). The other level which, as a simple exposition shows, figures prominently in the analysis of Poulantzas, is termed, following its author, that of '*place*' (a term that refers, as we shall see, to place within the social division of labour as a whole).

The analysis which Poulantzas himself conducts at the level of 'place' has been criticised, among other things, for its functionalism (Clarke 1977). However, the present article is not concerned with the adequacy of this particular analysis. Rather, it is concerned to draw attention to the general possibility that class relations can be analysed at this level; to suggest that this level is a different one to the more familiar one which is here called 'condition'; and to suggest also that the object and purpose of such an analysis means that the statistics appropriate to it (for instance those that relate to categories of productive and unproductive labour) necessarily differ from those likely to be relevant to official concepts of social class (which rest on assumptions about status) and from those likely to be considered pertinent to many studies of social class in sociology (which often have as their main object the investigation and description of differences in work, status and market situations).

THE STATUS OF SOCIAL CLASS IN THE CENSUS

In 1801, in the first of the ten-yearly Censuses, enumerators were required to answer the question: 'What number of persons in your parish, township or place are directly employed in agriculture, how many in trade manufactures or handicraft, and how many are not comprised in any of the preceding classes?' The question was deemed to be a failure and revisions were made, and continued to be made, until a predominantly industrial classification of seventeen classes, and sub-classes, was introduced in 1851. This classification included categories such as persons engaged in imperial or local government; in religion, law, medicine; and in agriculture. With some amendment and addition it continued to be used throughout the century, leading Charles Booth (1886: 318) to comment that 'generally there is such a want of fixity of principle or method, that even competent authorities have been seriously misled concerning the apparent results'. Certainly this is a verdict from which no social historian would dissent.[1] In 1911, though, the practice was instituted of summing birth and infant deaths into a number of groups 'designed to represent as far as possible different social grades'. These 'social grades' were very similar to the five 'social classes' used by the Registrar-General today: I. Professional Occupations; II. Intermediate Occupations; III. Skilled Occupations (split in 1971 into Non-Manual and Manual); IV. Partly Skilled Occupations; V. Unskilled Occupations. Table 4.1 shows the distribution of the population across these categories at the 1971 Census. (It also serves to draw attention to some of the different possible social bases to which this classification may be applied; husband's class or 'own class' for married women, etc.).

Apart from these 'social class' categories the Registrar-General provides a classification of 'socio-economic groups' (SEGs). Introduced in 1951, and modified in 1961, these constitute seventeen groupings of occupations, but in contrast to the Registrar-General's 'social classes' there is no pretension that the SEGs are ranked one to another in terms of social standing. The groupings distinguish manual and non-manual occupations, and separate out the Armed Forces and those in agriculture. Employment status (whether employed or self-employed) is used as a further differentiating factor. Although of relatively recent origin, the SEGs are particularly useful for plotting occupational shifts (as can be seen from the case of agriculture in Table 4.2). A source of confusion here is that a collapsed version of the SEG groupings (see Table 4.3) is used by the General Household Survey. These collapsed groupings are sometimes referred to as 'social classes'. But it is better to term them 'the GHS socio-economic groupings'. This is precisely what they are, and it leaves the way open to regard the Registrar-General's I–V hierarchy as the nearest thing we have to an official definition of 'social class'.[2]

Table 4.1 Social class composition of people aged 15 and over in Great Britain in 1971, for various groups (percentages and thousands)

	Men only			Women only			Men and women aged 15 and over		
				Married		Single, widowed and divorced			
	Economically active	Retired	Economically active and retired	Own class^a	Husband's class^b	Own class^c	Own occupation of economically active and retired	Head of family	Chief economic supporter
	(1)	(2)	(3)	(4)	(5)	(6)	(7)	(8)	(9)
% in each social class									
I	5.2	3.0	5.0	0.9	5.3	1.2	3.6	5.1	4.9
II	17.8	19.1	18.0	16.2	19.8	19.2	17.8	20.0	19.8
III Non-manual	11.9	12.1	11.9	35.4	11.3	41.2	21.1	11.9	14.2
III Manual	39.0	34.2	38.5	10.0	39.0	10.8	28.4	37.9	34.8
IV	17.8	20.3	18.1	28.2	17.5	22.7	20.9	18.0	18.6
V	8.3	11.2	8.6	9.4	7.1	4.9	8.2	7.3	7.7
thousands									
Total classified (= 100%)	15,368	1,911	17,279	5,697	12,365	3,834	26,809	13,150	15,907
Total unclassified^d	516	323	909	1,101	471	1,549	3,488	694	1,374
Total in GB	15,884	2,304	18,188	6,797	12,835	5,383	30,367	13,844	17,281

Source: Social Trends 1975 (data from 1971 Census).
Arithmetic errors in original.

Notes: a Economically active and retired married women by own social class.
b Married women enumerated with their husband by the social class of husband including both the economically active and retired, and those economically active.
c Economically active and retired single, widowed and divorced women.
d Unclassified persons: those for whom no occupation or inadequate information was reported in the Census. A large proportion of this group were out of work, retired, or inactive at Census date.

Table 4.2 Socio-economic groups of males, 1961 and 1971 in Great Britain

SEG	1961 (thousands)	1971 (thousands)
Employers and managers: large establishments	640	642
Employers and managers: small establishments	1,051	1,444
Professional: self-employed	144	155
Professional: employees	500	703
Intermediate non-manual	685	965
Junior non-manual	2,252	2,158
Personal service	162	174
Foreman: manual	595	647
Skilled manual	5,549	5,286
Semi-skilled manual	2,657	2,299
Unskilled manual	1,568	1,432
Own account (non-professional)	621	773
Farmers: employers	195	156
Farmers: own account	191	157
Agricultural	444	286
Armed Forces	336	254
Inadequately described	489	654
Total	18,080	18,187

Source: Census 1961 and 1971

Notes: Classification: own occupation of economically active and retired

To answer the question of what principle or method lies behind the Registrar-General's summing and ranking of occupations into 'social classes' it is appropriate to go back to a paper which Stevenson, Statistical Officer at the General Register Office, read to the Royal Statistical Society in 1928 (Stevenson 1928). In this we find Stevenson arguing against classification by income, and, *more importantly*, asserting that 'any scheme of social classification should take account of culture' – 'culture', as he construed it, being something that 'the occupational basis of social grading has a wholesome tendency to emphasise'. It is of course the very emphasis of this 'wholesome tendency' in the construction of the Registrar-General's *social* classes – rather than of the relationship to the means of production, which is central to Marxism – that continues to make these classes so many categories of *status* ('culture'). In fact, in the words of the Census, the basic criterion continues to be 'the general standing within the community of the occupations concerned'.

Table 4.3 Possession of consumer durables, in Great Britain, 1972 (percentages)

Economically active heads of household[a] Socio-economic grouping[b]	Television	Telephone	Washing machine	Refriger- ator	1 car	2 or more cars
Professional	94	85	77	94	65	25
Employers and managers	96	81	82	93	57	26
Intermediate	92	62	69	86	55	9
Junior non-manual	95	48	69	83	40	6
Skilled manual	97	37	76	81	49	7
Semi-skilled manual	95	25	67	69	28	3
Unskilled manual	94	14	60	56	16	2
All groupings	96	46	73	81	43	9

Source: General Household Survey 1972

Notes: a   All heads of household for cars
  b   Classification: GHS socio-economic groupings of head of household

Now it is obviously possible to point to the lack of continuity in the Census, to query the internal homogeneity of any class (status) category, to point to omissions and so on. In *Classifications of Occupation 1951*, for instance, the 'capitalist', the 'business speculator', the 'fundholder' and the 'landowner' were lumped into the same residual category as the 'expert (undefined)' and the 'lunatic (trade not stated)'. A rather pleasing coincidence perhaps, but one that serves to remind us that in the 'five social classes' of the Census the owners of capital are lost to sight, as are the self-employed.[3] Although therefore we may note that other systems of *grading* or *ranking* are possible, the essential fact is that the Census categories of 'social class' rest on a concept of class as status.[4]

THE DIMENSIONS OF SOCIAL CLASS IN SOCIOLOGY

In sociology, as in the Census, much work on social class is concerned in one way or another with status.[5] Two broad tendencies can be distinguished. The one relates to the granting of status in the sense of *esteem*. Apt to figure here are those interviewer's probes that seek to elicit the interviewee's own estimation of his or her class membership and that of other 'classes'. Never far away is that out-and-out psychologism, according to which classes do not exist if people do not say they do. The other way in which status enters in is evidenced by attempts to categorise by *status group*; that is, by actual style of life. A recent work on

71

class differences in Britain (Reid 1977) is probably sufficient introduction to both of these concepts of class as status. It contains information on what class people think they belong to; it is bedecked with tables akin to Table 4.3, and while 'prestige' appears in the index, 'property' does not. The ownership of television sets is documented, but not the ownership of the means of production of televisions or of anything else. Any account of class struggle as a structural dynamic is entirely absent. The nearest we get to this is a reported survey finding that 60 per cent of interviewees 'thought there was a class struggle'.

More sophisticated sociologists resist the assimilation of class and status; indeed Weber's work (Gerth and Mills 1948: ch. 7) made much of the distinction between them.[6] Even so, their theoretical work tends to reduce class to one factor among others in a multi-dimensional view of social stratification. Thus, in the case of C. Wright Mills (1953) a distinction is made between class (economic), occupation, status and power; and in the case of Goldthorpe and Lockwood (1963) reference is made to the economic, the normative and the relational dimensions of class stratification.

Occasionally, the multi-dimensional approach takes on a different form. In this version (Lenski 1966) each dimension itself becomes the basis for one of a number of *different* 'class systems', yielding, for example, an educational class system, a religious class system, a racial class system, an age-related class system and so on. But apart from such absurdities the multi-dimensional approach is generally adequate to its purpose. For to sum stratified positions and clusters of social attributes into 'social class' and then, as is often the case in empirical research, to treat occupation as an indicator of this, can illuminate many features of social life – infant mortality, electoral support for political parties, differential performance at school, or, as in Table 4.4, inequality of educational opportunity.

Nonetheless, as at least one sociologist (Dahrendorf 1959: 76) has made

Table 4.4 Percentages obtaining education of a grammar-school type among children of different classes born in the late 1930s

Father's occupation	at ages 11–13	at age 17
Professional and managerial	62	41.5
Other non-manual	34	16
Skilled manual	17	5
Semi-skilled manual	12	3
Unskilled	7	1.5
All children	23	10.5

Source: Banks (1968: 55)

a point of telling us, *class* should always be a category for purposes of the analysis of the dynamics of social change and its structural roots, and *stratum* a category for describing hierarchical systems at a given point in time. And from this standpoint much sociology must be said to be concerned with social stratification rather than with class.

Marxists criticise sociology because, among other things, they hold that it conflates class and status, that it is descriptive rather than explanatory, and that it concerns itself over-much with the origins and the social mobility of agents. In short, as we noted earlier, it is held to concern itself too much with effects and too little with causes of a fundamental kind. The most weightily expressed criticism, however, is the one which claims that to analyse class relations it is necessary to have a prior understanding of the labour theory of value and the processes of capital accumulation (see for example Stolzman and Gamberg 1973). The question obviously arises therefore of what a contemporary Marxist analysis, which does claim such an understanding, looks like. Is it really all that different?

In an attempt to shed some light on this we will take some of the arguments made in what has been one of the most influential recent books in this area, *Classes in Contemporary Capitalism* (Poulantzas 1975, see also Poulantzas 1973). From this we may, by way of contrast, learn something further about the approach to class in sociology. But we may also learn that problems remain in the analysis of class relations for Marxists, problems that, for them as for others, cannot be reduced to merely technical, statistical, issues.

THE PLACE AND CONDITION OF SOCIAL CLASS IN MODERN MARXISM

Observations about the large number of wage and salary earners employed outside manufacturing, together with ideas about increasing automation, a decline in wage and status differentials, and more recently the rise of white-collar unemployment and unionisation, have become standard ingredients for sociological and popular analyses of the class structure. Within Marxism itself a major focus of debate about class also now centres on the relationship between different elements of wage-labour, leading to theories of a 'new working class' (the technicians of Mallet 1975); to theories of a working class expanded through deskilling (as reflected in the work of Braverman 1974), to theories of one big working class (including pretty well everyone except for a handful of capitalists),[7] and to yet other formulations which posit the rise of 'intermediate social strata' (the middle ranks of the state apparatus and management, self-employed professionals, lawyers, etc.).

This last concept of 'intermediate social strata', which suggests the existence of strata without class, is from a Marxist point of view perhaps the most surprising. Yet the political strategy of the 'anti-monopoly alliance', which characterises the French Communist Party (the PCF), and also the British, is closely bound up with this.[8] And whereas Communist Party theorists may protest that they do not share the social democratic notion of a 'wage-earning class', their political conclusions do tend in this direction. Or so Poulantzas maintains. *Classes in Contemporary Capitalism* is therefore both an attempt to recover the ground he sees to have been lost by some modern Marxists, in particular by the PCF, and a warning against what he sees as the dangerous political conclusions to which they are led by such an analysis.

In what way, then, does Poulantzas break with much which claims to be Marxism? To begin to answer this question it is necessary to grasp three things, the first two of which will be explained at greater length below. These are: (1) that he grounds his class analysis on a labour theory of value; (2) that he uses a concept of 'place' in the social division of labour which is theoretically prior to any consideration of what is referred to here as 'condition';[9] (3) that for Poulantzas the 'position in the conjuncture' of any particular stratum (say, managers fighting redundancy alongside shop-floor workers) is not evidence of class membership. Were this to be so, the managers in our example would of course shift into and out of the working class in accordance with their support for workers.

Poulantzas holds that in the capitalist mode of production, productive labour is labour that produces surplus-value while directly reproducing the material elements that serve as the substratum of the relation of exploitation. Moreover, and this is fundamental, the working class is itself necessarily defined by productive labour. There can be no doubt, therefore, that a theory of surplus-value is crucial for Poulantzas.

This stress on the importance of productive labour has invited criticisms of Poulantzas for having an economistic concept of social class. This is something he disputes strongly.[10] For him, social class refers to the overall effect of the structure on the field of social relations and on the division of labour. Structured class determination therefore includes the place of a class in terms of the *political* and *ideological* relations of the social division of labour as a whole. Let us take two instances of this:

1 The wage labour of managers[11] and technicians. This labour is productive in so far as it performs the work of co-ordination. But Poulantzas argues that these managers and technicians occupy a controlling place in political relations, and that as 'mental labour' they occupy a dominant place *vis-à-vis* 'manual' productive labour in ideological relations (secrecy, monopolisation of knowledge and the mystique of qualifications being the constituents of their place in ideological relations, not ideology in the sense of the ideas that these

people have in their heads). It is because of the place they occupy in ideological and political relations that Poulantzas excludes managers and technicians from the working class.

2 Wage labour that is not productive. For Poulantzas the performance of such labour *always* spells exclusion from the working class. Indeed, he argues that such wage labourers belong to a *new* petty bourgeoisie which, in turn, is aligned with the traditional petty bourgeoisie (artisans, small shopkeepers, etc.). This conclusion, like that arrived at in (1), is again justified on ideological and political grounds, and despite the fact that the traditional and new petty bourgeoisies have a different relationship to the means of production. In the event then, this hardly amounts to an economistic analysis. In practice, ideological and political relations do play an important part in Poulantzas' analysis. Or to put it in his terms: structured class determination includes the place of a class in terms of the ideological and political relations of the social division of labour as a whole.

It can be seen from (1) above that according to Poulantzas it is not necessary to perform unproductive labour to be excluded from the working class. But to perform such labour is always sufficient for exclusion. This has the following consequence: that those who perform unproductive labour are still excluded from the working class even if the *condition* of their lives is substantially similar to that of those whom Poulantzas includes in this class. The cleaner at a bank or the woman on the cash register at Tesco, for example, may do work which is boring, insecure and badly paid as well, but they perform their labour in the spheres of circulation and commerce. Since only productive labour produces surplus-value, and since surplus-value is not produced in these spheres, they are not working class.

Now such a scheme of analysis is clearly informed by different principles to much other Marxist writing. For example, Wright's recent work on class boundaries in effect defines the working class as a class that is dispossessed (Wright 1976). It is a class which not only lacks effective economic ownership but lacks *possession*, both in the sense of control over physical means of production, and in the sense of control over the labour power of others. Poulantzas' analysis cannot be reduced to this. As far as he is concerned an official in the state apparatus, say a lowly tax collector, must be designated petty-bourgeois by virtue of the unproductive labour that he performs and the place that he occupies in the social relations of the division of labour as a whole. Tax collectors and their ilk – no matter how wretched their condition – are bearers of social relations which mark their place as a petty-bourgeois one. And they remain petty-bourgeois even if they do lack control ('possession') over the labour power of workers within their own administrative departments. It is in this sense that

Poulantzas' analysis of place is theoretically prior to an analysis of condition.

So far, though, we have not seen how Poulantzas takes account of the effects which Wright deals with so neatly in terms of his concept of possession; the effects which we have referred to as 'condition'. As a consequence of this it appears that Poulantzas includes bank managers within the new petty bourgeoisie as well as the bank cleaners instanced above, the supermarket middle manager as well as the woman on the cash register, and most types of state employees, and of course professors like himself. This is indeed the case, but Poulantzas argues that the new petty bourgeoisie contains within it certain fractions with a 'proletarian polarisation'. Amongst these fractions, which constitute the majority of the new petty bourgeoisie, are to be found those unproductive workers – like the cash register operative and the bank cleaner – whose *condition* approximates to that of his working class.[12] These, he argues, are prime candidates to be won over to the side of the working class – they have a 'proletarian polarisation'. But they are not *of* the working class; in fact they have to be *won*, and could be *lost*.

Theoretically, then, Poulantzas takes us a fair distance from the analysis of class in sociology, and in much modern Marxism. And this is so, to go back to our introductory comments, because he grounds his analysis directly on a theory of surplus-value, and because, following through the ramifications of the fundamental relation of exploitation, he treats the social division of labour as a whole as the primary matrix in which he only then proceeds to situate the effects that the condition of labour broadly defined – the various work, status and market situations, if you like, of neo-Weberian sociology.

CLASS, THEORY AND POLITICS

At this point it is perhaps useful to put forward some comments of a summary kind. Of the Registrar-General's 'social class' it may be said that it is a classification according to status. This itself is founded on a notion of hierarchy – of gradation rather than opposition – which, especially when taken in conjunction with ideas about social mobility (which are fostered by all the main political parties), is quite consonant with a dominant ideology of the 'national interest'. Of 'social class' in sociology, we may say that it operates primarily at the level of 'condition', and, as with the Registrar-General's classification, in so far as it concerns itself with hierarchic notions of social stratification (something which, incidentally, ties in with the stress on social mobility and studies of the recruitment to elites),[13] it does not treat class relations as historical forces of explanatory power. Sociology gives us 'social class' in plenty, but along with political parties, race/ethnicity and various status rankings (for instance those based on educational qualification) – in fact it gives us many potential and actual bases of power, without the prior situation of these into class relations.

As for Marxism? Marxism is a mixed bag. All Marxists agree that class location is not a matter of capitalists consuming more goods than workers, but of the relationship to the means of production. Yet this – at a fundamental level a two-class model – is the beginning of analysis only. Considerable room for dispute still exists among Marxists, and it is most certainly an error to assume that they can rest content once they have labelled the sociologist's approach to class as 'neo-Weberian'. Consider the work of British Marxists for example. Much of this has aimed to demonstrate the continued existence of inequalities in this society. It has attempted to expose the falsity of notions about the welfare state, and about widespread educational opportunity and social mobility. It has stressed the continued existence and concentrated ownership of private property. It has also exposed the oddity of those stratificational analyses in which there is a 'middle class', with a 'working class' underneath, and – a sort of bald class structure this – nothing on top. But, as with sociology, much of this work (e.g. the trojan work of Westergaard and Resler 1975) might well be claimed to be descriptive and to operate only at the level of 'condition'.

A case could be argued, of course, that analyses conducted at the level of 'condition' are to be valued precisely *because* they bear most closely on the level at which experience is given most directly to consciousness. Also that if Marxists, no matter how 'theoretical', really are concerned with social change (of which more shortly), they should not be too eager to deny the possible relevance and propaganda value of such analyses. However, the main point which concerns us here is that some Marxism looks remarkably like some sociology.[14] It is for this reason that special attention was paid above to the more explicitly theoretical, and different, work of Poulantzas.

Poulantzas' work itself is best seen as a significant contribution to the opening of a debate, the long-term consequences of which remain to be seen.[15] Already it is apparent that he is far from having everything his own way. His work is not free from epistemological problems (see Hindess 1977) or indeed empirical ones.[16] There are yet other rival theories, of the middle class for example, which like Poulantzas' also claim Marxist credentials (see Carchedi 1975). And, even the Marxist origin of his concept of productive labour, which is so fundamental to his approach, is open to dispute.[17]

Some Marxists, like Wright (1976: 18), challenge the very relevance of the productive/unproductive distinction for the determination of classes. Furthermore, some Marxists themselves are again now asking awkward questions about the labour theory of value,[18] the removal of which would put the skids under Poulantzas' entire, elaborate, theoretical structure.[19]

Yet it would be wrong to leave the discussion of the definition of class as if it were some arid, thoroughly aseptic, technical matter. As Glaberman (1975) reminds us about the working class, how this is defined relates to the problem of whether it is considered to be a viable instrument for social change. In fact, among Marxists such definitions are likely to carry within them notions about what sort of social change, and what sort of socialism, *are* viable.

The questions of *who?* and *what?* – what sort of socialism, and essentially for whom – are never far away. At the turn of the century for instance, discussion of the rise of a 'new middle class' – and in some versions the theoretical addition of this to the working class – was one of several attempts to characterise classical 'revisionism' (see Bernstein 1961, and for a commentary, Gay 1952: 210). And then, as now, the 'anti-revisionists' insisted that what was at issue was the question 'reform or revolution?': a question that was 'basically, in another form but the question of the petty bourgeois or proletarian character of the labour movement' (Luxemburg 1900: ix). Of course, the 'character' of the labour movement encompasses much more than the matter of its social composition. But generally it might be said that the looser the definition of the working class (or more precisely, the more the interests of the working class are considered to be similar to those of the traditional petty bourgeoisie, the various agents of social control, and even small and medium capital) the less the qualitative shift that the promise of socialism is held to represent. And vice versa: the more constricted the definition, the greater the shift.

To take the more constricted definition of the working class first, it would seem that, *theoretically,* this tends to rest today on a 'politicisation' of social relations (Poulantzas' reasons for the strict exclusion of managers and technicians can be considered in this light: although wage labour, they are excluded because they perform the work of control). And *politically,* partly because it is often associated with a view of the state as an irredeemably bourgeois institution, it tends to be shared by those who eschew a 'parliamentary road to socialism', who emphasise the importance of crises and workers' direct struggle (and thereafter, in socialism, workers' self-management, from below). By contrast, if we look now to the looser concept of the working class, it would seem that, *theoretically,* this takes the form of a relative lack of 'politicisation' of social relations (grossly so in formulations of the kind: the working class = all wage/salaried labour). And this meshes well with a *politics* that promises an 'administrative socialism' (rational planning of more or less conventionally structured state enterprises, from above). All of which – even though these compressed remarks are far from a definitive statement – should alert us to the fact that it is quite insufficient to conclude that the pertinent difference between Poulantzas and the PCF is that they 'classify' segments of the population differently. For the brunt of Poulantzas' analysis of the working class/new middle class boundary is to emphasise a *political* point: that monopoly capital is not the only enemy, and that the European Communist Parties had therefore better be *very* careful in allying themselves with non-proletarian elements, and in their related preference for a parliamentarian strategy.[20]

Of course, the above might suggest that various Marxist theorists first decide who they want to include in the working class, and then construct their 'theory' around this. The reality is that theory informs politics and politics theory, and that 'the definition of the working class' is all of a piece with this. In the case of Marxism and class, this means that at the very heart of the matter are questions about who is on what side in the dominant relations of exploitation, what the consequences of this are and what they can be made to be. The constraints and possibilities are theorised – but the theorisation itself serves political ends.

POSTSCRIPT

I am grateful for the opportunity to republish the above piece at the request of my colleagues. It was first published in 1979. This is to say it was written before the advent of Thatcherism; before what many seem to regard as the end of class politics; before many sociologists, who had quite suddenly found both Marxism and class analysis fashionable a decade before, ceased to do so; also before a plan was announced to abolish social class, officially. The latter was unfurled in 1987 when, as *The Times* reported:

> The working class is to be abolished, statisticians in the Office of Population Censuses and Surveys (OPCS) have decided. To ensure social equality, the middle and upper classes are being abolished too.
>
> (*The Times*, 30 October)

The plan to abandon the Registrar-General's classification had been favoured by Mr John Moore, a new Secretary of State at the DHSS, who, again according to *The Times*, was 'keen on the idea of a classless Britain'. Like many other rising stars of the Conservative Party since 1979, Mr Moore soon fell by the wayside – and, in the event, the social class classification was not abolished. Although it had been intended to replace it prior to the 1991 Census, a review continues to be conducted and the 'official' version of social class lives on.[21]

The social classes of the Census[22] continue to be of use, for example in the analysis of infant mortality. Despite the technical modifications to which all long-term time series are prone (e.g. in this case the disappearance since 1971 of certain occupational groups and the emergence of others) the Registrar-General's classification can also provide us with a rough guide to the changing shape of the occupational structure. Thus to compare the results of the latest Census that was available to me in 1979 (1971) and the most up to date information that is available now (1991) is to see that more men are now to be found in managerial occupations; and that a rather lower percentage is to be found in the skilled manual, partly skilled and unskilled categories (Figure 4.1). It can be seen that somewhat similar shifts have taken place for females: again an increase in the managerial category, and again decreases in the skilled manual, partly skilled and unskilled categories (Figure 4.2).

Of course, what these figures also tell us is that just as men remain heavily over-represented in the skilled manual category, so do women remain heavily over-represented in the skilled non-manual category. If the 'condition' of labour is to be reckoned by, the latter sphere is one that far from generally merits its apparent location, according to the Registrar-General's schema, between 'managerial' and 'skilled manual' work. Rather, it might be argued, these women should be reckoned part of the working class.

In the 1970s considerable amounts of ink were spent in discussion of a problem raised by the last remark. Namely, how the labour of those who were not employed on 'productive labour' (according to certain Marxist definitions, notably that of Poulantzas 1975) was to be theoretically

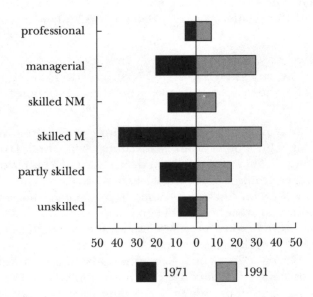

Figure 4.1 Registrar-General's social class: males 1971 and 1991 (percentages)

Source: *Census 1971 Great Britain Economic Activity*, Part IV, Table 29 and *Census 1991 Report for Great Britain*, Part II, Table 91

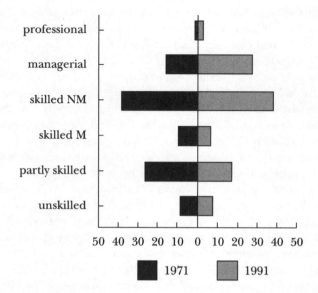

Figure 4.2 Registrar-General's social class: females 1971 and 1991 (percentages)

Source: *Census 1971 Great Britain Economic Activity,* Part IV, Table 29 and *Census 1991 Report for Great Britain,* Part II, Table 91

integrated into an understanding of contemporary advanced capitalist class structure. There can be little doubt that the rigorous exclusion of such workers from the working class has fallen out of favour. Different solutions to this problem have been adopted by different authors, who, whether Marxist or not, have still held to the fundamental proposition that class in capitalism is not about real or imaginary status differences (as in the Census) but about the production of a surplus (Miliband 1989: 38, Scase 1992: 21). However, the main tendency within sociology has been to shift away from Marxist toward Weberian formulations (cf. Crompton and Gubbay 1977: ch. 2, Crompton 1993, Wright 1976, 1985). As Carter (1995) has argued, there has also been a tendency to separate the analysis of class relations from that of the labour process. Such has been the turn of the political, as well as the theoretical tide, that it has become possible for even those researchers who have devoted decades of careful and valuable analysis to class-based inequalities and social mobility – but without any presupposition whatsoever that class relations are relations of exploitation (e.g. Goldthorpe and Marshall 1992) – now to find themselves under attack for subscribing to a 'hidden agenda of *marxisante* theory' (Pahl 1993: 257).

It was of course a key intention of the earlier piece, 'Social class: official, sociological and Marxist', to emphasise that the delineation of class categories and the analysis of class relations were not politically neutral activities and that all problems in the analysis of class relations were not reducible to technical ones. In hindsight, it is perhaps appropriate to add that the quite pronounced attention that sociologists paid to class in the 1970s, and in particular to Marxist theory, needs itself to be situated in the context of the balance of class forces which then prevailed.

It is undeniably the case that the long post-war boom had strengthened the resolve of labour against capital. Indeed, even today after a decade and a half in power, Tory ministers have not tired of claiming that, before they first gained office in 1979, the trade unions had too much power. No doubt, come another election, voters will be told yet again about how in the 1970s the nation was 'held to ransom' by 'militant' trade unionists and trade union 'barons' and that things were so bad, again because of trade union action, that it was not possible to bury the dead. Grossly exaggerated as these claims are, organised labour was strong in the 1970s, and most certainly it was strong as compared to today. But through the 1980s and into the 1990s the balance of power has shifted the opposite way: further toward employers and away from workers; yet further toward the rich and the owners of capital.

It is difficult to drive back the thought that when a heightening of class struggle takes the form of the strengthening of the position of the dominant class (in other words, as Miliband, 1989 has nicely put it, takes the form of 'class struggle from above') salaried middle-class intellectuals tend to keep their heads down; to engage, in the evocative title of a critique by Meiksins Wood (1986), in *The Retreat from Class*. This, it would seem, is an idea that 'reflexive' sociologists have yet to explore.[23]

However, the last decade and a half has served to highlight major problems for those whose analysis of class relations is primarily born out of identification with socialism. One problem concerns the fall of the Eastern Bloc countries. The problem here is not that, with the ending of these regimes, an ideal has been vanquished. The problem is that no matter how unpleasant it might have been to live in the Soviet Union – which large sections of the British Left would not dispute, and which they did not dispute in the 1970s either – the USSR did represent a possible, and likely to be necessary, source of support for a future Britain that had the temerity to make decisive steps down a socialist road. We are now of course far from the point at which such support against the destabilisation tactics of the United States and its allies would be necessary. Of much more pressing concern have been the problems sharply silhouetted by the actual historical development of what Marx once referred to as 'three cardinal facts of capitalist production' (Marx 1981: 375).

The three cardinal facts, as Marx saw them, were that a world market would be established; that the ownership of production would become concentrated in a few hands; and that labour would become social labour.

That the world market has been established is such an unassailable fact that it scarcely merits remark. Nor, given the dominance of the giant corporation, does the concentration and centralisation of capital need further comment (though it is perhaps worth adding that, in the face of this, and the massification of ownership into impersonal institutional forms, the much vaunted so-called 'wider share-ownership' is a total irrelevance). But the process of the organisation of labour into social labour is further from the mark today than it was in 1979 – at least in so far as this was expected to result in the objective sociological conditions for the overthrow of capitalism (the so-called 'gravedigger thesis'). Shipbuilding, dock work, steel, coalmining and other segments of the historically formed traditional core of the British working class have been gutted. Much of the hitherto unionised manufacturing base has been destroyed. Worldwide production has meant a worldwide division of labour, not its unification. The concentration of capital has outstripped the concentration of labour, and labour forces have become smaller, not larger.

On the back of the above developments ride some important questions. The first question bears directly on the matter of class struggle from above – something which so much contemporary literature about 'class' (as reviewed for example by Savage 1994) simply ignores. In the British case, which is the focus here, it concerns how the short-term policies and the economic destruction of the last decades are to be understood: exclusively as the unmediated and inexorable, impossible-to-mediate consequence of the operation of an external economic system? or in terms of an analysis of the nature of the dominant class (the class which, in Figures 4.1 and 4.2, is entirely lost to sight)?

The second question concerns the consequences of this destruction. Adversity has not only befallen the historically constituted core of what is often regarded as the traditional working class. As can be seen from Figure 4.3, it is the unskilled, semi-skilled and skilled workers who have borne the brunt of unemployment, but those in hitherto supposedly safe sectors like banking have also been affected. In fact, whole sectors of wage labour have been treated as honorary members of the working class – granted the benefits of work intensification, casualisation and the rest of it – whether this is recognised as their status in the Census classification of social class or not.

The first question directs attention to the issues: what sort of capitalism does Britain have? what sorts of capital and how do they relate to the state, and what are their interests in relation to state policy? The second question poses once again an issue which preoccupied those who wrote about class in the 1970s: how to understand the interests and potential for change of the working class and those others who also perform wage labour (and also, today, those unable to enter it). Such questions are more, not less, pertinent at a time when, as a welter of sources confirm,[24]

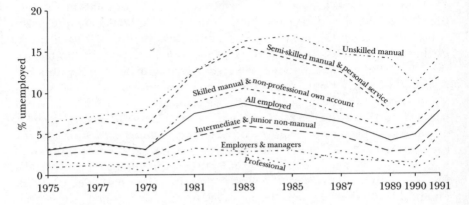

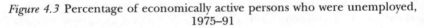

Figure 4.3 Percentage of economically active persons who were unemployed,
1975–91

Source: General Household Survey 1991: 84, Figure 5c

the concentration of wealth remains much the same as it did in 1979, with
10 per cent of the adult population still owning 50 per cent of marketable
wealth; when the pay gap between the wages of top earners and the lowest-
paid male workers is now bigger than at any time this century, and has
widened rapidly since 1977; and when poverty is yet more widespread than
it was in 1979, at which time 'only' 9 per cent of the population lived below
the unofficial poverty line (half average income after allowing for housing
costs) compared to just under 25 per cent of the population in 1991.

NOTES

1 See, for example, Armstrong (1972). Armstrong is useful on the development of
the Census, as is Marsh (1958: chs 5 and 6). For a critique of the 1951 Census see
Cole (1955: ch. 6).
2 For further details of the above and other classifications of social class in official
statistics see Reid (1977) and *Social Trends* (1975: 10–32, especially the
Appendix). Tables 4.1–4.3 above are drawn from the latter source.
3 The Census occupational classification was completely revised in 1961 when the
number of occupational unit groups was cut from about 600 to 200. As a
consequence 'the capitalist' has now been purged entirely. Note, though, the
political economy that informed the Census of 1861: there the 'unproductive
classes' – 'certain ladies (who) like the lilies of the field, neither toil nor spin',
and as many 'gentlemen', along with 'children', the 'infirm', and 'gypsies' were
contrasted to 'the greater part of humanity' – those who were employed 'during
the whole of their days in making articles of exchangeable value . . . supplying
our wants, executing *our* wishes, gratifying *our* tastes, edifying *us*, protecting *us*
from danger, preserving *our* property' (*1861 Census* 3, Appendix to Report: 225,
my emphasis).

4 For another system of grading see Hall and Jones (1950); for an example of the obvious point that some people rate the labour of, say, dustmen above that of advertising men – which raises the question of what it is that is being evaluated – see Young and Willmott (1956).

5 The present account does not claim to be comprehensive. In particular, we leave aside here the now largely discredited 'functional theory of stratification' (on which see Heller 1969, Part VIII) and Dahrendorf's (1959) distinctive attempt to translate Marx's classes into authority groups.

6 A view which, incidentally, has its supporters in high places, including, so it appears, Garter Principal King of Arms: 'Social classes', he tells us, meaning status groups, 'and economic classes are not the same thing and, though at times they coincide, often do not.' (See his letter to *The Times*, 24 December 1976.)

7 Seemingly a popular view with some currents of North American Marxism. See for example Freedman (1975) and Loren (1977). For two classic texts that make clear Marx's analysis was not exhausted by the dyad bourgeoisie and proletariat, see *The Eighteenth Brumaire of Louis Bonaparte* and *The Civil War in France.*

8 For the British Communist Party see the collection *Class Structure* (CPGB 1974). For an effective critique of the Party's old programme statement *The British Road to Socialism* (CPGB 1977); see Warren (1970). See also Hunt (1977a) for a slight change of emphasis.

9 'Condition' overlaps loosely with what Giddens (1973: 108) calls the 'proximate structuration of class relationships: the division of labour *within* the productive enterprise; the authority relations *within* the enterprise; and the influence of . . . "*distributive* groupings"', i.e. common patterns of *consumption*. (Giddens distinguishes the 'proximate' from the 'mediate structuration of class relationships' – seemingly the distribution of mobility chances – but this is not the same as Poulantzas' 'place'). Emphasis mine.

10 See his contribution to Hunt (1977b).

11 Top managers are excluded here. Like Wright (see p. 75), Poulantzas argues that these 'managers' have effective economic ownership and stand in the place of capital. Dahrendorf uses the split between juridicial ownership and effective economic ownership – the so-called 'separation of ownership and control' – as a key element in his attempted rebuttal of Marx. For a largely descriptive critique of this sort of managerialistic theory see Nichols (1969). For a concise theoretical statement, see De Vroey (1975).

12 In practice, these workers tend to be those wage/salary earners who lack authority. But note that for statistics to bear on even a concept of the working class which, unlike Poulantzas', *included* such workers, information would be necessary on 'possession' in both its aspects, and that the Registrar-General's social class classification does not give this. The SEG classification does of course have the advantage that it presents 'foremen' separately, and also the self-employed (but this conceals another problem since whereas workers on the lump constitute a separate juridical category, they are, in effect, wage labour). As for Poulantzas' concept of productive labour – to order official data on this would be an heroic, probably impossible, task.

13 For a guide to sociological treatments of elites and power in Britain see Crewe (1974), Stanworth and Giddens (1974), and Urry and Wakeford (1973).

14 The irony of this has not been lost on some sociologists: see Goldthorpe (1972).

15 For the opening shots see the exchange between Poulantzas and the British Marxist Miliband in Blackburn (1972).

16 An extensive – and readable – critique of Poulantzas is provided by Wright (1976).
17 The argument, I think a correct one, is that Marx did not define productive labour exclusively in terms of material production. See *Capital* 1 (1976: 644). For 'what Marx really meant' see Gough (1972).
18 Note for example the unsettled tone of Anderson (1976: 115).
19 For the beginnings of a recent attempt to rethink Marx, *minus* the labour theory of value, see Hodgson (1976). Fine and Harris (1976) usefully situate Hodgson's position and provide a guide to other recent tendencies in modern Marxist economic theory.
20 Although a recent interview with Poulantzas (1977) makes interesting reading in this context. One might suggest in the light of this that the implication of his theoretical 'politicisation' of class relations is not that an entire superincumbent strata of bourgeois society must be 'sprung into the air' but the very opposite – that the superincumbent strata now weigh so heavily on the working class that they *cannot* be 'sprung into the air', *have* to be worked with by the PCF and that it is just because of this that the PCF must be very careful. Be this as it may, this takes us a long way from any pretence that the analysis of class relations is merely a technical or statistical exercise.
21 An ESRC report on Phase 1 of a review of OPCS social classifications was published in June 1995. In response to the report, which spelt out that 'a person's employment situation is a key determinant of life chances' (Rose 1995: vl), OPCS accepted that government should continue to produce a social classification based on occupations and announced that it was prepared to fund research projects on the matter. The ESRC Report recommended attempting to produce one occupational classification which united the most important features of both the Registrar-General's Social Class and SEG. The importance of not losing such a long time-series was a prominent argument advanced in favour of retention of the Registrar-General's social class scheme. A description of the development of a new Standard Occupational Classification (SOC) to replace the 1980 Classification of Occupations (CO80) is provided by Thomas and Elias (1989).
22 Since the piece 'Social class' was published a more recent account of the origin of the Registrar-General's occupational classification has been provided by Szreter (1984).
23 In this context, Wright's Prologue to his most recent foray into class analysis – 'Falling into Marxism: choosing to stay' – is an exceptionally refreshing statement.
24 See for example Glyn and Miliband (1994), Goodman and Webb (1994), *Inland Revenue Statistics* (1993: Table 13.5, Statistical Appendix Figure 2.8b), Rowntree (1995).

REFERENCES

Anderson, P. (1976) *Considerations on Western Marxism*, London: New Left Books.
Armstrong, W. A. (1972) 'The use of information about occupation', in E. A. Wrigley (ed.) *Nineteenth Century Society: Essays in the Use of Quantitative Methods for the Study of Social Data*, London: Cambridge University Press.
Banks, O. (1968) *The Sociology of Education*, London: Batsford.
Bernstein, E. (1961) *Evolutionary Socialism: A Criticism and Affirmation*, New York: Schocken Books (first published 1899).
Blackburn, R. (ed.) (1972) *Ideology in Social Science*, London: Fontana.

Booth, C. (1886) 'Occupation of the people of the UK, 1801–81', *Journal of the Statistical Society* 49.

Braverman, H. (1974) *Labor and Monopoly Capital: the Degradation of Work in the Twentieth Century*, New York and London: Monthly Review Press.

Carchedi, G. (1975) 'On the economic identification of the new middle class', *Economy and Society* 4, 1.

Carter, B. (1995) 'A growing divide: Marxist class analysis and the labour process', *Capital and Class* 55, Spring.

Clarke, S. (1977) 'Marxism, sociology and Poulantzas' theory of the state', *Capital and Class*, Summer.

Classification of Occupations (1951) London: HMSO.

Cole, G. D. H. (1955) *Studies in Class Structure*, London: Routledge & Kegan Paul.

CPGB (Communist Party of Great Britain) (1974) *Class Structure*, London: CPGB.

—— (1977) *The British Road to Socialism*, London: CPGB.

Crewe, I. (ed.) (1974) *The First British Political Sociology Yearbook*, London: Croom Helm.

Crompton, R. (1993) *Class and Stratification: An Introduction to Current Debates*, Cambridge: Polity.

Crompton, R. and Gubbay, J. (1977) *Economy and Class Structure*, London: Macmillan.

Dahrendorf, R. (1959) *Class and Class Conflict in Industrial Society*, London: Routledge & Kegan Paul.

De Vroey, M. (1975) 'The separation of ownership and control in large corporations – the Marxist view', *Review of Radical Political Economy* 7, 2.

DHSS (1994) *Households below Average Income*, Department of Social Security, London: HMSO.

Fine, B. and Harris, L. (1976) 'Controversial issues in Marxist economics', in R. Miliband and J. Saville (eds) *The Socialist Register 1976*, London: Merlin Press.

Freedman, F. (1975) 'The internal structure of the American proletariat: a Marxist analysis', *Socialist Revolution* 5, 4.

Gay, P. (1952) *The Dilemma of Democratic Socialism: Eduard Bernstein's Challenge to Marx*, London: Collier Macmillan.

General Household Survey 1991, Office of Population and Surveys Social Survey Division, London: HMSO.

Gerth, H. H. and Mills, C. Wright (1948) *From Max Weber: Essays in Sociology*, London: Routledge & Kegan Paul.

Giddens, A. (1973) *The Class Structure of Advanced Societies*, London: Hutchinson.

Glaberman, M. (1975) *The Working Class and Social Change: Four Essays on the Working Class*, Toronto: New Hogtown Press.

Glyn, A. and Miliband, D. (eds) (1994) *Paying for Inequality: The Cost of Social Justice*, London: IPPR/Rivers Oram Press.

Goldthorpe, J. H. (1972) 'Class, status and party in modern Britain: some recent interpretations, Marxist and Marxisant', *European Journal of Sociology* 13.

Goldthorpe, J. H. and Lockwood, D. (1963) 'Affluence and the British class structure', *Sociological Review* 11, 2.

Goldthorpe, J. H. and Marshall, G. (1992) 'The promising future of class analysis', *Sociology* 26: 381–400.

Goodman, A. and Webb, S. (1994) *For Richer, For Poorer: The Changing Distribution of Income in the United Kingdom 1961–91*, London: Institute for Fiscal Studies.

Gough, I. (1972) 'Marx's theory of productive and unproductive labour', *New Left Review* 76.

Hall, J. and Jones, D. C. (1950) 'Social grading of occupations', *British Journal of Sociology* 1, 1.

Heller, C. S. (ed.) (1969) *Structured Social Inequality*, London: Collier Macmillan.
Hindess, B. (1973) *The Use of Official Statistics in Sociology*, London: Macmillan.
—— (1977) 'The concept of class in Marxist theory and Marxist politics', in
    J. Bloomfield (ed.) *Class, Hegemony and Party*, London: Lawrence & Wishart.
Hodgson, G. (1976) 'Exploitation and embodied labour time', *Bulletin of the
    Conference of Socialist Economists* 13.
Hunt, A. (1977a) 'Class structure and political strategy', *Marxism Today*, July.
—— (ed.) (1977b) *Class and Class Struggle*, London: Lawrence & Wishart.
Inland Revenue Statistics (1993) Inland Revenue Statistics and Economics Office,
    London: HMSO.
Lenski, G. E. (1966) *Power and Privilege: A Theory of Social Stratification*, New York and
    London: McGraw Hill.
Loren, C. (1977) *Classes in the United States: Workers against Capitalism*, California:
    Cardinal Publishers.
Luxemburg, R. (n.d.) *Social Reform or Revolution*, London: Merlin Press (first
    published 1900).
Mallet, S. (1975) *The New Working Class*, Nottingham: Spokesman Books.
Marsh, D. C. (1958) *The Changing Social Structure of England and Wales*, London:
    Routledge & Kegan Paul.
Marx, K. (1976) *Capital* I, London: New Left Review/Penguin.
—— (1981) *Capital* III, Harmondsworth: Penguin.
Meiksins Wood, E. (1986) *The Retreat from Class: A New True Socialism*, London: Verso.
Miliband, R. (1989) *Divided Societies: Class Structure in Contemporary Capitalism*,
    Oxford: Oxford University Press.
Mills, C. Wright (1953) *White Collar: the American Middle Classes*, New York: Oxford
    University Press.
Nichols, T. (1969) *Ownership, Control and Ideology*, London: Allen & Unwin.
Pahl, R. E. (1993) 'Does class analysis without class theory have a promising
    future?', *Sociology* 27, 2, May.
Poulantzas, N. (1973) *Political Power and Social Class*, London: New Left Books.
—— (1975) *Classes in Contemporary Capitalism*, London: New Left Books.
—— (1977) 'The state and the transition to socialism', *International* 4, 1, Autumn
    (an interview with H. Weber).
Reid, I. (1977) *Social Class Differences in Britain*, London: Open Books.
Rose, D. (1995) *ESRC Review of OPCS Social Classifications: A Report on Phase 1 to the
    Office of Population Censuses and Surveys*, Swindon: Economic and Social Research
    Council.
Rowntree (1995) *The Joseph Rowntree Foundation Inquiry into Income and Wealth*, 2 vols,
    York: Rowntree Foundation.
Savage, M. (1994) 'Review article – class analysis and its futures', *Sociological Review*
    42, 3, August.
Scase, R. (1992) *Class*, Buckingham: Open University Press.
Social Trends (1975) Article on 'Social commentary and social class', London:
    HMSO.
Stanworth, P. and Giddens, A. (eds) (1974) *Elites and Power in British Society*,
    London: Cambridge University Press.
Stevenson, T. H. C. (1928) 'The vital statistics of wealth and poverty', *Journal of the
    Royal Statistical Society* 61.
Stolzman, J. and Gamberg, H. (1973) 'Marxist class analysis versus stratification
    analysis as general approaches to social inequality', *Berkeley Journal of Sociology* 18.
Szreter, S. R. S. (1984) 'The genesis of the Registrar-General's Social Classification
    of Occupations', *British Journal of Sociology* 35: 522–4.

Thomas, R. and Elias, P. (1989) 'Development of the Standard Occupational Classification', *Population Trends*, Spring.

Urry, J. and Wakeford, J. (eds) (1973) *Power in Britain*, London: Heinemann.

Warren, B. (1970) 'The British road to socialism', *New Left Review* 63.

Westergaard, J. and Resler, H. (1975) *Class in a Capitalist Society*, London: Heinemann.

Wright, E. O. (1976) 'Class boundaries in advanced capitalist societies', *New Left Review* 98.

—— (1985) *Classes*, London: Verso.

—— (1994) *Interrogating Inequality: Essays on Class Analysis, Socialism and Marxism*, London: Verso.

Young, M. and Willmott, P. (1956), 'Social grading by manual workers', *British Journal of Sociology*, 7.

5

HEALTH FOR ALL?

Will Guy

In May 1994 it was announced that the government was to set up an inquiry into links between social inequality and ill health. The decision came only two years after the publication of *The Health of the Nation* White Paper (1992), which had outlined health strategy for the 1990s. In this document the government had refused to accept such a link, seeing improvements in health as a matter of individual responsibility rather than associated with structural problems within society. The announcement marked a recognition that social factors 'such as housing, unemployment, education and benefit levels have a bearing on the nation's health – a view denied during the Thatcher years' (*Guardian* 4 May 1995). The first Thatcher government had regarded with scepticism the findings of an important new study, known as the Black Report, when it strongly argued such a connection in 1980. Its recommendations had been dismissed as 'quite unrealistic in present or any foreseeable economic circumstances' (Townsend and Davidson 1982: 39).

MEASURING HEALTH

Health is often understood negatively to mean simply absence of any illness requiring medical treatment. A wider and more positive concept of health was adopted at the founding of the World Health Organisation (WHO) at the end of the Second World War when health was seen as a 'state of complete physical, mental and social well-being and not merely the absence of disease or infirmity' (quoted in Townsend and Davidson 1982: 42). This positive view of health corresponds to our lay usage of the term 'healthy'. It may then seem perverse that many subsequent studies of health turn aside from this broad definition and use mortality statistics as their main, or even sole, indicator of health. There are three reasons for this: the availability and reliability of mortality data, and the difficulties of using alternative measures.

All deaths have been officially recorded in England and Wales since the late 1830s and overall and disease-specific mortality statistics are published

90

on a regular basis, classified by age group, region and occupation. In this century deaths have also been grouped according to social class, a more problematic categorisation on which much of the subsequent debate on health inequalities has focused. In 1911, T. H. C. Stevenson, Statistical Officer at the General Register Office, looked at patterns in the Census by assigning all occupations to three broad groupings – 'professional, middle and working'. This classification was not made on the basis of income but by using the more nebulous concepts of the social standing and lifestyle associated with occupations. This meant, for example, that relatively impoverished clergymen were categorised as 'professional', a decision Stevenson justified by pointing to their low mortality. He argued that such cases demonstrated that 'the lower mortality of the wealthier classes depends less on wealth itself than upon the culture, extending to matters of hygiene, generally associated with it'. The mortality gradients resulting from grouping occupations in this way were regarded by Stevenson as 'an indication both of success in the social grading of the population and of the association of mortality with low status' (Stevenson 1928). Although the argument was circular, since mortality was originally among Stevenson's criteria for locating occupations in social classes (Marsh 1988: 272), a revised version of this scheme still remains a key analytical tool for the Registrar-General's Decennial Supplement on occupational mortality. It continues to generate similar mortality gradients to those noted by Stevenson.

Such mortality statistics are relatively straightforward as well as readily accessible. The fact that someone has died is clear-cut, though the cause of death may be less so. The difficulties of trying to measure morbidity or general state of health are much greater, and most available figures are both partial and hard to interpret. Using a positive definition like that of the WHO would require subjective measures of well-being; these would be vulnerable to social and cultural variation in expectations of health. A more precise epidemiological approach, focusing on specific diseases, is also highly problematic. While some data is collected nationwide, mainly for infectious diseases and cancers, this is very limited. Even cases of notifiable diseases are recorded only if the sufferer seeks medical help, and are therefore subject to under-reporting. Moreover, criteria for diagnosis and recording rates can differ. Statistics based on self-reported illness are also problematic, and provide serious underestimates of clinically identified disease (Blaxter 1985). Problems with measuring individual diseases are compounded when attempting to construct overall measures of general health. Morbidity can also be estimated from administrative sources, such as absences from work or use of medical services. Such proxies, however, necessarily reflect the administrative structures which generate them, and are particularly problematic as these change over time (Blaxter 1989). Despite these difficulties, the General

Household Survey (GHS) has since 1970 regularly asked about acute and chronic illness, as well as including occasional questions on health-related behaviour such as smoking and drinking. In 1971 the Longitudinal Study (LS) began a routine linking of birth, death and cancer registrations to Census data for a 1 per cent sample of the population. This new information was gathered from large nationwide samples, but in 1991 coverage was extended to the whole population once more, again through the Census.

The problems of measuring morbidity are such that mortality has often seemed an attractive choice as a proxy. Although serious doubts have been voiced about the validity of using mortality as a substitute for direct measures of health (Blaxter 1989, 1990), this chapter focuses initially on research making use of mortality statistics before broadening its scope to include investigations employing more complex indices of health. Studies of differential mortality have been central to the ongoing debate about the existence of a growing health divide in British society, and draw primarily on data from the Registrar-General's Decennial Supplement of occupational mortality and the Longitudinal Study. In spite of disputes about 'technical adjustments' affecting the Decennial Supplement of 1986 and the threat to the continuation of the LS posed by the 1980 Rayner review, these statistical series have remained key sources of information. The main issues have centred, therefore, on the interpretation of the data rather than its availability.

Governments in the 1980s actively discouraged the dissemination of major health research findings based on mortality data but, during this same period and continuing into the 1990s, eagerly promoted a mass of new statistics concerning health. This additional data concerned the radical restructuring of the health service and represented a new and aggressive, publicity-conscious use of statistics for political purposes. Evidence that the widening social inequalities of the 1980s and 1990s were damaging the health of the poorest was repeatedly countered with a plethora of figures about administrative reorganisation, patient treatment, hospital beds, waiting lists and public expenditure on the health service. It would require a separate chapter to discuss the validity of these new statistics but official claims that such figures represented a marked improvement in service delivery have been criticised as selective and misleading (Radical Statistics Health Group 1987, *Dispatches* 1989).

THE REDISCOVERY OF HEALTH INEQUALITY

The establishment of the National Health Service (NHS) in 1948 encouraged many people to believe that free and better health care, coupled with protective state legislation, would soon bring about a marked reduction in the unequal risks of serious illness or early death. But by the early 1970s there were worrying signs that any initial rate of improvement had slackened. The 'rediscovery' of health inequality can be linked to two main concerns: official dissatisfaction at Britain's failure to keep pace with the progress of other developed countries and suggestions that health differentials between classes were not decreasing (Blaxter 1990: 6). Between 1960 and 1978 Britain dropped from eighth to fifteenth place for the lowest infant mortality rate – behind Hong Kong and Singapore (Townsend *et al.* 1988a: 2). Discouraging statistics for the whole population masked the even worse condition of the least well off. In 1977 the Secretary of State for Social Services, David Ennals, acknowledged the seriousness of the situation:

> the crude differences in mortality rates between the various social classes are worrying. . . . when you look at death rates for specific diseases the gap is even wider . . . the first step towards remedial action is to put together what is already known about the problem . . . it is a major challenge for the next ten or more years to try to narrow the gap in health standards between different social classes.
>
> (Ennals, 27 March 1977, quoted in Townsend and Davidson 1982: 14)

That same year he established a research working group, chaired by Sir Douglas Black, to assess differences in health according to social class, investigate possible causes, make policy recommendations and suggest further research. The group submitted its report in April 1980 and the findings, now usually known as the Black Report (DHSS 1980), were received as an unwelcome legacy by the incoming Conservative administration. This major report was eventually 'published' by releasing 260 duplicated copies of the typescript with the minimum of publicity over the August bank holiday (Townsend *et al.* 1988a: 3). Nevertheless, it was to prove a landmark in research on health inequalities.

THE BLACK REPORT AND THE HEALTH DIVIDE

In investigating the extent of social class inequalities in health, the working group decided to rely primarily on mortality rates 'partly because of the problems of measurement [and definition of morbidity], but also because of the need for time-series statistics', so that trends, and especially any recent deterioration in the situation, could be detected (Townsend and Davidson 1982: 45). Standardised mortality ratios (SMRs) were used to compare the mortality of particular groups with the national rate. This common measure is calculated by dividing the number of actual deaths recorded for a given group by the number of deaths that would have been expected in a population of identical size and age structure and then multiplying this ratio by 100. In this way any SMR under 100 can be easily seen as indicating lower than average chances of death while SMRs over 100 indicate raised mortality risks.

The selection of an adequate indicator of inequality was more problematic but the concept of social class was chosen as the most commonly used. This was operationalised by adopting the Registrar-General's scheme of categories based on occupation, although the working group was fully aware of its limitations. The report listed the examples shown in Table 5.1, including the percentage of economically active and retired males in each of these categories.

The working group drew on the most recent relevant statistics, the Registrar-General's Decennial Supplement of occupational mortality, which compared occupations listed on death certificates between 1970 and 1972 with those recorded in the 1971 Census. As could have been expected, this revealed stark variations in social class life chances. Men and women in occupational class V had more than double the chance of dying before retirement age than those in class I. The differences formed a consistent pattern where mortality rates increased with descending occupational class. Similar gradients were found for all age groups, although they were steepest in infancy and childhood. They were repeated for specific causes of death, most dramatically for those closely linked to socio-economic environment. Amongst adults the greatest class differences were for respiratory diseases; among children, accidents, which caused 30 per cent of all childhood deaths, were the most unequally distributed. Put in crude terms these figures showed that, at whatever age, the lower the occupational class, the greater the chance of an early death. The working group also explored links with gender, ethnicity, region and housing tenure. The significance of gender and ethnicity are discussed briefly in later sections of this chapter.

At the heart of the Black Report was the chapter dealing with trends over time. While differences in health between classes were disturbing they were not unexpected, but the time-series data contradicted the belief

Table 5.1 Registrar-General's scheme of social categories – percentage of economically active and retired males

Category	Examples	%
I Professional	(accountant, doctor, lawyer)	5
II Intermediate	(manager, nurse, schoolteacher)	18
IIIN Skilled non-manual	(clerical worker, secretary, shop assistant)	12
IIIM Skilled manual	(bus driver, butcher, carpenter, coal face worker)	38
IV Partly skilled	(agricultural worker, postman, bus conductor)	18
V Unskilled	(cleaner, dock worker, labourer)	9

Source: Adapted from Townsend and Davidson (1982: 48)

that post-war Britain was becoming a more egalitarian society. In spite of the welfare state and the NHS, the gulf in life chances, as measured by mortality, was progressively widening and was actually greater than it had been at the start of the 1930s. These stark findings did not go unchallenged and over the following years there continued debate over problems of measurement and interpretation.

While recognising that health inequalities were the product of multiple causes, the working group saw the effects of economic and socio-structural factors as predominant. Consequently it recommended policy measures which, 'while practicable, in economic and administrative terms . . . [would] none the less, properly maintained, exert a long-term structural effect'. Foremost was the recommendation that 'the *abolition of child poverty should be adopted as a national goal for the 1980s*' (Townsend and Davidson 1982: 177, emphasis in original). It was this clear advocacy of a solution which the Conservative government saw as 'social engineering', as well as the total costs involved, that led to its official rejection as both ideologically repugnant and financially 'unrealistic'.

In 1986 the Health Education Council (HEC) commissioned a follow-up study from Margaret Whitehead to evaluate new research evidence and review progress in implementing Black's policy recommendations. This report was published in a limited number of copies as *The Health Divide* in March 1987 (Whitehead 1987). As had happened earlier with the Black Report, the launch was hampered by government obstruction. The press briefing was cancelled by the chair of the HEC an hour before its scheduled start, following a last-minute approach from the Department of Health and Social Security (DHSS) (Townsend *et al.* 1988a: 6–11). The new report set its findings in the context of both the Black Report and the 1985 WHO European *Targets for Health for All*, a programme endorsed in 1984 by all member countries including the UK. *The Health Divide* drew attention to advances in understanding the problems of health, but the outlook for solutions remained bleak. The first of the thirty-eight WHO targets was to reduce differences in health status by 25 per cent by improving the health of disadvantaged groups. Although recognising that there had been a drop in overall UK death rates since 1980, the report confirmed that marked inequalities had persisted into the 1980s, with the health gap continuing to widen. Between 1971 and 1981 the SMR for adult men in classes I and II had improved, from 77 to 66 and from 81 to 76 respectively, while those for classes IV and especially V had worsened, from 114 to 116 and from 137 to 166 (Wilkinson 1986: 2). In the meantime there had been little attempt to implement the proposals of the Black Report, other than by a limited re-allocation of NHS funds. Indeed, of Black's principal recommendation, it could be stated bluntly: 'The goal of abolishing child poverty is nowhere in sight.' On the contrary, there was evidence that conditions had worsened (Whitehead 1988: 332–3).

Some of the sharpest criticism in the report singled out the failure of government to make relevant information more widely available. There had been a marked deterioration in the quality of statistical data and the wording of the complaint implied that this had been deliberate.

None of the recommendations concerned with improving the collection of information or the monitoring of social inequalities in health has been adopted. In many cases the information required to carry out vital research is still not available. What is even more frustrating is the fact that in recent years the traditional sources of information on social class and health, and deprivation and health, have also virtually dried up. For example, many have relied on the Registrar-General's occupational mortality Decennial Supplements for authoritative information, but the latest supplement (1986) scarcely addresses the issue.

(Whitehead 1988: 354–5)

Researchers had been particularly hampered by the reclassification of some occupations for the 1981 Census. The Decennial Supplement claimed that for this, and other technical reasons, 'social class mortality in this study cannot validly be compared with earlier reports, particularly for Social Class V' (OPCS 1986: 45). To a lesser extent the publication of the major tables of the Decennial Supplement in microfiche form was also a hindrance. Although it was stated that '[t]he use of microfiche allows more data to be made available' (OPCS 1986: iv), in practice the most important data became less accessible. In spite of these and other difficulties researchers showed great ingenuity in continuing to investigate patterns of inequality in Britain's health, with the Decennial Supplements and Longitudinal Study remaining as essential analytic tools.

PROBLEMS IN RELATING GENDER AND ETHNICITY TO HEALTH

Both the Black Report and *The Health Divide* stressed the importance of under-researched aspects of health in Britain, particularly the health of women and of ethnic minorities. In each case a fundamental barrier to further investigation was the inadequacy of the basic measuring tools available. The most striking difference between the health of men and women in developed, industrial societies is that while women live longer than men, on average by six years, they report more acute illness and make greater use of medical services, especially for mental illness. Hart has argued that this marked gender differential in mortality is comparatively recent (Hart 1989: 109–10).

The exclusion of discussion of women's health from the mainstream debate on health inequalities is a facet of the general under-representation of women in official statistics (Macfarlane 1990: 20). In particular, the reliability of matching mortality statistics with social class has been undermined by problems in assigning women to occupations, both during their lives and at death:

Although most women are in employment for much of their working lives, at any one point in time a large proportion are housewives. The 1971 Census found that [only] 53 per cent of women in the 'working' age range 15–59 could be classified to an occupation and hence a social class.

(Pugh and Moser 1990: 94)

At death the information gap is even more extreme. The Decennial Supplement for 1970–72 revealed that for only 20 per cent of deaths to women aged 15–64 was the woman's own occupation recorded on the death certificate (Pugh and Moser 1990: 97). As recently as 1986, registrars in England and Wales were instructed that 'the occupation of a woman should not be recorded unless she was in paid employment most of her life' (OPCS 1986 quoted in Macfarlane 1990: 25).

Even if women's occupations are recorded, a further difficulty is that the classificatory scheme was devised for men's work and is very weak in dealing with major areas of women's paid employment. The manual/non-manual distinction is unhelpful for many occupations, and standard categorisation obscures differentiation. The 1970 occupational classification put 53 per cent of women in five of its 223 occupational unit groups and 24 per cent in one alone – clerical and secretarial (Dale *et al.* 1985). Other problems arise from regarding large numbers of disadvantaged women homeworkers and outworkers as among the independent and autonomous 'self-employed'.

Even though attempts have been made to construct a more sensitive scheme, extensive retrospective reclassification of women would prove impossible. Nevertheless Pugh and Moser took account of this approach when they looked at mortality in the period 1976–81, using the Longitudinal Study as a way of gaining fuller information about a sample of women aged 15–59. While their basic findings showed that, just as for men, high mortality was linked to factors such as manual occupations, rented accommodation and lack of a car, they also revealed that 'in order to accurately reflect the relationship between a woman's life circumstances and mortality it is necessary to use measures other than those based solely on occupation' (Pugh and Moser 1990: 111). Not only is the effect of women's own class on their mortality mediated by marital status (Moser *et al.* 1990), but disentangling the relative effects of causal influences is complicated by the multiple roles of women, combining intermittent participation in the labour market with unpaid work at home.

Leaving aside the difficulties of classifying women by their own occupation, the relevance of this for explaining health differentials was challenged by Arber (1989, 1990) in her examination of morbidity among women using the General Household Survey's question on 'limiting long-standing illness'. Following Hart she argued that 'life chances are influenced primarily by the social and economic circumstances of the household' (Arber 1989: 253); thus a household-based measure is more appropriate than an individualistic approach which makes every attempt to classify women according to their own current or last occupation.

The 'conventional' view advocated earlier by Goldthorpe, where married women are assigned to the social class of their husband (Goldthorpe 1983, 1984), is just such a household-based measure, although questionable on the grounds that 'it is no longer socially or politically acceptable for women to be considered an appendage of men, with their class position derived from their husband' (Arber et al. 1986). A more pragmatic reason for querying the 'conventional' view is that this may not be the most appropriate household-based measure for under-standing health. Arber preferred an alternative occupation-based measure where the class of both husband and wife was determined by that of the occupationally 'dominant' spouse. Apart from being free of gender bias, this 'dominance' approach had the advantage of revealing the effect of wives' occupational class on husbands' health, and findings using this method 'lend support to structural-materialist explanations of health' (Arber 1989: 276–7).

Research on the health of ethnic minorities in Britain has been hampered by a different and more basic gap in the information available from official statistics. It was noted by both the Black Report and The Health Divide that since ethnicity, as such, has not been recorded in the Census or on birth or death certificates, this essential variable must be inferred from proxies such as 'country of birth' (Whitehead 1988: 249–50). The unreliability of these proxies is discussed fully in Chapter 8. These problems may diminish as a result of the inclusion of a direct question on ethnicity in the 1991 Census, but this has problems of its own. As a consequence of these difficulties the limited research on the health of ethnic minorities has either reluctantly accepted inevitable and unknown levels of distortion or else has restricted itself to small-scale surveys, often of questionable representativeness due to incomplete sampling frames. The most common solution to the problem of such flawed data, taken by several major studies, has been to ignore the aspect of ethnicity altogether in the analysis. Although their analytic focus was directed elsewhere, the Health and Lifestyles survey (Blaxter 1990) made no reference to ethnicity and the same is true of research on the Northern Region (Townsend et al. 1988b).

ALTERNATIVE EXPLANATIONS OF HEALTH INEQUALITY

The findings of the working group raised the question of why class should continue to exert such a significant and damaging influence on health. In the search for an explanation, four separate theoretical approaches were considered. The first was that the relationship was illusory, a statistical artefact; secondly, that what was at work was a process of social selection; thirdly, that individual behaviour was to blame; and fourthly, that economic and structural factors exerted a real effect.

The artefactual explanation

Raymond Illsley, a pioneer in researching social aspects of health, found it unbelievable that the post-war period could have produced even a relative worsening of the situation between classes. Although Illsley did not deny that poorer groups suffered worse health and heightened mortality, he thought that improvements in health and living standards for the whole population must outweigh the importance of any differential effects between classes (Illsley 1987). He argued that the statistics on which claims for worsening inequality were based were limited and deceptive; to use the mortality rates for occupied males aged between 15 and 64 in this way was misleading, for a number of reasons.

First, the approach took no account of demographic changes, most importantly the significant alteration in class composition since the 1920s. Social class V, the unskilled, was much smaller and class I much larger. There had also been periodic reclassifications of occupations. This meant that high mortality rates for class V in the 1960s and 1970s were derived from a much smaller base than formerly and were consequently unreliable. Moreover, the crucial rates reflected only a minority of the adult population. They excluded males under 15 and over 64, those who had never been employed, and all women. In addition, increasing overall life expectancy made direct comparison unreliable. While in 1921 only 32 per cent of men survived beyond 65 years, by 1971 this proportion had doubled to 65 per cent. Consequently death rates for all classes were increasingly based on a smaller proportion of all deaths. For these reasons Illsley preferred to use survival rather than mortality rates as a measure of changes over time, and argued that inequalities had diminished. However, Illsley pointedly excluded the 1980s from his alternative account of narrowing health differentials since he was 'sure that the economic and social policies of the Thatcher government . . . [had] fostered true health inequality' (Illsley 1987: 17).

The Health Divide considered these and other criticisms of the Black Report. The charge of unreliability in using figures for the two classes at the extremes of the social range was countered by combining class I with class II and class IV with class V to produce larger and more comparable proportions over time (see Whitehead 1988: 230–1). When data from all Decennial Supplements since the Second World War was analysed using this regrouping the existence of a widening health gap was reconfirmed (Hart 1987: 17–18). A more radical regrouping into manual and non-manual groups also confirmed a widening of the health gap (Marmot and McDowall 1986).

The commentary to the Decennial Supplement for 1979–80, 1982–83 had discounted the validity of comparing SMRs for social classes because of technical deficiencies in the data, preferring the greater reliability of the OPCS Longitudinal Study in spite of its small sample size. While the LS data covered only 1 per cent of the population it had important advantages because it referred to tracked individuals. This ensured much greater reliability for classification by social class since Census details could be directly matched with those on death certificates, occasionally vulnerable to 'respectful desire among the next of kin . . . "to promote the dead"' (Wilkinson 1986: 3). Also, problems of comparison over time were minimised since the LS was a relatively recent survey. Results from this study, too, showed a similar divergence in mortality rates for manual and non-manual classes from 1971 to the early 1980s, both for all-cause mortality as well as for lung cancer and circulatory diseases (Goldblatt 1986). Further support for rejecting the artefactual explanation was provided by a number of research projects on specific types of employment, where categorisation of occupation was likely to be much more accurate (Marmot *et al.* 1984).

The Black Report had been criticised for excluding from its calculations all deaths of men aged 65 or over which constituted a steadily growing proportion of all deaths. This was countered by the argument that such premature deaths were of particular significance. Subsequently, reliable new evidence from the Longitudinal Study indicated that class mortality gradients for men after retirement age were similar to those for the later years of working life (Fox *et al.* 1986).

Concern about the implications for analysis of improving life expectancy had led Illsley to prefer to work with survival rates rather than mortality figures. This path was followed by Le Grand who calculated Gini coefficients, measuring the dispersion of age-at-death in the population as a whole without consideration of social class (Le Grand 1985). This method revealed a steady overall decrease rather than increase in inequality and consequently was regarded as supporting Illsley's position in opposing the findings of the Black Report. However, since this approach dealt with differences in mortality between individuals, rather than between social groupings, the contradiction was only apparent. It is quite compatible for steep falls in infant and child mortality

100

to have produced overall decreases in variation in the age of death while social class inequalities in mortality increased. Although Illsley saw the results of research based on survival rates as conflicting with findings based on mortality figures, Le Grand accepted that these methodologies measure different things and, as such, are complementary tools (Illsley 1987: 16, Le Grand 1986: 117–18, Townsend *et al.* 1988a: 15–16).

Social selection

The Black Report had briefly considered natural and social selection as a possible explanation of health inequalities but had discounted it for lack of conclusive evidence. Such explanations accept that health and social class are causally linked but see the causality operating in the reverse direction. As Wilkinson put it: 'Instead of saying people are less healthy because they are in lower social classes, it suggests they are in lower classes because they are less healthy' (Wilkinson 1986: 4). Illsley (1955, 1986) had favoured such an explanation, and it had been argued theoretically that social mobility could generate the observed effects (Stern 1983). Indeed, the greater the social mobility, the more the effect would be magnified, giving the illusion of a widening health gap, although the phenomenon being measured in reality would be mobility rather than health inequality.

While it is clear that health status can and does affect social mobility directly, for example when someone suffering long-term illness might have to leave demanding full-time employment for a less prestigious part-time job, there could also be an indirect association through the operation of health-related factors such as height, diet and education. The existence of a direct link is not at issue; the problem is to estimate how much this contributes to health inequality. Once more the Longitudinal Study was able to provide valuable additional evidence since its linked records made it possible to use the occupational classification in the 1971 Census together with the same individuals' death certificates. In this way a study looking at deaths during the period 1976–81 was able to control for mobility when ill health could be expected to have its greatest effect on employment – in the five to ten years before death. The new social class gradients derived from LS data resembled the original mortality gradients from the 1970–72 Decennial Supplement, which indicated that social mobility was relatively unimportant in explaining differential class mortality rates during the period of the life-cycle when most deaths occurred (Fox *et al.* 1986). A similar, later study, using LS data for a broader period, confirmed this conclusion by failing to find any clear association between mobility and mortality (Goldblatt 1988, 1989). More general studies of social mobility showed that this occurs most frequently in the early years of working life, when both morbidity and mortality rates are relatively low, casting further doubt on social mobility as a significant

101

explanation. Furthermore, specific studies of earlier periods of life suggested that other factors were more important than health in determining social mobility (see Wilkinson 1986, Blane *et al.* 1993). Thus:

> although there is evidence that social mobility is affected by ill-health and/or health potential, its contribution to observed class differences in health is probably always small in relation to the overall size of the mortality differentials. At older ages, the contribution may become almost insignificant.
>
> (Wilkinson 1986: 10)

Cultural and behavioural explanations

The Black Report listed cultural/behavioural explanations of health inequalities separately from materialist/structuralist ones while recognising that many 'see behaviour which is conducive to good or bad health as embedded more within social structures – as illustrative of socially distinguishable styles of life, associated with, and reinforced by, class' (Townsend and Davidson 1982: 118). Similarly *The Health Divide* acknowledged the force of arguments that the two approaches were closely linked if not inseparable since behaviour should be interpreted and understood within its social context. Nevertheless it is worth trying to assess to what extent the behaviour and lifestyle of individuals within different social groups can affect health. Aspects of behaviour most commonly studied – smoking, alcohol, diet and exercise – are those seen as strongly associated with major causes of ill health and death and yet regarded as largely a matter of individual choice.

If academic critics of Black's findings tended to favour artefactual explanations of the apparently widening health gap, political opponents have preferred to seek an explanation for health inequalities in the variation of individual behaviour. Although the overriding emphasis on personal responsibility and corresponding denial of the relevance of social factors can be recognised as an integral part of the ideological thrust of the Conservative governments of the 1980s, this approach has obvious attractions for any political party in power. Stressing the primacy of individual choice implies that government policy should be directed towards exhortation and education rather than the far more challenging task of achieving fundamental structural change. For example, *Prevention and Health: Everybody's Business*, a consultative document produced under a Labour government in 1976 argued that

> many of the major problems of prevention are less related to man's outside environment than to his own personal behaviour; what may be termed his lifestyle. . . . To a large extent, it is clear that the

weight of responsibility for his own health lies on the shoulders of the individual himself.

(quoted in Graham 1990: 195)

This general theme of individual responsibility reached its apogee in 1986 when the Junior Health Minister, Edwina Currie, disagreed with the findings of a newly published report linking health inequalities in the north of England to material deprivation and poverty. After commenting on 'the problems . . . of high smoking and alcoholism', as well as that of poor diet, she offered her preferred solution:

People need to look after themselves better. That is something which is taken more seriously down south . . . I honestly don't think the problem has anything to do with poverty. . . . The problem very often for people is, I think, just ignorance and failing to realise that they do have some control over their lives.

(*Guardian* 24 September 1986)

Marked regional differences in mortality gradients had been noted in the Black Report. Studies using broader measures of health confirmed the persistence of such geographical inequalities, with the health gap between the highest and lowest social classes at its greatest in the North (Townsend *et al.* 1988b, Blaxter 1990). Regions are not simple, homogeneous wholes, however. Any assumption that variations in mortality and morbidity can be explained by localised 'regional cultures' is contradicted by evidence indicating greater heterogeneity within regions than between them (Blaxter 1990: 75). *The Health Divide* had suggested that the presence of the greatest concentrations of deprivation in the North and in Scotland might explain the well-established regional differences in health. This general approach is supported by small area analyses at the level of districts and electoral wards which found material deprivation to be extremely closely associated with poor health (see Whitehead 1988: 247–9).

Yet personal choice of lifestyle cannot be discounted as a factor in determining health outcomes. There is convincing evidence – which fits with popular understanding – that certain types of 'voluntary' behaviour directly affect health. In particular, smoking, alcohol, diet and exercise are seen as closely linked to the two commonest causes of death, coronary heart disease and cancer, and all display roughly corresponding patterns to mortality differentials across the social classes. There is no space here to review the abundance of supporting evidence but there is little dissent from the view that higher proportions of people from lower social classes act in a way damaging to their health. In Hilary Graham's words: 'it is those whose health is already at risk through the cumulative effects of social and economic disadvantage who are most likely to pursue unhealthy

103

patterns of behaviour' (Graham 1990: 218). This prompts two obvious questions:

What explanation can be given of these kinds of self-damaging behaviour?
How much of the poorer health of lower social classes can be explained by lifestyle?

The first of these two questions is by far the harder to answer. Why, for example, do more people with the least resources, such as the poorly paid and unemployed, spend greater amounts – both absolutely and relatively – of their meagre disposable income on smoking (Marsh and McKay 1994, Smith 1987: 58–9)? Is it that they are less aware of studies warning of the risks? The Heath and Lifestyles survey discovered that 'the public had learned well the lessons of health education' and, if anything, 'it was those *with* the relevant "unhealthy behaviour" who were most conscious of the links with disease' (Blaxter 1990: 153, 157, emphasis in original). In discussing the specific examples of heavy smoking and unhealthy diet amongst white, working-class women Graham offered a more plausible, functional account. She explained such behaviour as a consciously adopted, rational coping strategy, providing psychological respite for women to help them better sustain family welfare, even at the known cost of their own health. For these women '[h]ealth choices are experienced more as health compromises which, repeated day after day, become the routines which keep the family going' (Graham 1990: 219).

It can be argued that research findings on the extent to which lifestyle contributes to the poorer health of lower social classes significantly reduce the importance of this first question. A longitudinal study of Whitehall civil servants concluded that behaviour was not a major factor in explaining the markedly unequal mortality patterns of different occupational grades (Marmot *et al.* 1984). Similarly the British Regional Heart Study found increased heart disease and raised mortality among the unemployed after controlling for factors such as age, class, smoking and drinking (Cook *et al.* 1982). The Health and Lifestyles survey concluded that:

circumstances, including social support, have been shown to carry more weight for health outcomes than behaviour . . . [and for the] great majority, it seems that health is *primarily* affected by the environment, and by the characteristics – occupation, income, housing – subsumed under the broad description of 'social class'.
(Blaxter 1990: 230–1, emphasis in original)

However, this study revealed a strange and vicious twist for poorer sections of society. Not only was health-threatening behaviour more prevalent in lower social classes but changed habits were unlikely to have more than minimal remedial effects as they could not compensate for multiple social disadvantages. The message was that the poor might as well smoke and drink themselves to death since social class was their main killer – not their own unwise behaviour. The survey put this more circumspectly:

> If circumstances are good, 'healthy' behaviour appears to have a strong influence on health. If they are bad, behaviours make rather little difference. . . . Only in favourable circumstances is there 'room' for considerable damage or improvement by the adoption of voluntary health related habits.
>
> (Blaxter 1990: 216, 233)

Materialist or structuralist explanations

Following exhaustive investigation of the contributory effects of voluntary behaviour to ill health, the 1986 Health and Lifestyles survey supported the unequivocal stance taken in the Black Report that in trying to explain variations in health 'it is in some form or forms of the "materialist" approach that the best answer lies' (Townsend and Davidson 1982: 122). This preferred approach was not new but similar to that adopted by Victorian pioneers. Nevertheless it seemed strange that, in spite of the vast and undeniable improvements in living and working conditions since the time health statistics were first collected systematically, the effects of social class should still produce marked health differentials in post-war Britain. Even stranger, the relative differences appeared to be both under-estimated by the official statistics of the Decennial Supplement and on the increase. Reviewing research findings, including studies since the publication of the Black Report such as those arising from the Longitudinal Study, Wilkinson concluded:

> It is now possible to say, without risk of serious challenge, that the differences in life-expectancy associated with socio-economic posi-tion are larger than the figures of class differences in mortality suggest and that these differences have been increasing since 1951.
>
> (Wilkinson 1986: 19)

Further confirmation of this alarming situation was provided by a detailed study of the Northern Health Region which found a wide health divide with 'the differences in levels of deprivation or privilege between [electoral] wards in each town and city in the North . . . generally mirrored by differences in the health of their populations' (Townsend *et al.* 1988b: 158). This study broadened the approach taken in the Black Report, which had concentrated on mortality and social class, by constructing overall indices of health and deprivation. The health index reflected morbidity by including levels of permanent illness and disability, as declared in the 1981 Census, and the proportion of low birth weight as well as using the conventional indicator of mortality rates. The study also found that its deprivation index was more effective in explaining variations in health than the relatively crude measuring instrument of social class.

A continuation of this same study, which looked at changes in mortality in the Northern Health Region between 1981 and 1991, charted a worsening situation for the poorest areas, not just relatively but even absolutely for certain age groups. While it was not unexpected that mortality rates at all ages for the poorest fifth of wards had deteriorated in comparison with others, it was a shock to discover that life expectancy for some of these groups was actually worse than it had been ten years earlier. Among men and women aged 45–64, the mortality rates in the poorest 10 per cent of wards for 1989–91 resembled national levels for England and Wales prevalent in the late 1940s and early 1950s. The researchers saw this as 'striking . . . evidence of the poorest areas increasingly coming adrift from the experience of the rest of the population' (Phillimore *et al.* 1994: 1127).

The study also provided counter-evidence to alternative explanations of health inequalities. Against Illsley's artefactual argument, that apparent inequalities are the illusory product of concentrating on the high mortality of the small and diminishing proportion of people in the lowest social classes, the new evidence showed that mortality rates of richer and poorer had not drawn closer, even when the most deprived 20 per cent of wards were excluded from the analysis. Similarly, the researchers pointed out that their findings gave no support to behavioural explanations, hinting wryly that advocates of such an approach were often inclined to adopt double standards, for 'if historical improvements in health throughout the population are generally attributed to rising living standards and improving material conditions, so worsening health among some groups and widening differentials must be related primarily to changes in the same factors' (Phillimore *et al.* 1994: 1128). To emphasise the point the single main conclusion of the research was stated in blunt terms: 'These results re-emphasise the case for linking mortality patterns with material conditions rather than individual behaviour' (Phillimore *et al.* 1994: 1125).

The relatively poor health in the North was linked in the findings to the recession of the 1980s, which this region experienced with particular severity. Appropriately, one of the four components of the overall deprivation index was unemployment, to which considerable attention had been paid in earlier research. Raised mortality rates among unemployed men had been found in the British Regional Heart Study and in the OPCS Longitudinal Study, even after controlling for social class (Moser *et al.* 1984), and 'the General Household Survey [had] consistently shown higher rates of declared "long-standing illness" among the unemployed' (Blaxter 1990: 87). The 'social selection' argument – that men had become unemployed because of their ill health rather than vice versa – was not supported as the major explanatory factor by evidence from the Longitudinal Study (Moser *et al.* 1986). Further confirmation came from a later British Regional Heart Study report, based on a survey of 6,000 men in Britain who became unemployed or took early retirement, which found an increased risk of mortality among middle-aged men that could not be explained by previous ill health (Morris *et al.* 1994). Raised mortality rates were also found for wives of unemployed men (Moser *et al.* 1986) and the health and development of children of the unemployed was poorer (Macfarlane and Cole 1985).

THE SOCIAL CREATION OF HEALTH DIFFERENTIALS

The initial preference of Black's working group for a materialist explanation seemed to have been vindicated by subsequent research. In addition, later investigations had lent further support to Black's most contentious finding – not just that a marked health divide existed but that it was increasing. Now new evidence from the Northern Health Region, an area with 'the highest proportion of households in low income categories in England and Wales', had suggested that the situation of the poorer classes was not just worsening in relation to that of the more affluent but was beginning to show signs of deteriorating in absolute terms (Phillimore *et al.* 1994: 1128).

The Northern Health Region study had considered the 1980s, a period of widening income differentials and increasing relative poverty in Britain; its findings provided the strongest case for a growing health gap unequivocally associated with material deprivation. This localised investigation provided detailed confirmation of what seemed to be happening on a wider scale. In a series of studies Wilkinson found significant correlations between mortality and income distribution, both nationally within the UK and internationally, using OECD and other data (Wilkinson 1993). For Britain he found a close relationship between long-term trends in social class differentials in mortality and relative poverty (Wilkinson 1989).

> Class difference in death rates reached their narrowest on record in the early 1950s when relative poverty was reduced to an all time British minimum. Since then relative poverty has increased at an accelerating rate and mortality differences have widened decade by decade.
>
> (Wilkinson 1993: 15)

It was not unexpected that growing differences in income should have adversely affected the mortality of the poorest, but the figures revealed a surprising outcome – that the damaging effects appeared to extend beyond the most clearly disadvantaged. International comparisons with other developed countries showed that higher overall life expectancy was associated with narrower income differentials rather than absolute levels of affluence, suggesting 'that the degree of socio-economic inequality in developed societies is a key determinant of the *average* standard of health of their populations' (Wilkinson 1993: 7, emphasis in original). In other words the health of many who are not among the very poorest is also harmed and indeed the proportion of those in absolute poverty in the developed countries would be too small, in any case, to greatly affect the national average mortality rates. Leaving aside the political difficulties, a flattening of income differentials might therefore seem the most direct way of eliminating the worst of health inequalities. Moreover there is evidence suggesting that income redistribution could significantly improve the health of the poor without noticeably affecting that of the rich (OPCS 1978, Wilkinson 1986, Blaxter 1990: 69–74).

However, a problem remains. While the destructive impact of absolute destitution is self-evident, it is far less easy to show how inequality can injure health on a sufficiently wide scale to produce such results. One solution is to argue that the extent of real penury is masked by using simple income figures as the sole measure, since this procedure carries the implication that limited resources are used in the most effective ways. And some of the most interesting research both before and after Black indicated that the influence of psycho-social risk factors might compound the direct physical effects of poverty. The Health and Lifestyles survey had emphasised the complexity of the relationship at the outset, arguing that 'the evidence of mortality suggests that the issue is not simply one of the disadvantage associated with extreme deprivation, but of a general structured association between prosperity and privilege and health experience' (Blaxter 1990: 60). The survey concluded that conventional measures of health masked the extent of differentiation in subjective experience of health between social classes, especially 'in the prevalence of common symptoms, in feelings of positive healthiness [and] in psycho-social well-being' (Blaxter 1990: 235).

In advocating further research, Wilkinson (1993) pointed to studies which stressed the importance to health of social relations, particularly 'social support', 'confiding relationships' and 'social participation'. In one study, the combination of income and social relations appeared to exert such a strong mediating influence that they counteracted known, highly damaging risk factors, for higher administrators who smoked regularly were less likely to contract heart disease than lower grades such as messengers who had never smoked (Marmot 1986). These findings appeared to confirm the view of Antonovsky (1979), who had suggested that exposure to risk factors was less important for mortality than the availability of coping resources such as social support.

As well as the important social contacts surrounding work, the labour process itself was likely to be a major source of psychological solace or harm, given the central location in perceived identity of paid employment. Phillimore drew attention to the principal, male working-class occupations in trying to explain the wide divergence in mortality between equally deprived areas in two apparently similar northern industrial towns. In Sunderland, with its dramatically lower mortality rates, 'shipbuilding and coal mining have tended to give comparatively greater autonomy and control to the workforce than steel and chemical production' in Middlesbrough, where men were characteristically process workers (Phillimore 1993: 173). In a similar vein a study of 14,000 Swedish workers, men and women, found that 'disease was twice as common among people with high job demands, low control and low social support, even after controlling for other pertinent factors' (Wilkinson 1993: 24).

As for those without work, the unemployed, material circumstances did not, in themselves, fully explain their demonstrably worse health. Growing evidence challenged the idea that the damaging effects of unemployment were simply due to the resulting low income. A small-scale but revealing long-term study showed that the onset of worsening health among the workforce at a single Wiltshire factory occurred two years prior to becoming unemployed and losing income (Beale and Nethercott 1986). This was fully compatible with other studies of stress-related illness where the perceived threat of an event, rather than the actual event itself, triggered the decline into ill health. The Health and Lifestyles survey found that for unemployed men over 30 'some additional "effect" of unemployment is demonstrated: the unemployed were more likely to be unfit and to have long-standing chronic conditions than other men with low incomes. At all ages they were more likely to have poor psycho-social health' (Blaxter 1990: 91).

Reflecting on alternative ways of understanding how poor health is generated, and the role of human agency, Phillimore condemned the limitations of the fashionable concept of lifestyle:

> The difficulty with lifestyle . . . lies with the reluctance to bring to bear on health a more complex understanding of how people act as they do. In place of a vision of how social activity and the decisions we make reproduce the structures which in turn constrain us, we resort to a concept – lifestyle – with inescapable connotations of the idioms of 'consumer choice' and 'individual responsibility'. No amount of stressing that lifestyles are socially constructed and not simply freely chosen evades the individualism of the concept.
>
> (Phillimore 1993: 173–4)

Instead he advocated a broader understanding of how people act in relation to the control and autonomy they have over their lives, seeing, like Graham, that what appear to be 'health choices' are really 'health compromises' for those in adverse conditions. This kind of approach could be extended to include the wide-ranging and damaging psycho-social effects not of just material deprivation but of inadequate incomes relative to others in the same society, such as stress, demoralisation and lack of self-esteem. Wilkinson argued that although relative inequalities had long been regarded as socially divisive at all levels, now the evidence suggested that these were actually harmful to health so that instead of 'thinking of individuals as healthy or unhealthy, it looks as if we must think more in terms of healthy and unhealthy societies' (Wilkinson 1993: 23–5). Durkheim would have felt vindicated by these developments.

THE FUTURE OF BRITAIN'S HEALTH

In Britain, as in many other countries, the scale of the excess mortality associated with lower social status dwarfs almost every other health problem. . . . If risks as great as [those arising from the social causes of disease] . . . resulted from exposure to toxic materials then offices would be closed down and populations evacuated from contaminated areas.

(Wilkinson 1994: 1113)

This bleak assessment was made in a *British Medical Journal* editorial in the issue which revealed that 'life expectancy for some groups in Britain [had] worsened for the first time in 50 years' (*Guardian* 29 April 1994). Less than a week later a governmental working party on links between poverty and ill health was announced at a British Medical Association conference on social inequalities and health. However, there is little sign of any commitment to action. Tom Sackville, Minister of Health, reiterated the preference for seeing health as a matter of individual responsibility:

It's fairly obvious that people who are in very unstable surroundings and in and out of employment are less likely to look after their health and take a positive approach to it. . . . Some people claim that poor housing, for example, leads, of itself, to bad health. I think it's more [a matter of] lifestyle, much of which, actually, could be controlled by the individual concerned.

(*File on Four,* 9 August 1994)

He went on to blame poor health on 'ignorance' and 'lack of education'. But perhaps the real ignorance is that displayed by those who make policy decisions affecting health in this country, regardless of advances in understanding the social causes of ill health. Richard

110

Wilkinson commented sceptically on the proposal to set up the new working party:

> Providing money for research is not the same thing as doing something about it. . . . In fact we know how to tackle deprivation. It is clear that the Department of Health is not the most important in terms of policies to tackle health inequality.
>
> (*Guardian* 4 May 1995)

The authors of a 1995 King's Fund report (Benzeval *et al.* 1995) made the same point: that any serious attempt to begin to close the health divide would require 'radical changes to economic and social policies' rather than new health service policies. They were scathing in their condemnation of continuing government inaction:

> It is nothing short of a national scandal that so much avoidable death, disease and disability is caused by growing social and economic disadvantages. *Tackling Inequalities in Health: An Agenda For Action* shows that this health divide could be significantly reduced if the political will existed to promote fairer policies that would create healthy life expectancy opportunities for the whole population.
>
> (Benzeval and Judge 1995)

Wilkinson went further. For him 'what matters to health in the developed world is no longer where we stand in terms of any absolute standards, but simply how we stand in relation to each other' (Wilkinson 1993: 20). As in the case of environmental pollution, where the ill–effects cannot be limited to those most immediately affected, a grossly unequal society damages the health not just of the poorest but of us all.

REFERENCES

Antonovsky, A. (1979) *Health, Stress and Coping: New Perspectives on Mental and Physical Well-Being*, San Francisco: Jossey-Bass.

Arber, S. (1989) 'Gender and class inequalities in health: understanding the differentials', in J. Fox (ed.) *Health Inequalities in European Countries*, Aldershot: Gower Press.

—— (1990) 'Revealing women's health: re-analysing the General Household Survey', in H. Roberts (ed.) *Women's Health Counts*, London: Routledge.

Arber, S., Dale, A. and Gilbert, G. N. (1986) 'The limitations of existing social class classifications for women', in A. Jacoby (ed.) *The Measurement of Social Class*, London: Social Research Association.

Beale, N. and Nethercott, S. (1986) 'Job-loss and morbidity: the influence of job tenure and previous work history', *Journal of the Royal College of General Practitioners*, 36: 560–3.

Benzeval, M. and Judge, K. (1995) 'The unequal struggle', *Guardian* 26 April 1995.

111

Benzeval, M., Judge, K. and Whitehead, M. (eds) (1995) *Tackling Inequalities in Health: An Agenda For Action*, London: King's Fund.

Blane, D., Davey Smith, G. and Bartley, M. (1993) 'Social selection: what does it contribute to social class differences in health?', *Sociology of Health and Illness* 15, 1: 1–15.

Blaxter, M. (1985) 'Self-definition of health status and consulting rates in primary care', *Quarterly Journal of Social Affairs* 1: 131–71.

—— (1989) 'A comparison of measures of inequality in morbidity', in J. Fox (ed.) *Health Inequalities in European Countries*, Aldershot: Gower Press.

—— (1990) *Health and Lifestyles*, London: Routledge.

Cook, D., Bartley, M. J., Cummins, R. O. and Shaper, A. G. (1982) 'Health of unemployed middle-aged men in Great Britain', *Lancet* 1: 1290–4.

Dale, A., Gilbert, G. N. and Arber, S. (1985) *Alternative Approaches to the Measurement of Social Class for Women and Families*, report to the Equal Opportunities Commission, Guildford: University of Surrey, Department of Sociology.

Department of Health and Social Security (1980) *Inequalities in Health: Report of a Research Working Group Chaired by Sir Douglas Black*, London: DHSS.

Dispatches (1989) 'Is the government cooking the books?', London: Channel 4.

File on Four (1994) 9 August, Manchester: BBC Radio 4.

Fox, A. J., Goldblatt, P. O. and Jones, D. R. (1986) 'Social class mortality differentials: artefact, selection, or life circumstances', in R. G. Wilkinson (ed.) *Class and Health: Research and Longitudinal Data*, London: Tavistock.

Goldblatt, P. (1986) 'Social class mortality differentials of men aged 16–64 in 1981: a note on first results from the OPCS Longitudinal Study for the period 1981–83', working paper 42, London: Social Statistics Research Unit, City University.

—— (1988) 'Changes in social class between 1971 and 1981: could these affect mortality differentials among men of working age?', *Population Trends* 51: 9–17.

—— (1989) 'Mortality by social class, 1971–85', *Population Trends* 56: 6–15.

Goldthorpe, J. H. (1983) 'Women and class analysis: in defence of the conventional view', *Sociology* 17, 4: 465–88.

—— (1984) 'Women and class analysis: a reply to the replies', *Sociology* 18, 4: 491–9.

Graham, H. (1990) 'Behaving well: women's health behaviour in context', in H. Roberts (ed.) *Women's Health Counts*, London: Routledge.

Hart, N. (1987) 'The health divide: social class still reigns', *Poverty* 67: 17–19.

—— (1989) 'Sex, gender and survival: inequalities of life chances between European men and women', in J. Fox (ed.) *Health Inequalities in European Countries*, Aldershot: Gower.

The Health of the Nation: A Strategy for Health in England (1992) White Paper, (Cm 1986), London: HMSO.

Illsley, R. (1955) 'Social class selection and class differences in relation to stillbirths and infant deaths', *British Medical Journal* 2: 1520–4.

—— (1986) 'Occupational class, selection and the production of inequalities in health', *Quarterly Journal of Social Affairs* 2, 2: 151–65.

—— (1987) 'The health divide: bad welfare or bad statistics', *Poverty* 67: 16–17.

Le Grand, J. (1985) *Inequalities in Health: the Human Capital Approach*, LSE welfare state programme discussion paper 1, London: London School of Economics.

—— (1986) 'Inequalities in health and health care: a research agenda', in R. G. Wilkinson (ed.) *Class and Health: Research and Longitudinal Data*, London: Tavistock.

Macfarlane, A. (1990) 'Official statistics and women's health and illness', in H. Roberts (ed.) *Women's Health Counts*, London: Routledge.

Macfarlane, A. and Cole, T. (1985) 'From depression to recession – evidence about the effects of unemployment on mothers' and babies' health 1930s–1980s', in

L. Durward (ed.) *Born Unequal: Perspectives on Pregnancy and Childbearing in Unemployed Families*, London: Maternity Alliance.

Marmot, M. G. (1986) 'Social inequalities in mortality: the social environment', in R. G. Wilkinson (ed.) *Class and Health: Research and Longitudinal Data*, London: Tavistock.

Marmot, M. G. and McDowall, M. E. (1986) 'Mortality decline and widening social inequalities', *Lancet* 2: 274–6.

Marmot, M. G., Shipley, M. J. and Rose, G. (1984) 'Inequalities in death: specific explanations of a general pattern?', *Lancet* 1: 1003–6.

Marsh, A. and McKay, S. (1994) *Poor Smokers*, London: Policy Studies Institute.

Marsh, C. (1988) *Exploring Data*, Cambridge: Polity Press.

Morris, J. K., Cook, D. G. and Shaper, A. G. (1994) 'Loss of employment and mortality', *British Medical Journal* 308: 1135–9.

Moser, K. A., Fox, A. J. and Jones, D. R. (1984) 'Unemployment and mortality in the OPCS Longitudinal Study', *Lancet* 2: 1324–8.

—— (1986) 'Unemployment and mortality in the OPCS Longitudinal Study', in R. G. Wilkinson (ed.) *Class and Health: Research and Longitudinal Data*, London: Tavistock.

Moser, K., Goldblatt, P. and Pugh, H. (1990) 'Occupational mortality of women in employment', in P. Goldblatt (ed.) *Longitudinal Study: Mortality and Social Organisation*, Series LS 6, pp. 129–44, London: HMSO.

OPCS (Office of Population Censuses and Surveys) (1978) *Occupational Mortality: the Registrar-General's Decennial Supplement for England and Wales 1970–2*, Series DS 1, London: HMSO.

—— (1986) *Occupational Mortality: the Registrar-General's Decennial Supplement for Great Britain 1979–80, 1982–83*, Series DS 6, London: HMSO.

Phillimore, P. (1993) 'How do places shape health? Rethinking locality and lifestyle in North-East England', in S. Platt, H. Thomas, S. Scott and G. Williams (eds) *Locating Health: Sociological and Historical Explorations*, British Sociological Association, Aldershot: Avebury.

Phillimore, P., Beattie, A. and Townsend, P. (1994) 'Widening inequality of health in northern England, 1981–91', *British Medical Journal* 308: 1125–8.

Pugh, H. and Moser, K. (1990) 'Measuring women's mortality differences', in H. Roberts (ed.) *Women's Health Counts*, London: Routledge.

Radical Statistics Health Group (1987) *Facing the Figures: What Really is Happening to the National Health Service?*, London: Radical Statistics.

Smith, R. (1987) *Unemployment and Health*, Oxford: Oxford University Press.

Stern, J. (1983) 'Social mobility and the interpretation of social class mortality differentials', *Journal of Social Policy* 12: 27–49.

Stevenson, T. H. C. (1928) 'Vital statistics of wealth and poverty', *Journal of the Royal Statistical Society* 91: 207–30.

Townsend, P. and Davidson, N. (eds) (1982) *Inequalities in Health: the Black Report*, Harmondsworth: Penguin.

Townsend, P., Davidson, N. and Whitehead, M. (1988a) *Inequalities in Health: the Black Report and the Health Divide*, Harmondsworth: Penguin.

Townsend, P. Phillimore, P. and Beattie, A. (1988b) *Health and Deprivation: Inequality and the North*, London: Croom Helm.

Whitehead, M. (1987) *The Health Divide: Inequalities in Health in the 1980s*, London: Health Education Council.

—— (1988) 'The health divide', in P. Townsend, N. Davidson and M. Whitehead, *Inequalities in Health: the Black Report and the Health Divide*, Harmondsworth: Penguin.

Wilkinson, R. G. (1986) 'Socio-economic differences in mortality: interpreting the data on their size and trends', in R. G. Wilkinson (ed.) *Class and Health: Research and Longitudinal Data*, London: Tavistock.

—— (1989) 'Class mortality differentials, income distribution and trends in poverty 1921–81', *Journal of Social Policy* 18, 3: 307–35.

—— (1993) 'The impact of income inequality on life expectancy', in S. Platt, H. Thomas, S. Scott and G. Williams (eds) *Locating Health: Sociological and Historical Explorations*, British Sociological Association, Aldershot: Avebury.

—— (1994) 'Divided we fall: the poor pay the price of increased social inequality with their health', *British Medical Journal* 308: 1113–14.

World Health Organisation (1985) *Targets for Health for All: Targets in Support of the European Regional Strategy for Health for All by the Year 2000*, Copenhagen: World Health Organisation Regional Office for Europe.

6

PROBLEMS IN MONITORING SAFETY IN BRITISH MANUFACTURING AT THE END OF THE TWENTIETH CENTURY

Theo Nichols

This short account considers the official administrative statistics on industrial injury which are produced by the Health and Safety Executive (HSE). In particular, it looks to the future and considers whether, in the 1990s, a point has been reached when none of these statistical series – for fatalities; for major injuries; and for three day and over injuries – can provide satisfactory monitoring of improvements or otherwise in safety for employees in UK manufacturing. First, the fatality rate is briefly discussed, then the rate for major injuries, then the rate for over three day injuries. The importance of the special trailer to the 1990 Labour Force Survey (LFS) is also briefly considered.

FATALITY RATE

The technical virtue of the fatality rate, apart from the fact that until recently it has provided the longest run of years for which data on comparable injuries is available, and that such statistics do unequivocally relate to injuries at work, is that we can be reasonably sure that the injuries it is intended to count are actually recorded. There are at least two different sorts of problem that arise in using time series for the fatality rate, however.

The first is that, even in order to construct a time series which stretches back from 1985 to 1960, as has been attempted in some previous work, it is necessary to make various adjustments to the official published statistics. Problems arise for example because of changes in the definitions of manufacturing industry and of the individuals deemed to be at risk (only direct operatives or also, as currently, managers, salespeople, etc.). Such difficulties can in principle be overcome (Nichols 1990: 337–8, 1991b: 583). But the closer we come to the present day, and the further we move into the future, the greater a second problem becomes, and this is a problem that there is no way round.

The second problem is one of which anyone who has looked at fatalities in manufacturing over the past few decades cannot help but be aware. It is that the progressive collapse of the manufacturing base has proceeded so far that the number who lose their lives through injury is now so small as to make further analysis of this rate exceptionally difficult. By 1985 for example, at the end point for the time series that has been used in my own previous work, the figure was thankfully as low as 124. Back in 1960, at the start of that series, it had stood at over 300.

It has been suggested elsewhere that, especially toward the end of the above period, a certain volatility in the fatality rate, as opposed to the rate for major injuries, might have been a function of the small number in the numerator (Nichols 1989b: 544, 1990: 327 Figure 6). Whether or not this is so, the small number of fatalities currently does not of course necessarily invalidate research that uses the manufacturing fatality rate for the two decades or so up to 1985. What it does suggest, on the other hand, is that it will be foolhardy to use a time series for fatalities in manufacturing as a proxy for temporal shifts in safety for the period after 1985. Provisional HSC data for 1993–94 (the most recent that is available) puts fatal injuries in British manufacturing at 64, and since then the manufacturing base has contracted yet further.

MAJOR INJURY RATE

Very briefly, from 1981, when the rate for major injuries was first introduced under the Notification of Accidents and Dangerous Occurrences Regulations (NADOR) it included injuries which took the form of various fractures, amputations, loss of sight and other injuries which resulted in admittance to hospital as an in-patient for more than 24 hours, unless for observation. The major injury rate then underwent a change in 1986 when new Reporting of Injuries, Diseases and Dangerous Occurrences Regulations (RIDDOR) were introduced. RIDDOR widened the definition of injuries which there was a duty to report. For instance, amputations of fingers, thumbs or toes were now included, not only of a hand or foot; penetrating injury and hot metal burns to the eye were included, not only loss of sight; further categories were also added, including *inter alia* loss of consciousness from electric shock, and acute illness from exposure to a pathogen or infected material (H&SS 1988: 58–9).

The introduction of RIDDOR made for a break in the series for major injuries. After 1986 HSE statisticians provided only broad estimates of what the rate would have been had the earlier reporting requirements remained in force. Moreover, there is no continuity between the NADOR major injury rate and another earlier series for 'serious injuries'. This had been abandoned in 1979 after it had become apparent that it was subject to under-reporting (this being the very deficiency of the over three day rate that the serious rate had initially been intended to overcome).

The technical virtue of the major injury rate has often been assumed to be that whilst it avoids the small number problem of the fatal rate it is also more likely to be a valid indicator of safety than the rate for over three day accidents. None of the discontinuities noted above are incompatible with such a view. They simply mean that if the major rate were to serve as an indicator of safety for manufacturing then it would be best for any long-term time series to start in 1986–87.

There is a further difficulty, however. For although doubts have been expressed over the last few years that the major rate, like the serious rate before it, may be subject to under-reporting (Aw and Harrington 1989: 68 citing Hashemi 1989, Nichols 1991a: 575, 589n), it has commonly been assumed (including by the present writer) that the major rate did not suffer from marked under-reporting and that it could therefore be used as a proxy for safety in a way that the over three day rate could not. Recent evidence from the Labour Force Survey has now put it beyond doubt that the major rate is under-reported, and that the extent of the under-reporting is very substantial indeed.

On the basis of evidence from the LFS it is now estimated that only about *one third* of all reportable non-fatal injuries at work are actually reported under RIDDOR (HSC 1991: 55). There is some variation between sectors, with as many as 70 per cent of such injuries reported in the energy sector as against a mere 15 per cent in agriculture. But it is no consolation that the level of reporting in manufacturing lies between these extremes, for it stands at only around 37 per cent. The LFS sample size makes for difficulty in arriving at more precise information about the reporting of specifically 'major' non-fatal injuries (as opposed to over three day ones, to which the above figures refer). But it is considered that the reporting level for the major injury category is actually lower than for non-fatal reportable injuries as a whole (HSC 1991: 56 and Table A).

The LFS investigation means that it cannot be assumed that the major rate is a valid index of changes in safety in British manufacturing. The nature of its limitations will only become apparent when HSE has concluded its investigation into the determinants of this under-reporting and more is known about its variability over time. But once HSE has digested the results of its ongoing inquiry into under-reporting another revision to the reporting requirements for the major rate may ensue. If so, this could introduce another discontinuity into the figures. (RIDDOR is currently under review anyway.)

Reporting of over three day accidents effectively ceased after 1982 and only resumed in 1986–87. This makes for a specific problem with continuity. But it has long been thought that decisions made by workers about whether to take time off for relatively slight injuries, and how much time they take off, are socially mediated (*Annual Report of the Chief Inspector of Factories for 1945*: 8, *Annual Report of the Chief Inspector of Factories for 1967*: x). This is one reason why it is held that the series for over three day injuries should not be used as an index of safety performance over time (H&SS 1987: 58; Nichols 1989a: 64). Another reason is under-reporting.

A decade ago Beaumont cited a Department of Employment estimate of under-reporting in manufacturing of the order of 15–25 per cent. His view then was that this and other weaknesses 'appear to be of major concern to researchers examining changes in the aggregate accident rates through time' (Beaumont 1981: 20).[1] Given that the LFS investigation puts under-reporting of non-fatal injuries in manufacturing at over 60 per cent, not 15–25 per cent, this applies *a fortiori* today. It is true enough that minor accidents have the potential to transform into major or even fatal ones, but there is no warrant to use official statistical records of these as a proxy for safety performance over time when under-reporting exists to such a remarkable extent. It has been seen, though, that not only is there still reason to believe that 'over three day injury statistics are intrinsically unreliable as a measure of safety performance', but that the reliability of the major rate ('the much smaller group of reported injuries which are both severe and unambiguously the direct result of an accident at work') which was designed to assess safety (H&SS 1987: 58) is now also open to question. And, again as noted above, the rate for fatal injuries is now likely to prove volatile because of the small number of cases in the numerator.

It would seem that, for various reasons, at the end of this century greater difficulties will almost certainly stand in the way of using official time series on injuries in British manufacturing as proxies for safety performance, over say the previous two decades, than was the case in the 1980s. Even if a consistent time series for major injuries can be fashioned for future use this will only be for a limited number of years before the end of the century.

It remains to be seen whether or not employers can be persuaded better to fulfil their legal duty to report injuries and thus increase the usefulness of the HSE administrative statistics. But even success in this regard could bring its own problems, for in future much thought will have to be given to whether increases in either the over three day rate or the major rate are a function of a deterioration in safety or of improved reporting.

There is a good case to put considerably greater resources into surveys such as the special one recently conducted by the LFS (Stevens 1992) so that estimates can be made of the extent of under-reporting. The information provided by the LFS also represents an important step forward in our knowledge about work and health in Britain in several respects. For example, it provides evidence on the extent of those injuries which are *not* required to be reported to the HSE. There are probably one and a half fold more of these than of injuries that should be reported, and at least five times more of them than the number of reportable injuries that actually are reported (H&SS 1991: 59, Diagrams 3a and 3b).[2] But work injuries, although they most certainly merit attention in their own right, are only one aspect of health and safety at work – one which, as we have seen, is often poorly reported. Another important feature of the LFS inquiry is that it also provides 'for the first time, a comprehensive workers'-eye view of the scale and make-up of work-related illness' (HSC 1991: 56). This was sorely needed,[3] as, in future, will be much-improved work injury statistics.

NOTES

1 Beaumont's focus in this article (Beaumont 1981) is, in contrast to mine, predominantly on the uses of industrial accident statistics in cross-sectional rather than temporal studies, for example inter-industry ones.

2 Further independent evidence of the substantial under-reporting of the HSE major injury rate comes from an analysis of other data on injury which was collected as part of the 1990 Workplace Industrial Relations Survey. This was examined at length in Nichols and Guy (1994).

3 Work ill health must be distinguished from work injuries. Readers interested in ill health should certainly consult the data on self-reported work-related illness in Hodgson *et al.* (1993).

REFERENCES

Annual Report of the Chief Inspector of Factories for 1945 (1946) London: HMSO.

Annual Report of the Chief Inspector of Factories for 1967 (1968) London: HMSO.

Aw, T.C. and Harrington, J. M. (1989) 'Industrial accidents: underreported and not improving', *British Medical Journal*, 298 (14 January): 68.

Beaumont, P.B. (1981) 'Industrial accidents: a useful indicator of working life?' *Industrial Journal of Manpower*, 2, 2: 19–25.

Hashemi, K. (1989) 'Hazards of the forklift truck', MD thesis, University of Birmingham.

HSC (1991) *Annual Report 1990/91*, Health and Safety Commission, London: HMSO.

H&SS (1987) *Health and Safety Statistics 1984–85*, Health and Safety Executive, London: HMSO.

—— (1988) *Health and Safety Statistics 1985–86*, Health and Safety Executive, London: HMSO.

—— (1991) *Health and Safety Statistics 1987–89*, Health and Safety Executive, London: HMSO.

Hodgson, J.T., Jones, J.R., Elliott, R.C. and Osman, J. (1993) *Self-reported Work-related Illness: Results from a Trailer Questionnaire on the 1990 Labour Force Survey in England and Wales*, London: HSE Books.

Nichols, T. (1989a) 'On the analysis of size effects and "accidents"', *Industrial Relations Journal* Spring: 62–5.

—— (1989b) 'The business cycle and industrial injuries in British manufacturing over a quarter of a century: continuities in industrial injury research', *Sociological Review* August: 538–50.

—— (1990) 'Industrial safety in Britain and the 1974 Health and Safety at Work Act: the case of manufacturing', *International Journal of the Sociology of Law* 18: 317–42.

—— (1991a) 'Industrial injuries in British manufacturing industry and cyclical effects: continuities and discontinuities in industrial injury research', *Sociological Review* February: 131–9.

—— (1991b) 'Labour intensification, work injuries and the measurement of Percentage Utilisation of Labour (PUL)', *British Journal of Industrial Relations* December: 569–92.

Nichols, T. and Guy, W. (1994) *The WIRS3 Injury Rate*, Colchester: ESRC Archive, WIRS Users Group.

Stevens, G. (1992) 'Workplace injury: a view from the HSE's trailer to the 1990 Labour Force Survey', *Employment Gazette* December: 621–38.

7

FIGURING OUT WORKING WOMEN

Jackie West

This chapter reviews some of the main uses of official statistics for understanding gender and employment, with reference both to published primary sources and secondary analyses. Data on women and work has increased exponentially since the 1970s, partly because of the introduction of equality legislation and the need to monitor its effects, partly because of major secular changes in the gender composition of the labour force. The feminisation of employment has undoubtedly been one of the most profound developments of the twentieth century, throughout Europe, North America and Australasia as well as within developing economies. But the extent of change and the forms it has taken have varied enormously even within advanced capitalism (Rubery 1988, Jensen 1988). Patterns in Britain are in many ways quite specific – for example in respect of the growth of part-time work – yet they illustrate rather well some of the intrinsic difficulties that surround interpretation of change.

The chapter concentrates on economic activity, part-time work and sex segregation, since these three dimensions of employment are of particular significance. Historically it has been economic activity rates which have characterised women's specific ('secondary') relationship to the labour market, and part-time employment remains as important for this relationship as for an understanding of what is distinctive about employment trends in Britain. Sex segregation is not only a core component of gender differences in work but also provides an excellent example of secondary analysis of official employment statistics. This is the subject of an extended discussion in the second part of the chapter. More generally, I argue that the data themselves and their interpretation have tended to obscure the terms on which women's integration has been secured and have often exaggerated the extent to which gender inequality was eroded during the 1980s.

There are pitfalls in interpreting even simple descriptive statistics on gender differences, which have to do, for example, with the criteria for counting activities in certain ways, or for including or excluding certain workers. But there are also problems with the level of analysis or aggregation, and with the variables by which disaggregated data can be analysed. Of particular sociological significance is the contrast between data sources which tap demographic variables, such as household circumstances, and those which might better allow investigation of economic factors, because of their different role in the determination of gendered work patterns, and hence their implications for theories on the greater significance of 'the family' or 'economy' in shaping gender inequalities. So, what are the main data sources available and the hazards to watch for in their interpretation?

DATA SOURCES: THEIR SCOPE AND USES

The main primary sources on employment are the Labour Force Survey (LFS), the Census of Population, the Census of Employment and its linked surveys. The following section describes their scope and highlights the particular uses of the LFS, which has recently assumed the greatest relevance for examining gender issues. The LFS and Population Census, which are household based, are the main source of data on labour force participation, while the employer-based Census of Employment and related surveys are used, in conjunction with the LFS, as the main source of data on employment patterns.

The *Census of Employment* counts jobs not people and, though biennial, has a long time series. It is, importantly, supplemented by two further sources: (1) panel surveys of employers, monthly for production industries (that is manufacturing and utilities) and quarterly for the whole economy; plus (2) centralised returns from government departments and from large organisations in industries such as banking and coalmining. It is these sources (along with the claimant count of the unemployed) which provide most of the labour market 'update' data published in the *Employment Gazette*, the monthly journal of the Employment Department (ED).[1] As well as being the most current data available, some of the tables provide gender breakdowns. One of these is particularly comprehensive: that on employees in all industries and services, which separates full- and part-time jobs by sex for all industrial groupings (a classification which is very detailed) and includes comparable data from previous quarters and the previous year.

The industry data is especially reliable since it is based on employers' own reports, and the coverage of the panel survey (around 30,000 units) includes all large workplaces (those employing 250 or more) and, altogether, over 25 per cent of all employees. However, because the panel is mainly selected from the Census of Employment (with adjustments for closures and new firms) and this is only biennial, the panel data is subject to periodic revisions in the light of the subsequent Census. An important example of this is the initial underestimates of employment in the early 1990s. The panel drawn from the 1989 Census did not adequately reflect employment growth in small firms and the scale of the shift to services. This period of recession (from a peak in June 1990 till late 1993) certainly produced employment decline, but less, according to the ED, than originally thought. The revised estimates (Curtis and Spence 1994) also suggest lower falls in manufacturing and in full-time work for both men and women.

These difficulties in tracking employment shifts may partly explain the growing discrepancy between estimates derived from Employment Census sources and from the alternative source, the LFS. Estimates of the number of employees in work used to be very close indeed but began to diverge markedly after 1990, especially from early 1992, with the LFS suggesting almost half a million more people in work than employer-based surveys, and thus a less depressed labour market. Differences in coverage between these sources have always existed but balance out, at least at aggregate level, so the growing gap is only partly due to these (Spence and Watson 1993). But these differences of coverage are in any case especially pertinent to women's work and to gender differences.

The *LFS* is a survey of individuals (about 150,000) from a representative sample of around 60,000 households, and, since 1992, covers people resident in NHS accommodation and in education establishments (though not in other institutions, whatever their role in the labour force). Importantly, it includes at least three types of employment which are excluded from the remit of employer-based surveys: domestic servants, outworkers and people employed by firms not part of the PAYE system. Private domestic service is clearly important for women, though estimated to account for less than 0.1 million workers (there are around 11 million employed women in total). Homeworkers on piece rates are excluded from employer-based surveys and are estimated at at least 0.3 million, the overwhelming majority of whom are women. Non-PAYE firms employ an estimated 0.4 million workers. Recent panel revisions to employer-based surveys have increased the number of small firms covered (in the light of their previous under-representation), but the PAYE criterion still excludes workplaces which might disproportionately recruit casual workers, many of whom will be women. Although the LFS itself excludes one source of casual workers (anyone under 16 years of age), there are other respects in which the LFS counts a great deal of marginal work, a factor of particular importance for women's economic activity rates as discussed below. In addition, the LFS covers self-employment and indeed is now recognised as the most reliable source of information on this. Of growing significance in recent years, this form of employment is highly gendered, women accounting for only a quarter. Around 17 per cent of male workers but only 7 per cent of women are self-employed (Sly 1994a).

123

The wider LFS coverage of paid work, whatever its forms and extent, is one of the major reasons why the LFS has assumed such significance in recent years. But there are other reasons too. First, it is a survey directly comparable to others undertaken in each EU state (and indeed was initiated by the EC), although the scope of individual surveys is variable and the UK survey is now more frequent and comprehensive than most (Hakim 1991a). This comparative feature of the LFS makes it of special interest for the study of gender inequalities in Western Europe (Dale and Glover 1990), the more so since the EC has played a large part in inducing improvements to UK equality legislation (Gregory 1992). The LFS time series is not that long (dating in the UK from 1973) but it was annual from 1984 and, in Britain, has been quarterly since 1992. This has hugely increased its currency and some of the other ways in which it has been enhanced are of particular relevance to gender issues as we shall see. It is highly specialised on labour market questions and allows far more detail than either of the other household surveys which include employment information (such as the GHS) or the decennial Population Census. And, corresponding to the significance with which it is regarded by the Employment Department, there has been a considerable increase in both the quantity and quality of information published from the LFS. Like all survey data, however, it must be treated with caution, as indicated below and in Chapter 3.

Annual LFS reports have often been supplemented by regular *Gazette* articles on women in the labour market, published in the autumn, with trend data from earlier surveys and, since 1992, increasingly up-to-date results. These features have provided valuable overviews, whose scope is discussed shortly, but there is a growing number of more specialised LFS analyses which include a gender dimension. Features on lone parents (Bartholomew *et al.* 1992), mothers (Sly 1994c) and part-time workers (Naylor 1994) provide obvious examples, but others, such as those on union density (Beatson and Butcher 1993) and redundancies (Cockerham 1994), are equally important. So too are *Gazette* features arising from other national surveys, like the new British household panel which has generated valuable data on, for example, carers and employment (Corti and Dex 1995a) and on qualified women (Corti and Dex 1995b).

Although the *Gazette*'s articles are extremely accessible, another source of LFS data with a substantial public profile is the *Quarterly Bulletin*, new in 1992. This presents the main results for the latest survey along with selected trend data for earlier quarters and years. In some cases there is annual trend data from 1984. The *Bulletin* is a model of clear presentation, but the gloss and readability of the data, especially in the summary reports, inevitably oversimplifies. For example, summary economic activity rates published here do not always distinguish by gender; or tables with separate sex breakdowns (e.g. on activity rates by ethnic group) may

124

include the entire adult population, not just those of working age. It is crucial to use other more detailed tables supplied in both the *Bulletin* and the *Employment Gazette*. Detailed comparisons over time may also require examination of the LFS *Historical Supplement* (that published in 1993 covers the years 1979–91). The *Bulletin*'s coverage has itself been enhanced, partly in response to user requests, and examples of new tabulations from June 1994 which are relevant to gender include an occupational and sectoral breakdown for part-time workers; a time series breakdown for men and women separately on job-related training; and household population characteristics. But there is some loss of information in the summary tables and more need, compared with previous editions of the *Bulletin* to extract it from the detailed tables.

ECONOMIC ACTIVITY

'Economic activity', synonymous with participation in the work or labour force, is problematic both conceptually and in terms of its measurement. This is particularly true for women. Overall economic activity rates for all adults will inevitably be lower than those for the population of working age, even though an increasing number of people continue to work after the age of retirement. Activity rates among the older population are affected by differences in generational expectations and opportunities, and attitudes to women's work have altered greatly since the post-war period (Martin and Roberts 1984). So crude overall rates for men and women overstate contemporary differences. In fact economic activity rates have grown closer as paid employment has become the norm for women while less expected – and certainly now less available – for men. For example, in 1993 73 per cent of all men and only 53 per cent of women were active (Employment Department 1994a). But for those of working age, the rate for men fell between 1979 and 1993 from 91 to 86 per cent, whereas that for women rose from 63 to 71 per cent (Sly 1993).

Economic activity conventionally refers to those in paid work or counted as unemployed. This excludes domestic labour, which in many developing economies neglects some productive work (Benaria 1988), though its exclusion in largely market economies is more appropriate since the relationships of domestic consumption, however unequal, are not equivalent to production relations, even including those which obtain for paid domestic labour, as Graham (1990) rightly argues. This is not in any way to imply that unpaid caring is not work; indeed it is only by distinguishing it from paid care work that its oppressive character and its role in relation to the economics of health and community care can be appreciated. A more important omission from past conventional data on economic activity is unpaid work in family enterprises, but this has been addressed in the UK LFS since 1992, bringing it into line with other EU states. The LFS thus distinguishes a separate category of the economically active who are in employment: those who do 'unpaid work for their own or a relative's business'. Though fairly small in number overall (well under 0.2 million) the gender difference is substantial: around 30–40,000 men of working age but 100,000 women (with a further 15,000 men and 4,000 women over retirement age). Women thus account for almost three-quarters of such workers. Some of this work would have been reported previously as self-employment, some as 'economic inactivity' (Sly 1993).

There are specific problems with assessing unemployment among women, as Levitas discusses in Chapter 3, problems arising from women's eligibility for benefit and, under some circumstances, from self-definition as a housewife even when made redundant (Coyle 1984). But in addition, the category of 'economically inactive: looking after home/family', may conceal outwork. Homeworking is often unreported in official surveys, for reasons which include fear of exposure to tax and benefit offices where the work is undeclared, or fear of reprisals from employers who are operating illicitly or from male relatives where, as in the case of some Muslim women, wives' participation in the public realm is proscribed. Attempts have been made in recent years to secure more reliable national estimates of homeworking through the design of special large-scale surveys (Hakim 1987, Huws 1994) but analysis has sometimes blurred the crucial distinction between workers based at or working from home (including self-employed consultants and freelance professionals) and those who work at home (including childminders, machinists, program-mers and others working for a single employer). This conflation of the production relations in different types of 'homework' is sociologically misleading and has led to exaggerated accounts of the decline of traditional homeworking. Population Census estimates in particular suggest a much more even gender and social class composition among homeworkers today than in the past. But these estimates are highly problematic because they treat as equivalent 'homeworking' undertaken by employers and managers, professionals, service workers, those in farming and all manual workers (Felstead and Jewson 1995).

All these issues draw attention to ways in which women's labour force activity can be under-represented, but there are also issues of over-representation since the LFS, at least, counts as employed anyone who reports any paid work however few their hours ('work, of one hour or more for pay or profit'). It is this which largely lies behind the lower economic inactivity rate for women in the LFS (8 per cent lower) than in the Population Census, a differential that also exists for men, though to a lesser degree (5 per cent). Significantly the Census is based on self-report and how individuals see their own circumstances in relation to the questions asked, while the LFS relies on interviewers trained to probe and to encourage respondents, through a sequence of questions, to include any job-related activity, however minor. In some cases, as Sly (1994a: 90) observes, 'when filling in the Census form, they or their partner did not report [such] activity because they saw it as less relevant than their homekeeping activity'. This, as Levitas also notes, is a particular problem with proxy respondents, but whereas Census forms are often completed by men (Sly 1994a), LFS respondents are frequently women and it is likely that interviewing them directly will produce more valid responses than relying on husbands' reporting or assessment (especially since some husbands still disapprove of their wives' employment). Equally, the LFS reports many more people working under sixteen hours a week than does the Census (3 per cent of men and 20 per cent of women in the LFS; only 1 per cent of men and 16 per cent of women in the Census). It is clear that the Employment Department regards the LFS as more accurate since it 'may provide a more complete measure of the number of people in employment than the Census': work is seen as contributing to the economy, no matter how few the hours or its difference from a person's past or future work (Sly 1994a: 94).

In theory, then, the LFS should be more reliable than the Population Census as a source on casual employment, particularly the kind of jobs which women, because of their domestic circumstances, are often constrained to take, jobs of very limited duration, such as domestic cleaning, bar or canteen work or shop work. However, it is this which leads Hakim (1993a) to argue that measures of economic activity should be redefined since they include, at least potentially, the most marginal work and the most marginal workers. It is of course important to distinguish different levels of employment commitment, but there is a danger of throwing the baby out with the bath water by disregarding certain kinds of work because they are so far removed from even 'standard' part-time employment. It is, after all, crucial to assess the extent to which very casualised work has been increasing while conventional forms of full- and part-time work may have declined. But Hakim argues that more appropriate measures are needed precisely to assess the growth of non-standard work, and it is absurd, as she notes, to treat all forms of employment as equivalent. Because this is what the LFS measure of economic activity does, it allows for over-optimistic interpretations of post-war employment growth in Britain, a point to which I return below in discussing the significance of part-time work, as well as underestimations of unemployment as discussed in Chapter 3.

Despite all these drawbacks to LFS data, the LFS is nevertheless especially useful on the labour market participation of *women* since it distinguishes rates of economic activity according to the variables of marital status and age of youngest child, the latter being a major factor differentiating women's labour market experience and of generally greater significance than the number of children. Crude activity rates, even for women of working age, are precisely that. Even in the 1970s it was clear that economic activity rates were high among women in their mid-thirties and forties, that is among those whose children were in primary or secondary school. The LFS seeks quite comprehensive information on this aspect of household circumstances and annual analyses focus heavily on it. For example, the overall activity rate in 1993 of 71 per cent averages or aggregates figures which range from 51 per cent among those with their youngest child of pre-school age to 80 per cent among those whose youngest is aged 11–15. Importantly, this latter rate is higher than that (76 per cent) among women with no dependent children (Sly 1993). More interesting relationships are clear from further cross-tabulations, showing for example that while the highest overall rate of women engaged in 'family care' (45 per cent) is among those with a pre-school child, it is the youngest women in this group (and single mothers especially) who have the highest rate of all, at over 60 per cent (Sly 1993: 496, Employment Department 1992: 452).

The LFS has become an important resource for studying more detailed aspects of women's relation to employment. Changes in the timing of women's return to the labour market following the birth of children have been a critical factor in explaining the rise in participation rates in recent decades. The greatest increase has been among mothers of under-fives (Sly 1994c). Women increasingly return earlier, and between the birth of children, rather than wait until their families are complete (Martin and Roberts 1984, McRae 1991). LFS data shows that of those inactive for domestic reasons, one-fifth tend to re-enter the labour market within a year, mostly in part-time work (Employment Department 1992, 1994b). Significantly, the data also shows that while over a third of unemployed women in 1990 were still unemployed by 1991, this was true for over half of men. The new quarterly basis of the LFS will permit more detailed analysis of individual movements in and out of work and connects to the ED's interest in labour market flows and training provision, especially for women returners (Employment Department 1994b).

'Working mothers'

The picture of 'women in the labour market' that emerges from all this data is, however, both over-homogeneous and over-domesticated. There are two principal lacunae, those of social class and ethnicity. The variables which are typically used to disaggregate the totals in published analysis of women and employment are chiefly familial in character. Cross-tabulations based on these can be extremely informative, as indicated, and much is made within the LFS of relationships between domestic constraints and 'outcomes', such as the length of time in present job and usual weekly hours according to employee or self-employed status. But there are factors which differentiate women *other* than those which distinguish their relation to men and children. And while the latter are undoubtedly important determinants of women's relation to paid and unpaid work, other social structural determinants (especially economic ones) are overlooked or underplayed. There is a general focus on domestic influences but this is exacerbated by *Gazette* articles explicity focused on 'mothers in the labour market' (Sly 1994c) or by a whole issue devoted to 'The family at work' (March 1995).

Although data on ethnicity is collected and the LFS is an important source for this (see Chapter 8 below), it is not typically integrated with general analyses of women's position in the annual *Gazette* features. Paradoxically, perhaps, it does appear in *Bulletin* reports, but is limited by the summary and highly aggregated presentation of data. For example, economic activity rates are given for men and women separately by a fourfold 'ethnic' breakdown. These show wide differences between minority women despite an overall rate which is virtually identical to that for 'white' women (see Table 7.1). But among women of working age it is white women who have the highest rates, something actually highlighted by the specialist *Gazette* feature on the ethnic minority labour force (Sly 1994b: 149). Yet we have to consult a further *Gazette* feature on lone parents (Bartholomew *et al.* 1992) to discover that 'black' women have the highest rates of labour force participation *despite* responsibilities for children. They are also much less likely than white women to work part-time, and this too is concealed by broad comparisons of economic activity between white and ethnic minority women (Bruegel 1994). The general contrast in unemployment rates is, however, striking, as Table 7.1 also shows, with that among minority women over double that of white women. Most striking of all is the fact that while activity rates for Pakistani and Bangladeshi women are very low, their risks of unemployment are the highest of all. Even in periods when the recession was less deep in 1993 and 1994, there were similar differentials.

Ethnic differences demonstrate, then, that women's relation to employment is far from simply determined by their domestic circumstances; or rather, that the significance of these varies considerably according to ethnicity. But this is a function less of cultural difference than of labour market opportunities, migration and racism (West and Pilgrim 1995).

Questions of social class are even more complex. One of the few official sources which does highlight this is that which demonstrates the more skewed distributions among ethnic minority groups (Sly 1994b). 'Black' men have the highest proportion of skilled manual, and Pakistani/ Bangladeshi men the highest proportion of semi-skilled workers. South Asian women are also more likely than others to be skilled or semi-skilled manual workers, and 'black' women have the highest proportion

Table 7.1 Economic activity and unemployment among women by ethnicity, spring 1993 (percentages)

	Economic activity		Unemployment rate[b]
	women of working age	women aged 16 and over	women aged 16 and over
White	72	53	7
All ethnic minority	54	51	17
Black[a]	66	62	20
Indian	61	57	11
Pakistani/Bangladeshi	25	24	29

Sources: Sly (1994b), Employment Department (1994a: Table 20)

Notes: a Black includes Afro-Caribbean and all other black-identified.
 b International Labour Organisation (ILO) unemployment rate.

unskilled. Social class differences, however, also play an important role in women's labour market behaviour. The highest rates of early return to work and of remaining at the same level are found among professional women, with those in managerial and administrative occupations also well placed. Downgrading is most likely for women in part-time work (McRae 1991, 1993).

It is important to emphasise that difference and diversity among women are often glossed over in data on gender differences, precisely when the focus is on simply comparing all women with all men. These differences between women do not lie only in their varied domestic circumstances; indeed they are often obscured by the focus on those alone.

PART-TIME WORK

As already indicated, it is part-time work which mainly accounts for the higher activity rates of white compared to ethnic minority women. The same is true of the highest rate of 80 per cent among women aged 40–50. The LFS has been an invaluable source for tracking the significance of part-time work for women. It accounts for 43 per cent of all employed women (including the self-employed), for approximately half those in their forties, and for two-thirds of employed mothers (Sly 1993, 1994c). In 1979 part-time work accounted for only 38 per cent of all women in employment.

The growth in part-time work has long been recognised as the main reason for women's increased role in the labour force and has led Hakim (1993a: 101–2) to argue that 'the much trumpeted rise in women's employment in Britain consisted entirely of the *substitution of part-time for full-time jobs* from 1951 to the late 1980s' (emphasis in original). She shows that long-term rates of female economic activity were actually very stable from at least 1851 to 1971 – varying from around a third to 44 per cent, the lower rates distinguishing the Censuses after 1881. As she observes, recent patterns can be made to look quite substantial by comparing them with those at the turn of the century rather than earlier. Elsewhere Hakim (1991b) has argued that part-time women workers really are a distinct category with less attachment to paid work. And the LFS is often used for evidence that most people, especially women, work part-time out of choice.

This is often interpreted to mean that part-time jobs are no less desirable, no less 'real' or 'proper', than full-time jobs, and as such has provided further fuel to government claims since the early 1980s that employment growth in the UK has been substantial. The LFS has been used to support this, but Hakim's (1993a) scepticism is based on Population Census data and she argues too that the overall rise in employment for women and men from 1951 to 1991 is largely 'illusory' since declining full-time work was 'concealed and cancelled' by rising part-time work. If employment is measured in terms of full-time equivalents, then '1988 was the first recent year in which the workforce grew larger than it was in 1951', and the recent peak in 1990 was little more than that reached thirty years earlier in 1961 (Hakim 1993a: 103).

Whether or not part-time work compensates for the decline in full-time work depends on where part-time work is concentrated and with what other factors it is associated. Since the LFS in particular allows analysis of the relationship between part-time work and household circumstances, it might be tempting to conclude that part-time work and its growing popularity is largely a function of domestic variables. But this is belied, not only by ethnic variation, but also by comparative data, since rates of part-time work are internationally quite variable. Full-time work among women is more common in, for example, the USA, France and Finland largely because of better child-care provision, not differences in family formation (Dex and Shaw 1986, Beechey 1989, Pfau-Effinger 1993).

The significance of part-time work in Britain – that which makes employment patterns in the UK so distinctive – arises from the role it plays within the economy. The LFS and Employment Census give us a limited purchase on this and reflect rather than reveal the causal processes involved.

The association between part-time working and the service sector is very clear. For example, the LFS shows that while 43 per cent of all employed women work part-time this is true of 60 per cent in personal service occupations and three-quarters or more of those in sales (Sly 1993: 491 and Table 7). Fewer than 10 per cent of men work part-time but their numbers grew considerably in the 1980s, virtually doubling in the ten years to 1994 (Employment Department 1995). It is more common (at one-fifth) among the self-employed (which includes much of the building trade). But it is the service sector which accounts for the increase, and most of the growth for men is accounted for by students who make up four in ten of all male part-timers (Naylor 1994: 477). For women it is traditional kinds of service sector work which have expanded most.

The substantial rises in part-time work are especially clear from the Census of Employment time series. However, many published LFS sources now include data only from 1984 when the survey became annual. This neglects the employment trough of the early 1980s when part-time work was the sole source of employment growth (West 1991). Even more recently its significance has been rather greater than sometimes indicated. Showing the percentage increase in part/full-time work separately for men's and for women's employment (as the *LFS Bulletin* and many *Gazette* commentaries tend to do) tends to understate the contribution of women's work generally and of part-time work to total employment growth within the economy.

In Britain, the proportion of jobs that are part-time almost doubled between 1971 and 1994, from 15 to 28 per cent. While the growth was especially rapid in the early 1990s, growth over the past two decades has been 'fairly steady . . . regardless of the different stages of the economic cycle' (Naylor 1994: 479). Undoubtedly, the increase has much to do with the changing industrial structure alone, the shift to services (Beatson 1995: 7). But the biggest growth in the number of part-time jobs (by around two-thirds in the ten years to 1994) has been in postal services, national government, retail food and transport, with growth in other retail and health services also very significant. These sectors are mostly ones where part-time jobs have markedly increased their *share* of total employment (in contrast to education and refuse services, for example) (Naylor 1994), and there appears to be a generally strong relation between declining full-time and rising part-time work. Only business services, which saw a growth in both, is an exception.

The real role of part-time work within the economy has to do with its structural significance in the expansion of the service sector and more generally in the part it plays in employers' 'labour-use' strategies. Employer recruitment policies and employment practices are, however, not accessible from household-based surveys of individuals (nor from the published Census of Employment, whose main purpose is a count of jobs). An altogether different survey is needed, and the recent Workplace Industrial Relations Survey (WIRS) is an important national source of this. It was carried out by the Employment Department in 1984, 1987 and 1990 with panel data providing for change over time within specific workplaces. Increased use of part-time and even temporary labour has actually been related to traditional rather than new rationales of flexibility (Hakim 1990, Hunter and McInnes 1991), though weakened labour market regulation in the 1980s is also relevant (Beatson 1995). But there is scope for greater exploration of part-time work and its relationship to the characteristics of establishments (workplaces), such as their sectoral and market position and industrial relations (Millward 1992).

The character of part-time work is also crucial to questions about the terms on which women have been integrated into the economy. There are indications of a limited increase in high-status part-time work (Sidaway and Wareing 1992), and some evidence of rising skill levels in recent years among part-timers. But it is not clear how far this simply reflects involvement with new technology or formal training in tasks that rarely form part of employees' actual jobs, as in retail. It is also very evident that differentials of skill and prospects between part- and full-time workers generally remain marked (Gallie 1994). This has important implications for the conclusions we can draw about sex segregation in the workforce.

SEGREGATION

Occupational segregation by sex has been an important issue since the late 1970s, largely because of growing awareness that it is this which forms the principal barrier to equal pay. It is also highly relevant to theories of labour market segmentation, and feminism has placed special emphasis on segregation as a key mechanism whereby men have retained their privileged position in work.

In Britain, it became clearer following the Equal Pay Act (EPA) of 1970 that women earned less than men mainly because their work was non-comparable and women were concentrated in low-paying occupations or industries. It was also clear that employers often evaded the Act by segregating workers who had before worked alongside each other (Snell 1979, Armstrong 1982). Men frequently supported these and other measures too, since they protected the gender gap in earnings. It has proved remarkably difficult to tackle this persisting or increased segregation via the 1975 Sex Discrimination Act or the 1983 equal value amendment to the EPA (Gregory 1992), so the facts of segregation remain as important as ever. Occupational segregation has in addition become a principal indicator of comparative gender equality, that is both of historical changes over time within a given economy and also of cross-national variation. It has been the subject of major reviews, as we shall see, and high-profile international reports on the position of women (OECD 1985).

The facts of occupational segregation are, however, far from unequivocal once it is recognised that widely differing conclusions are drawn from the data, depending on the kinds of measures used. These differences are, then, not a product of the official statistics as such but of the analytical operations performed on them, but they add to the difficulties of interpretation. What follows is a brief guide to some of the methodological issues which need to be appreciated along with a recognition of the uses and limitations of the data sources themselves. The primary sources in question, in Britain at least, are Population Census and LFS statistics.

Some 'facts' are indisputable, although their significance is more problematic. For example, most people work in effectively 'same sex' occupations. Hakim (1992: 134) shows that in Britain over eight in ten men work in occupations where they outnumber women, and a similar proportion of women are found in occupations where they outnumber men. Indeed, almost half of all men work in occupations where they form 90 per cent of the workforce. Athough this may seem very high it was true of almost six in ten male workers only eleven years earlier, in 1979. Women, by contrast are less likely to be found in heavily feminised occupations, 'only' a quarter in 1990 being in those where they outnumbered men by nine to one.

Hakim uses this and other measures, including detailed biennial data, to argue that segregation did in fact decline in the 1980s, and that there are therefore grounds for greater optimism than is generally believed, especially by comparison with the 'glacial' pace of change over most of the century and the lack of substantial progress in the 1970s. In particular, she identifies four further indicators of declining segregation: (1) greater proportional representation of women in many occupational groups; (2) a decline in women's over-representation in low-grade, less well paid occupations; (3) women's increased share of higher-status occupations; (4) the growth of integrated occupations. The significance we can attach to these is, however, somewhat problematic on account of the methodology and the available data.

Measures of segregation

The first two of these indicators are derived from the use of the Sex Ratio Index (SRI). This (or a variant of it) is one of the most widely used measures of occupational segregation and is relatively straightforward. Essentially segregation is defined in terms of women's (or men's) under- or over-representation in given occupations or sectors of the economy. That is, their share of an occupation is compared with (divided by) their share of the workforce as a whole.[2] Measured this way, segregation declined in many professional and managerial occupations, as well as in sales, catering and personal services, and overall segregation fell more in the 1980s than in any other post-war decade (Hakim 1992: Tables 7.2 and 7.3).

Similar measures have been widely adopted in comparative research too. They enable us to detect broad differences between economies in gender (in)equality and differing progress over time. For instance, it is on this basis that Dale and Glover (1990) concluded that women in the USA, compared to those in France and the UK, were less over-represented in service jobs and also had a greater presence in both administrative and managerial occupations and in extractive, processing, transport and communication industries.

The great advantage of Hakim's SRI is that it is independent of changes in the size of occupations and industrial restructuring. This is of particular importance in assessing trends in gender equality because of the relationship between female employment and the expansion of the service sector. Change in the index is a measure of real change in levels of segregation. And comparisons between countries are not affected by differences in the sizes of occupational groups. However, the SRI is not independent of the sex composition of the workforce; indeed it is not meant to be. It can, in its defence, be argued that an occupation which retains an identical sex ratio over a decade while women's general share of the workforce increases actually indicates conservatism and the SRI precisely captures this by being a measure of relative or comparative representation. Nevertheless, many critics such as Siltanen and Blackburn (e.g. Blackburn *et al.* 1993) see this as a major flaw. As Jacobs (1993: 326) puts it (in relation to another measure), a researcher wishing to assess whether segregation declines as more women enter the labour force needs a measure independent of the growth in women's numbers. A further problem is that any sex ratio index by definition can only be computed separately for women and men, but this means the level of segregation varies according to which version we use (Blackburn *et al.* 1993).

Another measure of segregation, one which is perhaps even more widely used especially in the USA, is the Index of Dissimilarity (ID). This essentially depicts the proportion of men or women in an occupation who would have to shift out of it to achieve an equal gender distribution. It thus measures the degree to which men and women are distributed unevenly across occupations. But this index is especially sensitive to the size of the occupational classification used. The higher the level of aggregation, the lower the index. Where categories are very broad, widely differing degrees of segregation at work cancel out. Industrialisation is associated with detailed occupational distinctions within manufacturing and services. Using this index in particular, as the OECD (1985) has often done, levels of segregation are higher in most industrial than in developing economies, and higher too in many of those countries which have pioneered sex equality laws. The index thus has major drawbacks for international comparisons, especially of countries at different stages of economic development, though it may be useful to assess trends within an economy over a fairly short time period, providing classifications remain the same.

The level of aggregation is relevant for other purposes too. In Hakim's view, another important measure of vertical segregation is women's share of high-status occupations (in addition, that is, to their representation in low-paid and low-status work). She is certainly right that much can be learned from the very detailed occupational classifications which are used in the UK Census and LFS. The LFS uses 550 separate occupational units (unlike the European LFS which has only eight broad groups). In this sense the UK classification is very disaggregated and permits analysis to distinguish doctors from nurses, chemists from laboratory assistants, architects from draughtsmen and so on. Hakim is able to demonstrate some interesting shifts in women's share of key higher occupations. However, the virtues of a national classification are also its weaknesses. Hakim claims that a national analysis is necessary since 'managing directors, parliamentary representatives and judges are thinly distributed at workplace level' (1992: 134). But, as she goes on to note, occupational classification does not in fact permit identification of MPs, nor even of those directors and executives who head up large companies in the private sector and 'who are men almost without exception' (1992: 137). Their invisibility in this respect is, for the study of gender inequality, arguably as critical as for studies of class inequality and the concentration of economic power (see Chapter 4 above). An even more significant drawback is that the analysis does not distinguish finer levels or grades *within* occupations and yet it is this which has generally been identified as the principal indicator of vertical segregation, that is the distribution of men and women within occupational hierarchies. It is extremely clear from case studies undertaken of certain occupations that women typically remain concentrated at the lower levels, and men tend to have a disproportionate share of higher-grade posts. School teaching is a classic example, as is medicine where the pattern of segregation also needs to take account of men and women's distribution within differentially prestigious specialities (Stacey 1988).

Alternative indices

Problems with the use of conventional indices have generated a literature all their own and attempts to devise alternatives. Blackburn *et al.* (1993: 339) show that conventional measures applied to the same data produce contradictory results, for example declining segregation using one index, an increase using the other, or a difference in the pace of change, or in the rank order of countries according to levels of segregation. It is generally agreed, though, that no one ideal measure is possible, and that different measures are needed for different purposes.

A fairly recent arrival on the scene is a measure of integrated occupations, which is especially useful in capturing those areas of work where women have successfully made inroads (Reskin and Roos 1990). Hakim (1993b) finds this a much more reliable measure for assessing the differential impact of the increase in women's full- and part-time employment. In her case the measure is, like the SRI, in effect a measure of representation. Defining 'integrated' as an occupation where women form 30–50 per cent (that is those falling within a 20 per cent band around the average 40 per cent female share of the workforce), such occupations are still a very small minority, accounting for only 12 per cent of all women workers and 16 per cent of men. But there has been some movement since 1979 and 'greater erosion of male monopolies than of occupations monopolised by women' (Hakim 1992: 139).

There are, however, serious drawbacks to such conclusions. The first is that these 'integrated occupations' vary considerably in size and status, as Hakim is well aware, including as they do farm workers, bakers, barristers, authors, shelf-fillers and fishmongers, for example. More critically, this measure again provides no purchase on vertical segregation. Pharmacy is a particularly apt example since women have made substantial inroads into this erstwhile male-dominated field. But they have done so in lower-status branches of the profession, partly as a consequence of rapid changes in retailing and the decline of an independent entrepreneurial career route which was especially attractive to men. These developments are as true of the USA as of Britain (Reskin and Roos 1990, Crompton and Sanderson 1990).

There are problems, too, with the criteria for integration. Paralleling the sex ratio index, Hakim's criteria are relative and so shift with the changing sex composition of the labour force. As already noted, this is both a strength and a weakness, depending on the kinds of question one is trying to answer. But in this case relative criteria have a particular disadvantage. Where women's labour force participation is low, say 20 per cent, an integrated occupation would be one where women formed say 10–30 per cent. In absolute terms such an occupation would be extremely male-dominated. Furthermore (and again paralleling the SRI), Hakim's criteria are different for men and women. By defining integration as within a 20 per cent band around the average female share, anomalies are created. An integrated occupation is one where women form 30–50 per cent of the workforce, so a female-dominated one has a female share of over 50 per cent, a male-dominated one has a female share of under 30 per cent.

Symmetry is no virtue in itself. The imbalance lies in the fact that this yardstick narrows male-dominated occupations to those where men form 70 per cent or more of the workforce. Hakim uses a different banding in a later analysis (1993b), namely 30 per cent around the average female share of 40 per cent (i.e. where women form between 25 and 55 per cent). Aside from inconsistencies, this more generous criterion arguably overestimates the decline in segregation achieved in the 1980s. It is also similarly uneven in its treatment of men's and women's work, since female occupations become those where women form over 55 per cent, male occupations those where men are 75 per cent of the workforce. These problems parallel those found with the SRI.

These kinds of inconsistencies are what lie behind the fixed measures of integration used by American researchers, by Reskin and Roos (1990) for whom women's share should be 40–60 per cent, and by Jacobs (1993) for whom it is the even simpler 50 per cent. As already indicated, many of these problems do not lie in the data themselves but in what is done with it, in the measures or methodologies concerned. But it is evident that interpretation is often contentious or at the very least far from straightforward.

One problem inherent in the data, however, has to do with levels of analysis. Findings on segregation will inevitably differ depending on the population base used, whatever the index or measure (Hakim 1992: 131). In particular, it is widely recognised that national occupational data provide no guide to segregation at the level of the workplace, which is typically far greater. This is for several reasons: because of vertical segregation within occupational grades or levels; because the job structure of individual workplaces and organisations is far more specialised; and because any national occupational picture aggregates establishments which can be at opposite poles on a continuum of segregation. Yet it is workplace-level segregation that is of particular sociological significance. And again it is absolute rather than comparative levels of segregation that matter for social behaviour. As Jacobs (1993: 327) notes, following Kanter (1977), there is a need to assess 'not . . . women's representation versus their labour force representation but their representation versus men'. It is absolute ratios which are likely to shape the reactions of male and female workers to each other, their social interaction and industrial co-operation, indifference or antipathy. Changes in segregation within a given workplace such as a factory will have far more influence on industrial relations or organisational culture than whether or not these changes are typical of what is happening elsewhere (Armstrong 1982, Cockburn 1984, 1991). Employers also adopt different strategies according to the gender composition of their workforce.

Another crucial example of the way in which aggregated data can be sociologically misleading has to do with full-time and part-time work. Hakim (1992, 1993b) argues that there have been two opposing trends, cancelling each other out, with real change in the full-time workforce being masked by stable or increasing segregation among part-timers, who have borne the brunt of casualisation, flexibility and 'atypical' working.

She found that integrated occupations were far more common among full-timers, one in five of whom by 1991 were in such work (1993b: 297). This is twice the proportion of that among part-timers.

Moreover, an increasing proportion of workers in female-dominated occupations are those who work part-time (30 per cent of workers in such occupations in 1971 but 43 per cent by 1991). Hakim (1993b: 298) further estimates that by the year 2000 'fully half would be part-timers . . . at which point conceptions of female-dominated and casualised occupations start to merge'. In view of this, her conclusion that future analysis should focus on full-time workers is perverse, except in the sense that it is only here that greater equality is likely to be found.

Nevertheless, the segregation data adds further weight to more general arguments on polarisation of the female workforce, as Hakim herself observes. There are, as discussed earlier, a number of other dimensions to this. Women are succeeding in breaking into male-dominated areas, even the higher echelons of managerial, administrative, professorial or consultancy work. Yet however small a minority they are among such post-holders, they are an even tinier minority of working women. Studies of vertical segregation need to pay closer attention to such divisions among the female workforce within occupations, professions and organisations. Another crucial dimension of difference within the female workforce is that of ethnicity. But difference is not just that, it is also inequality.

CONCLUSION

Inequality is often obscured by the presentation of official statistics on employment trends over the past fifteen years or so: both inequalities between women and men and inequalities among women themselves. The dominant picture is one of growing integration, a largely smooth rise in overall labour force participation and a gradual, if slow, increase in representation at all levels. This picture – of a benign economy to whose growth women are also directly contributing – is an artefact of certain conventions in the production and presentation of data.

Problems in the conceptualisation and measurement of economic activity among women are far from new, but the greater mapping of this in recent years has largely highlighted women's role in a traditional division of labour. The LFS, for example, which has assumed such importance, is a vital source of data on people's personal circumstances and their work, and hence of factors associated with the supply-side determinants of economic activity and employment patterns. These factors have been of particular importance in labour market trends among women, but the almost exclusive concern with them overstates domestic constraints on such trends and there is scope, as I have indicated, for much greater attention to social class and ethnic differences between women. The

139

increased data available in the past decade or so is not necessarily in a form most useful to sociologists. The emphasis on individual or household-based data generates problems in understanding the dynamics of part-time employment. Part-time work has remained the main growth area over the past decade, even when general levels of unemployment were falling, as have other forms of so-called 'non-standard' work to which men especially are increasingly subject. Yet the significance of these in the UK economy can only be fully grasped from workplace data and case study research which can chart the complex processes involved in decisions to restructure company employment profiles.

The popularity of 'individuated' survey sources also extends to research on gender segregation in the workforce and the resulting focus on national, aggregate occupational data tends to neglect many dimensions of the gendered division of paid labour and the processes that reproduce them. This chapter has outlined the scope and limitations of several leading measures in this area, in particular the work of Hakim. While her challenges to conventional feminist wisdom are to be welcomed, her own findings on declining segregation in the 1980s are problematic. And as she herself has shown, the polarisation of the female workforce appears to be growing rather than diminishing.

NOTES

1 Following the creation of the new merged Department for Education and Employment, the *Employment Gazette* has been retitled *Labour Market Trends*.
2 Coefficients of less than unity indicate under-representation, and degrees of that, coefficients of more than unity indicate the opposite, namely over-representation. The SRI itself is the difference between these and the closer to unity, the less the segregation.

REFERENCES

Armstrong, P. (1982) "'If it's only women it doesn't matter so much'", in J. West (ed.) *Work, Women and the Labour Market*, London: Routledge and Kegan Paul.

Bartholomew, R., Hibbett, A. and Sidaway, J. (1992) 'Lone parents and the labour market: evidence from the Labour Force Survey', *Employment Gazette* November: 559–78.

Beatson, M. (1995) *Labour Market Flexibility*, Research Series 48, London: Employment Department.

Beatson, M. and Butcher, S. (1993) 'Union density across the workforce', *Employment Gazette* January: 673–89.

Beechey, V. (1989) 'Women's employment in France and Britain', *Work, Employment and Society* 3, 3: 369–78.

Benaria, L. (1988) 'Conceptualising the labour force: the underestimation of women's economic activities', in R. Pahl (ed.) *On Work: Historical, Comparative and Theoretical Approaches*, Oxford: Basil Blackwell.

Blackburn, R. M., Jarman, J. and Siltanen, J. (1993) 'The analysis of occupational gender segregation over time and place: considerations of measurement and some new evidence', *Work, Employment and Society* 7, 3: 335–62.

Bruegel, I. (1994) 'Labour market prospects for women from ethnic minorities', in R. Lindley (ed.) *Labour Market Structures and Prospects for Women*, Manchester: Institute of Employment Research/Equal Opportunities Commission.

Cockburn, C. (1984) *Brothers: Male Dominance and Technological Change*, London: Pluto Press.

—— (1991) *In the Way of Women: Men's Resistance to Sex Equality in Organisations*, London: Macmillan.

Cockerham, J. (1994) 'Redundancies in Great Britain: results from the spring 1992 to spring 1993 Labour Force Surveys', *Employment Gazette* January: 11–18.

Corti, L. and Dex, S. (1995a) 'Informal carers and employment', *Employment Gazette* March: 101–7.

—— (1995b) 'Highly qualified women', *Employment Gazette* March: 115–22.

Coyle, A. (1984) *Redundant Women*, London: Women's Press.

Crompton, R. and Sanderson, K. (1990) *Gendered Jobs and Social Change*, London: Unwin Hyman.

Curtis, S. and Spence, A. (1994) 'Revised estimates of the workforce in employment in Great Britain', *Employment Gazette* May: 161–70.

Dale, A. and Glover, J. (1990) *An Analysis of Women's Employment Patterns in the UK, France and the USA: the Value of Survey-based Comparisons*, Research Paper 75, London: Employment Department.

Dex, S. and Shaw, L. (1986) *British and American Women at Work: Do Equal Opportunities Policies Matter?*, London: Macmillan.

Employment Department (1992) 'Women and the labour market: results from the 1991 Labour Force Survey', *Employment Gazette* September: 433–59.

—— (1994a) *Labour Force Quarterly Bulletin* 8, June.

—— (1994b) 'Women and training: data from the Labour Force Survey', *Employment Gazette* November: 391–402.

—— (1995) *Labour Force Quarterly Bulletin* 11, March.

Felstead, A. and Jewson, N. (1995) 'Working at home: estimates from the 1991 Census', *Employment Gazette* March: 95–9.

Gallie, D. (1994) 'Patterns of skill change: upskilling, deskilling or polarisation?', in R. Penn, M. Rose and J. Rubery (eds) *Skill and Occupational Change*, Oxford: Oxford University Press.

Graham, H. (1990) 'The concept of caring in feminist research: the case of domestic service', *Sociology* 25, 1: 61–78.

Gregory, J. (1992) 'Equal pay for work of equal value', *Work, Employment and Society* 6, 3: 461–74.

Hakim, C. (1987) 'Homeworking in Britain: key findings from the National Survey of Home-based Workers', *Employment Gazette* 95: 92–104.

—— (1990) 'Core and periphery in employers' workforce strategies: evidence from the 1987 ELUS survey', *Work, Employment and Society* 4, 1: 157–88.

—— (1991a) 'Cross-national comparative research on the European Community: the EC Labour Force Surveys', *Work, Employment and Society* 5, 1: 101–17.

—— (1991b) 'Grateful slaves and self-made women: fact and fantasy in women's work orientations', *European Sociological Review* 7, 2: 101–21.

—— (1992) 'Explaining trends in occupational segregation: the measurement, causes and consequences of the sexual division of labour', *European Sociological Review* 8, 2: 127–49.

—— (1993a) 'The myth of rising female employment', *Work, Employment and Society* 7, 1: 97–120.

—— (1993b) 'Segregated and integrated occupations: a new approach to analysing social change', *European Sociological Review* 9, 3: 289–314.

Hunter, L. and McInnes, J. (1991) *Employers' Labour Use Strategies – Case Studies*, Research Paper 87, London: Employment Department.

Huws, U. (1994) *Home Truths: Key Results from a National Survey of Homeworkers*, Leeds: National Group on Homeworking.

Jacobs, J. (1993) 'Theoretical and measurement issues in the study of sex segregation in the workplace: research note', *European Sociological Review* 9, 3: 325–30.

Jensen, J. (ed.) (1988) *Feminisation of the Labour Force: Paradoxes and Promises*, Oxford: Polity.

Kanter, R. M. (1977) *Men and Women of the Corporation*, New York: Basic Books.

McRae, S. (1991) 'Occupational change over childbirth: evidence from a national survey', *Sociology* 25, 4: 589–605.

—— (1993) 'Returning to work after childbirth: opportunities and inequalities', *European Sociological Review* 9, 2: 125–37.

Martin, J. and Roberts, C. (1984) *Women and Employment: a Lifetime Perspective*, London: HMSO.

Millward, N. (1992) *Workplace Industrial Relations in Transition*, Aldershot: Dartmouth.

Naylor, K. (1994) 'Part-time working in Great Britain: an historical analysis', *Employment Gazette* December: 473–84.

OECD (1985) *The Integration of Women into the Economy*, Paris: OECD.

Pfau-Effinger, B. (1993) 'Modernisation, culture and part-time employment: the example of Finland and West Germany', *Work, Employment and Society* 7, 3: 383–410.

Reskin, B. and Roos, P. (1990) *Job Queues, Gender Queues: Explaining Women's Inroads into Male Occupations*, Philadelphia: Temple University Press.

Rubery, J. (ed.) (1988) *Women and Recession*, London: Routledge.

Sidaway, J. and Wareing, A. (1992) 'Part-timers with potential', *Employment Gazette* January: 19–26.

Sly, F. (1993) 'Women in the labour market', *Employment Gazette* November: 483–502.

—— (1994a) 'Economic activity results from the 1991 Labour Force Survey and Census of Population', *Employment Gazette* March: 87–96.

—— (1994b) 'Ethnic groups and the labour market', *Employment Gazette* May: 147–59.

—— (1994c) 'Mothers in employment', *Employment Gazette* November: 403–13.

Snell, M. (1979) 'The Equal Pay and Sex Discrimination Acts: their impact in the workplace', *Feminist Review* 1.

Spence, A. and Watson, M. (1993) 'Estimating employment: a comparison of household and employer-based surveys', *Employment Gazette* October: 465–70.

Stacey, M. (1988) *The Sociology of Health and Healing*, London: Routledge.

West, J. (1991) 'Women's working lives: current labour market patterns in Great Britain', in W. R. Heinz (ed.) *The Life Course and Social Change: Comparative Perspectives*, Weinheim: Deutscher Studien Verlag.

West, J. and Pilgrim, S. (1995) 'South Asian women and employment: the impact of migration, ethnic origin and the local economy', *New Community* 21, 3: 357–78.

8

COUNTING ETHNICITY: SOCIAL GROUPS AND OFFICIAL CATEGORIES

Steve Fenton

A central character in the film *My Beautiful Launderette* was questioned about his social and political allegiances and, in some exasperation, retorted 'Look . . . I am a professional businessman, not a professional Pakistani!' Taking our cue from this example, 'ethnic identification' may seem to be primarily a matter of choice. The question becomes 'How does a person identify himself or herself?' But it would be wrong and misleading to view all ethnic and racial identifications as chosen. As Lowry says, 'there is something fundamentally wrong with the notion that ethnic status is elective' (1982, cited in Killian 1983: 78). In social life and in official reporting identities are subject to constraints. Throughout the 1980s in the United Kingdom, for example, statistics on the ethnic origin of the population were largely derived from a 1981 Census question which recorded the birthplace of the head of household. All those in a household where the head was born in, say, India were recorded, in effect as 'Indian'. In a wider grouping they were counted as part of the New Commonwealth and Pakistan ethnic minority population. As the decade wore on it became possible to refer to the ethnic origin question used in the Labour Force Survey and this *was* based on a kind of self-assignation to categories provided by the survey and with a category 'other, specify' on the list. This was the first time in official recording practices in Britain that ethnic origin was recorded and was, in a sense, regarded as something 'chosen'. Where a respondent fills out a return for a household, he or she also 'chooses' on behalf of others.

But 'choice' of ethnic identification by contrast with the answer to a question about, for example, place of birth of self or parents, is by no means the only dimension along which measurement varies. The form of measure used and the type of question asked has varied very greatly from time to time and country to country. This is because just as historical and political circumstances have varied, so have ideas about what kind of thing should be recorded. We need to be clear about the different measures used and the concepts underlying them.

ETHNIC GROUP AND RELATED CONCEPTS

We could confine ourselves to describing how 'ethnic group' membership has been recorded in Britain. But this would be imprudent for two principal reasons. First, membership of an 'ethnic group' has never been recorded in a British Census until the most recent 1991 enumeration. Second, both in practice and in theory, ethnic group is a concept closely allied to an array of related modes of identification. A discussion of these is essential to grasping the complexities of interpreting official data on 'ethnicity'.

A part of the population may be considered to constitute an *ethnic group* when its members share certain characteristics of ancestry and culture (Killian 1983: 77). For sociological purposes, which differ from Census-recording purposes, the members of such a group are usually thought not only to share a measure of common culture often exhibited by religion and language, but also to participate together in social institutions, to have a certain shared social organisation and purposeful 'membership' which the members, in some sense, assert. This collective institutional definition of an ethnic group is not at all represented in Census recording. Here, group statistics are only an aggregation of all the individual responses. From Census data we may speak of the ethnic group 'Indian' without regard to the degree to which Indians in Britain constitute an ethnic group in a collective or socio-political sense. The only connection lies in the fact that if the collective 'ethnicity' were weak one would (eventually) expect the individuals to cease to record themselves as 'Indian'. It should also be noted that ethnic group has meaning at law, since the 1976 Race Relations Act forbids discrimination on grounds of ethnic origin. To bring a case an individual must not only belong to an (ethnic) group but also show that the group to which he/she belongs is properly an ethnic group in the eyes of the law. All these things considered, social science and official records do display a good measure of agreement about what 'ethnic group' and 'ethnic origin' mean. The core of the concept is common ancestry, often national such as Polish, or sub-national such as Tamil, and common culture, frequently of language or religion, with all of these in some degree 'accepted' or 'chosen' by the individual.

The term *race* is no longer accepted as valid by social science. This is largely because of its history, in which this term, purporting to classify divisions of humankind, became part of now discredited theories of behaviour, character, and indeed of all human social organisation (Banton 1977b, Miles 1982). The term 'racism', referring to theories based on 'race', survives because that mode of thinking survives despite the discrediting of what was considered to be the science of races. The connotations of the term are principally physical (in technical language, phenotypical) so that appearance marked by skin colour and other physical characteristics has been, and remains, central to the concept of race (compare Sillitoe and White 1992: 143). Even some social scientists hang grimly on to the term race, merely placing it in inverted commas, presumably to signify that it is not real. But like Tariq Modood 'I find it a waste of ink to put race in scare-quotes' (1992c: 10). If it is not a real or useful sociological designation why retain it at all? The only sensible course is to replace race by ethnic group as the Census has striven to do. But the term race is still heard and seen often enough that it is wise to understand its antecedents. It is also interesting to note that visibility has been seen as a reason for recording ethnic group (Sillitoe 1987).

Nationality is, above all, a legal concept denoting formal membership of a nation state. A person may be described as a British 'national' because they have a legally recognised status as a citizen of Great Britain, usually acquired by birth (in Britain) sometimes by naturalisation, and sometimes because British citizenship has been held by persons living in some parts of the Commonwealth.

All British Censuses since 1841 have recorded the *place of birth of individuals* and, in some Censuses, additional information has been derived from recording the place of birth of an individual's parents and/ or the *place of birth of the head of household* in which an individual lives. Place of birth is closely allied to ethnic origin since country of origin is frequently the source of the shared ancestry, language and culture which themselves are constituent elements of ethnicity. Until the British Census recorded ethnic origin in 1991, data about place of birth was the main source of information of a kind which approximated to the notion of ethnic origin. But of course they are by no means the same thing. Place of birth may be misleading as a guide to ethnic origin, as in the case of people born in East Africa who are 'ethnically' Indian or Asian or Gujarati. And as long as ethnic identity survives the first generation of an in-migrant group, the birthplace of subsequent generations in Britain may be said to conceal their ethnic origin.

We have then ethnic group, race, nationality, and country of birth, which are quite closely linked concepts and/or demographic character-istics; and all of them have been measured by surveys and Censuses both in Britain and in other countries. Although they are linked, they must not be confused one with another. Race is an obsolete term and concept deriving from a discredited theory of racial differences. It has survived by a kind of historical inertia in some classifications, or as an element of a classification. It also survives in its derivative forms where ideas of racial difference form the basis of discrimination or of political ideologies, that is in such terms as racial discrimination and racism (Sillitoe and White 1992: 143). It continues to be used loosely as a kind of alternative to ethnic group. However, the term racial discrimination requires the existence of a group (a race) to which the victim of discrimination can be seen to

145

belong. Ethnic group, unlike race, refers to something sociologically real; and ethnic identity has a social reality both at a collective and individual level. Its principal referents are shared culture, language and religion, often deriving from shared national or sub-national origin. Nationality is a legal concept expressing the idea of the nation-state to which an individual belongs by way of legal status. Country of birth, and the country of birth of parents or of the head of household, are simple demographic facts about an individual, which are frequently recorded in official statistics and sometimes used as a proxy for ethnic origin.

The next question to address is how and why these population factors have been the subject of official recording. We shall be looking in detail at the case of Britain, but different countries have developed different and changing modes of recording facts relevant to one or more of the above demographic measures. This is partly because there are important variations in the reasons why ethnicity-relevant demographic facts have been recorded.

Many Censuses began recording race or ethnic origin before the discrediting of the term race, and so terms which reflect the belief in discrete races of the world have continued to appear in official recording practices. In the USA, race, expressed as physical appearance (i.e. colour), has long been part of public records and this is also true in some countries of the Caribbean (Sillitoe and White 1992: 142, Killian 1983). In South Africa prior to the downfall of apartheid, a belief in discrete racial groups was at the very heart of state administration and all people were assigned to a racial category. The rationale for recording race was either that it was taken to be self-evident that racial differences were among the most important that could be measured, or, as in South Africa, the social system was so thoroughly racialised that racial classification was the central element of public administration and policy.

In nineteenth-century Hawaii (later to become an American territory in 1901 and a state in 1959), native Polynesians were recorded as Hawaiians, white Europeans and Americans as Caucasian (a classic nineteenth-century racial category) and others by their immigrant origins such as Chinese and Japanese. They were in some doubt about Portuguese, who were sometimes included with Caucasians, and sometimes recorded separately. Once Hawaiians began inter-marrying in considerable numbers with Chinese, 'Caucasians', Filipinos and Portuguese, they were recorded as part-Hawaiians. In other words the non-Hawaiian part was 'lost'; just as the non-Maori part of part-Maoris has been 'lost' in official records in New Zealand (Lind 1967, Spoonley 1988).

In Canada the measurement of ethnic origin has been seen to be important because immigration has been such an important element of both population and labour policy (Richmond 1967). For over a century Canada has accepted immigrants as a source of needed labour and as an instrument of population policy. The latter was long predicated on the idea that the balance of population found in the first half of the twentieth century would be perpetuated, that is, it would remain mostly European in origin and predominantly British (Richmond 1967). By the 1970s this pattern was not being sustained and a growing proportion entered Canada from such areas as the Caribbean, Mexico and Asia. Immigration and ethnic ancestry were important for another crucial reason in Canada – their relevance to the balance of French and English in Canadian society and culture.

By contrast, in several European countries the concept and fact of nationality, particularly in measuring immigration, appears to take on social significance and an important place in recording practices. As one writer has expressed it:

> European countries collect and analyse their migration statistics by nationality – distinguishing 'foreigners' from 'nationals' by their country of citizenship. A number of countries maintain population registers from which the statistics are obtained, and a few countries, such as Switzèrland, operate a special register for foreigners.
>
> (Haskey 1992: 39)

But, Haskey continues, with respect to Britain,

> the large majority of those who immigrated from the Common-wealth countries into Great Britain are no longer 'foreign'; and it is this consideration which renders 'nationality' of limited use when attempting to measure the extent of past immigration, or the number of those of foreign origin living in Britain. It has largely been for this reason that nationality has not been asked as a Census question in the United Kingdom since 1961.
>
> (Haskey 1992: 40)

THE BRITISH CENSUS

In the remaining portion of this chapter I will present an account of recording practices in Britain, especially since the 1961 Census. In so doing I shall pay attention to the following questions. What ideas lie behind what is measured in Censuses? How do the measures relate to the concepts I have outlined? Why are particular dimensions measured? What can we learn from the results, or how can we be misled by them?

The 1961 Census was the last one to record nationality. Earlier anti-immigrant agitation had been couched as concern about *foreign* and *alien* incomers (Holmes 1988), and in 1906 Britain had passed the Aliens Act which restricted entry into Britain (Foot 1965). Through much of the nineteenth century and into the twentieth century, popular and political venom had been directed towards Irish, Jewish, Lithuanian and other incoming groups (Holmes 1988). Large numbers of Europeans, especially Polish, had entered Britain after the Second World War and the Irish continued to do so in larger numbers than any other single group. From 1950 onwards Britain began to accept considerable numbers of immigrants from the Caribbean (the majority from Jamaica), and from South Asia. Although these immigrants filled vacant positions in a full-employment economy (Peach 1968), by the late 1950s there were the beginnings of some popular and organised political opposition to what was often called 'coloured immigration'. Voice was given to the view that Britain was and should remain a 'white man's country' (Miles and Phizacklea 1984). Immigrants who had been seen, and had seen themselves, as temporary residents became long-term settlers, partly in response to increasingly restrictive immigration legislation. In the 1960s racist and anti-immigrant sentiments grew, culminating in the speeches of Enoch Powell whose view, that the England we knew and loved (Smithies and Fiddick 1969) was being radically altered, received widespread support. Immigration control was prominent on the political agenda, successive Acts were passed (1962, 1968, 1971) and arguments about the numbers who had entered and were deemed likely to enter were regular and often shrill (Moore 1975, Moore and Wallace 1975).

The 1961 Census could only provide country of birth data but, in the climate I have just described, the Home Office issued estimates of numbers of 'coloured immigrants' in Britain (Booth 1988). The International Passenger Survey provided another guide to the country of origin of people entering Britain (Booth 1988). The 1971 Census recorded not only country of birth but also the birthplace of a respondent's parents. There was increasing use of the term 'New Commonwealth' (later New Commonwealth and Pakistan) as distinguished from 'Old Commonwealth'. The latter meant Canada, New Zealand and Australia. New Commonwealth referred to those countries which had gained independence in the 1960s. With reference to migration to Britain and country of birth statistics, New Commonwealth was mostly made up of Jamaica and other Caribbean countries, South Asian countries India, Pakistan, Sri Lanka and Bangladesh, and some (East) African countries, especially Kenya and Uganda from where many people of Indian ethnic origin were expelled in the late 1960s and early 1970s. Given that the great majority migrating from these latter areas were either African, Caribbean of African descent, or South Asian, and that the Old Commonwealth was almost all white, the Old and New Commonwealth distinction was tantamount to a vulgar distinction between white and coloured. From the 1971 Census it was possible to estimate the New Commonwealth population from the data on parents' birthplace which augmented the simple country of birth data.

Through the later 1970s it began to be argued that the British Census ought to have an 'ethnic origin' or 'ethnic group' question. This met with opposition from varied quarters, including minority groups who were suspicious of the reasons for collecting such data (Booth 1983, 1988). With the added difficulty of constructing an acceptable question, after several trials which produced unpromising results (Sillitoe and White 1992), the proposal to ask about ethnic group was abandoned for the 1981 Census. Soon after the 1981 Census was completed, further trials and plans were set in motion which would lead to an ethnic group question being asked in the 1991 Census for the first time in British history. The 1920 Census Act had originally permitted the Census to inquire about 'nationality, race and language' (Sillitoe and White 1992), and this was now put into practice.

However, the Labour Force Survey, initiated in 1979, included a question about ethnic group. The LFS was conducted throughout the 1980s and continues to the present; but after 1991 it incorporated the Census form of the ethnic group question (discussed in Teague 1993; for other important surveys see Brown 1984, Daniel 1968, Rose *et al.* 1969, Smith 1977). The question asked in the LFS had been 'To which of these groups do you consider (x) belongs', with the respondent potentially answering for all household members. The options provided on the accompanying flashcard permit the following categories: White; West Indian or Guyanese; African; Indian; Pakistani; Bangladeshi; Chinese; Arab; Mixed or Other origin. Those choosing (or having chosen for them) the 'Mixed or other' category are asked for more detail:

> As a result, it was possible to reclassify many of these answers in terms of the main categories listed in the question. A small number of people initially classified as being of mixed descent, who further described themselves solely in terms of European ancestry, have been reclassified as White.
>
> (OPCS 1991: 24–5)

The LFS is based on interviews with approximately 150,000 persons and contains a substantial number of 'ethnic minority' respondents (about 7,000). It has therefore been a principal source of estimates about characteristics of the ethnic minority population in the last decade. But although it is a large sample survey it cannot be used for *local* estimates of population characteristics. For this reason, particularly at the local level, social scientists and administrators had to 'make do' with the 1981 Census results for a whole decade. The 1981 Census did not record the parents' country of birth in the manner of the 1971 Census. But it did record and present in national and local tables population characteristics in which the population was classified by the *country of birth of the head of household*. This classification is also available in the 1991 Census but it is much less reliable as a proxy for ethnic group than it was in the 1981 Census. Users of this data must be careful about what it means; this is especially true for anyone looking back to the 1981 data which has been so widely used as an approximation to ethnic group measurement.

A person enumerated in the Census can be classified according to the country of birth of the head of the household in which they reside. So if we have a household in which there are four persons, John (father) and Olive (mother) and Angela and Roy (both children of John and Olive) *and*, for the purposes of the Census, John is enumerated as the household head, *and* John was born in Jamaica, then John himself and Olive and Angela and Roy are, for this variable, listed as Jamaican. To be precise, each of the four is enumerated as living in a household in which the head of household was born in Jamaica. If this measure is to be a proxy for ethnicity or for a white / non-white classification then the assumption was that John was probably not only Jamaican born but also of Caribbean-African descent; that Olive was probably Caribbean-African too and that their children were Caribbean-African in ancestry though, maybe, British born. If John, Olive, Angela and Roy had been asked to describe their own ethnic group in their own terms a range of responses would have been possible: John might have said 'Jamaican', Olive 'African-Caribbean', Angela 'British' or maybe 'Black British' and Roy 'Black'. In 1981, in so far as 'ethnic origin' was measured, John, Olive, Angela and Roy were all classified by John's birthplace, Jamaica. In data grouped under wider headings this would have become part of the total New Commonwealth and Pakistan population which was widely used as a proxy for ethnic minorities.

It was recognised that even in 1981 this was unsatisfactory, for two reasons. First, up to 15 per cent of those classified in this way may have been 'white', belonging to families who had returned from former colonies, especially India. Second, it excluded from the minorities count those of, say, Black Jamaican descent who were born in Britain. In other words it is possible that John above was born in Jamaica as the son of a white British landowner settled there and has subsequently come to Britain, and that he and his white family would have been 'wrongly' classed as ethnic minority; and had Angela, born in England of Black Jamaican parents, moved from her parental home and set up her own household of which she was head, she and all in her household would not in 1981 have been classified in the (proxy) ethnic minorities category. It was readily recognised that by 1991 the second type of error, of undercounting, would have become very considerable indeed, rendering the proxy measure virtually useless.

Political opposition to the Census directly recording ethnic origin continued to be expressed to some degree in trials in the 1980s, especially by African-Caribbean ancestry groups and individuals (Booth 1988, Sillitoe and White 1992). There was also continued concern with the more technical and conceptual problem of how to ask the question and what form of classification to use, while suspicions about the purpose and confidentiality of the recording of ethnic origin continued to be voiced. Detailed accounts of the different formats and of the tests and trials can be found in articles in *Population Trends* (Sillitoe and White 1992, Sillitoe 1987) and other sources (Booth 1988). However, a format was agreed and adopted for the 1991 Census, and was announced in the House of Commons by Kenneth Clarke on 13 November 1989 as an important step forward in policy and practice:

> We hope this decision will be welcomed by the many people and organisations who have expressed a need for the kind of statistical information the question and others will provide. Statistical information on ethnic groups, together with that on, for example, housing, employment and age structure, will help central and local government and health authorities allocate resources and plan programmes taking account of the needs of each group. It will also help employers and those providing services identify and tackle areas of racial disadvantage. . . . I am delighted that it has been possible to take this important step. The government is firmly committed to playing its part in eliminating racial discrimination and promoting equal opportunities for all ethnic groups. The Census question will provide valuable help with this work.
>
> (White 1990: 12)

The question finally asked in the 1991 Census was one where respondents were asked to assign themselves to one of a series of categories, or, if none of these was appropriate, to write in a self-description under the category 'Other'. The question merely asked the person completing the form to tick the appropriate box, but adds:

> if the person concerned is descended from more than one ethnic or racial group, please tick the box to which the person considers he/she belongs, or tick the 'Any other ethnic group' box and describe the person's ancestry in the space provided.
>
> (OPCS 1993: 474)

The categories given, in the order in which they appear on the form, are: White; Black – Caribbean; Black – African; Black – other (please describe); Indian; Pakistani; Bangladeshi; Chinese; Any other ethnic group (please describe) – thus distinguishing between 'Black – other' and 'Any other'.

THE 1991 CENSUS: INTERPRETING THE RESULTS

The result was that the 1991 Census contains three of the kinds of measure we have discussed: ethnic group in response to the new question;

151

population classified by the birthplace of head of household; and country of birth statistics. These indicators give different pictures of the numbers and composition of minority populations in the UK. Tables 8.1 and 8.2 show the population classified by the birthplace of the head of household, and by the birthplace of each individual. Three different delineations of minorities are possible from this data, and a fourth from the new question on ethnicity. If we take responses to the direct question about ethnic group, of the 54,888,844 persons in Great Britain, 51,873,794 were categorised as 'white', and 3,015,050 (or 6 per cent of the total) were 'non-white'. Table 8.2 shows that the number born outside the UK was 3,746,122 (of whom almost 600,000 were born in Eire), or 6.9 per cent of the total population. Table 8.1, however, shows that 4,908,493 people lived in households headed by someone born outside the UK, some 9.1 per cent of the (resident in household) population. It also shows that 2,635,431 (or 4.9 per cent) were born in a household where the head of household was born in the New Commonwealth.

Table 8.3 shows the summary ethnic classification of those 3 million people who did not answer 'White' to the Census question. A close examination of one group, 'Indian', illustrates what can and cannot be learned from Census data. First, the 840,255 who are identified as Indian includes 352,448 persons who were born in the UK. This is 42 per cent of the total, part of that growing proportion of all ethnic minorities who are born in this country. The Census reports 487,807 Indians, as defined in response to the ethnic group question, who were born outside the United Kingdom. The overwhelming majority of these (475,391) were born in what are termed the New Commonwealth countries. Of these, 30 per cent were born in (East) Africa, and 66 per cent in India. This is an important distinction, since we know that, as well as some similarities, there are broad differences between these two groups. Many of the former are Gujaratis and Hindus. They share the experience of having lived in Uganda or Kenya and other East African countries. Many came as a result of strong pressures to leave, including expulsion, and there is among them a higher

Table 8.1 UK population classified by birthplace of household head, 1991

Population in h/hold where head of h/hold born in:	*Residents in household*
Total persons	54,055,693
United Kingdom	49,147,200
Not UK, of which:	4,908,493
Irish Republic	780,479
New Commonwealth	2,635,431
Rest of world	1,492,583

Source: OPCS (1993, vol. 1: 304, Table 3)

Table 8.2 UK population by birthplace, 1991

Country of birth	No. of persons
Total persons	54,888,844
United Kingdom	51,142,722
Outside UK, of which:	3,746,122
Irish Republic	592,550
New Commonwealth	1,688,396
EC (not incl. above)	493,890
Remainder of Europe	174,146
Turkey	26,597
Old Commonwealth	177,355
Africa (not incl. above)	146,869
Asia (not incl. above)	231,045
America (not incl. above)	185,033
USSR	27,011
Other	3,230

Source: OPCS (1993, vol. 1: 136, Table 2)

Table 8.3 UK persons not describing themselves as 'white', 1991

Chosen description	No. of persons
Black Caribbean	499,964
Black African	212,362
Black (other)	178,401
Indian	840,255
Pakistan	476,555
Bangladesh	162,835
Chinese	156,938
Other Asian	197,534
Other	290,206

Source: OPCS (1993, vol. 1: 405, Table 5)

proportion of people with business and professional experience (Robinson 1988). They also to some extent constitute a group in the sociological sense, and not just a Census category, and retain some collective institutional forms in the UK (Barot 1987).

Whilst these are the two large groups, there are interesting small groups beyond them. The ethnic group question enables the Census for the first time to enumerate the Indo-Caribbean population, the 4,815 people of Indian ancestry whose antecedents lived, worked and settled in the Caribbean (Dabydeen and Samaroo 1987) and who have now come to live in Britain. The year 1995 is the 150th anniversary of the arrival of Indians in the Caribbean, a century and a half of life in the diaspora. Again, their life experience marks them off in some degree as a sociologically distinct group.

If we turn to the Indians born outside the United Kingdom but *not* born in the New Commonwealth countries, we find 2,217 from South Africa, who may have lived quite a significant part of their lives under the apartheid system, 3,969 were born in parts of Africa not within the New Commonwealth. Over 1,000 were European-born – 705 from countries in the European Union, and 316 from elsewhere in Europe. These figures include 163 born in Norway, twenty-eight in Turkey, seventeen in the USSR – quite different social, cultural and political backgrounds from, say, Kenya. And somewhere in Britain are two people who are enumerated Indian and were born in Albania. Although the numbers are quite small (in some cases tiny!) it is enough to remind us of the great diversity in human experience, migration and life trajectories which can be concealed within broad categories. Whilst the Census can enumerate people as 'Indian' it does not by that simple enumeration say anything about the social constitution of a group or about the extent to which it is a group at all rather than a mere category. But further exploration and cross-tabulation does assist us in this respect, and it reveals both commonality and considerable diversity.

Finally, under ethnic group data there are some categories that could possibly *include* people of Indian ancestry (as well as many others of different ancestries) who did not respond 'Indian'. They are most likely to be included in the 'Black – other than mixed' category. This is where the ethnic group question was answered by ticking the 'Black – other' box and adding some elaboration. Excluding those who wrote in 'mixed', the responses, totalling 88,236, have been subdivided by the Census analysts into four groups: Black British (58,106); Black – East African, Asian or Indo-Caribbean (1,271); Black – Indian Sub-continent (Not Elsewhere Specified) (4,005); and Black – Other Asian (24,854). All of these categories may include people of Indian ancestry.

The category Black British does not, however, necessarily contain all those (of whatever ancestry) who prefer to think of themselves in this way. The Census form does not offer this as a category, and the only scope for variation from its seven categories is in write-ins in the 'Black – other' and the 'Any other ethnic group' boxes. But it is clear that a very small proportion of all those who returned the Census form utilised the 'write-in' boxes. Almost certainly any category (perhaps particularly Black British) would attract more responses if it were a provided category; but only further research and question testing would tell us *how much* more.

To remind us of the extent to which the information we get from the Census depends on the categories utilised, we can look at the category

'Indian' using two different methods from the Census: 'country of birth' and 'persons by birthplace of head of household'. These tables were still presented in 1991. Looking simply at country of birth, there were 409,022 people born in India, and 220,605 born in East Africa. This data excludes all those enumerated as Indian on the basis of the ethnic group question but born in the UK. It also includes, however, a considerable number of people who were born in India but were enumerated as 'white' (62,895 or 15 per cent), as well as those from East Africa who are of African rather than Indian ancestry. These groups of people show how birthplace data is an imperfect proxy for 'membership' of an ethnic minority, and its weaknesses in further classifying the ethnic minority population.

We can look at the relationship between place of birth of head of household, and place of birth of individuals, for the two main groups of 'Indians' in Britain; that is, where the head of household was born in India or in East Africa. When the data is in the form of persons in a household where the head was born in India, it 'catches' more, probably most, of the people born in Britain of Indian ancestry. Most, because many (but by no means all) Indian-British young people will still be in their family household – where the head was born in India or East Africa. Compared with 840,255 identified as Indian on the basis of the ethnic group question, this data shows 692,692 people living in households where the head of household was born in India; of these nearly half (305,091) were themselves born in the UK. If we look at households headed by someone born in East Africa, they contained 312,155 people in 1991, of whom 117,628 were born in the UK. The more that the British-born ethnic minority young people establish new households, the more this form of data becomes an unreliable proxy. In fact the 1981 Census, though itself unreliable in this respect (counting in whites and not counting new households of British-born minorities), was probably the only and last one where this proxy was even roughly usable in this way. But had the ethnic group question, with all its limitations, not been introduced, this probably would have been the proxy for ethnic group on the 1981 model. We can see that it is almost 150,000 less than the total enumerated as Indian by ethnic group.

The illustration of the category 'Indian' shows the way in which Census data is collected and presented and demonstrates the tenuous relationship between enumeration categories and possible social realities. As argued at the outset, a number of contested ideas lie behind the term ethnic group and other terms which are in theory or practice related to it. In particular, we must distinguish between three levels of analysis. First, there is the social reality of people's lives and the actual constitution of society. Second, there is a whole range of sociological concepts which are designed to grasp this reality, ethnic group among them. Third, there are specific questions asked in the Census for a variety of administrative and other purposes which approximate in some ways to sociological concepts and, if we exercise great care and attention, give us some guide – but no more than that – to social realities of individuals and society in Britain in April 1991. Unless we understand how the questions and categories are constructed we may risk jumping injudiciously from Census measurements to presumed social realities. This is especially so as the social reality changes when, for example, more Black people or Asian people are born in Britain and establish their own households, since we have seen that the different measures, although all bearing upon ethnicity, produce different results.

Furthermore, we have stressed that what the Census calls a group is really only an aggregate of individuals making the same response to the Census, not a group in any sociological sense. The official statistics do not tell us anything directly about the social constitution of Indians in Britain. In the Census, there is a sense in which the 840,255 Indians are simply 840,255 people who checked 'Indian' in the box on the Census form. Even this is not quite true, because Census forms are filled in by people taking on the role of head of household who answer for others in the household. Thus the 'ethnic group' of probably about two-thirds of the people enumerated as Indian was nominated for them by someone other than themselves. And clearly there is a strong attraction of the categories offered to the respondent. Few people choose to elaborate by way of write-in in the 'Other' categories. All these are among the things which need to be considered by social scientists in using Census data.

THE CENSUS CATEGORIES

The most outstanding feature of the ethnic group question is that one category is chosen by 94 per cent of the population. If we really think that ethnic differentiation is an important dimension of a society such as Britain, then this is an extraordinarily skewed conceptualisation. It has two overwhelmingly important implications. First, the category white is utterly undifferentiated. Secondly, the 6 per cent of the population choosing non-white categories are the ones effectively regarded as ethnic minorities. This is to confirm a popular conception, a political conception, and previous categories utilised by the Census, especially the category 'New Commonwealth'.

The Census and the Census reports do not use the term ethnic minority groups. But in discussions closely allied to the production of the Census (Sillitoe 1987, Sillitoe and White 1992), construction of the ethnic groups categories was clearly based on a conception of ethnic minorities as constituted by Black Caribbean and Asian populations. In that sense the Census record is not about ethnic groups but about a much older conception – colour. The 94 per cent/6 per cent split is a white/non-white split, and to this degree corresponds to the older New Commonwealth and Pakistan classification. Since very few people make use of the 'Other' category which could differentiate whites, we have no data by ethnic group on a whole host of potentially relevant categories. Among these would be all those with continental European origins, those from America and the Old Commonwealth, and above all the Irish ethnic group. About all these groups, we have in effect only birthplace data. And the birthplace data tells us that there are in Britain almost half a million people born in countries in the European Union, another 174,146 born elsewhere in Europe, 26,597 born in Turkey, 177,355 born in the Old Commonwealth and almost 600,000 born in the Irish Republic. Using the bare birthplace data as a guide this is approximately 1.5 million people.

If we consider the Irish by the 1981 standard measure of ethnic origin, birthplace of head of household, in 1991 we have 780,479 people living in households where the head was born in the Irish Republic. Of these, 444,905 were UK born and would not 'count' in simple birthplace statistics. At almost 800,000 Irish we have the second largest ethnic group in Britain, Indians being the largest. Indeed, when all Ireland, North and South, is the basis of the head of household measure, the 1991 Census records over a million Irish people. In the ethnic group question where respondents wrote in their definition it is estimated that only 20,000 wrote in Irish. The Census omission of Irish from 'ethnic group' seems all the more curious if we accept that the purpose of enumeration of ethnic group is to measure disadvantage and, by implication, discrimination. There is abundant evidence (as we shall see below) that the Irish in Britain experience a disproportionate share of poor material circumstances and, for example, poor health which would make information about them valuable for exactly the same reasons as those given for the current classification. This brings us to two important questions: how were the categories constructed, and why do we have such a question at all?

The Census question as it appears on the form delivered to households actually contains no guidance as to what the term 'ethnic group' is intended to cover. Strictly speaking it is not even a question, since the only instruction in the section of the form is 'Tick the appropriate box'. As we have seen, there are seven substantive options: white, Black – Caribbean, Black–African, Indian, Pakistani, Bangladeshi, Chinese. These categories are a mixture. One (white) is an unequivocal 'colour' category. Four (Indian, Pakistani, Bangladeshi, and Chinese) are national origin categories. They are ethnic group categories in the sense that Polish or Polish-American is a common-sense ethnic group in the United States. They are not however simple nation-state categories because people considering themselves Indian or Chinese may have come from Uganda, Malaysia, Singapore or Hong Kong. It is clear that in the 1991 Census people of Indian origin coming to Britain from, say, Kenya, have described themselves as Indian. The other two categories (Black – Caribbean and Black – African) combine within the categories themselves both a 'colour' designation and a national, regional or continental origin. After these two categories there is a Black – Other category with the invitation to please describe. The positioning of this 'please describe' box effectively creates a break between the top and the bottom section of the box. The category 'Any other ethnic group' is positioned at the bottom and is an invitation to anyone not, so to speak, satisfied with the offered categories to write something in.

The Census format is exactly the same as that recommended by the Commission for Racial Equality in a press release of 7 December 1988. But before that, for the purpose of ethnic monitoring by employers, the Commission had been recommending ethnic origin categories which differed significantly from this. In a guide for employers first published in June 1978 and still issued (in a revised form) in August 1987 the classification was boldly based on two categories, Black and White, which headed two quite discrete boxes. Furthermore, the category 'Asian origin' appeared within the box 'Black', a form of identification which was rejected by many Asians and resisted, it seems, in the end successfully (Modood 1988, 1992a, 1992b, Banton 1977a). The 'White' box also suggested, within it, 'European origin (including UK origin)' with the write-in instruction below, 'Other – please specify' (Commission for Racial Equality 1987: 12). This invited more differentiation within the white category, as well as including the evocative, controversial and ambiguous category 'European'. This form of classification stems from the 1980s when the difference between the Black/White format and the ethnic origin format was much contested. In fact the 1991 Census steps away from the stark Black/White distinction but retains the terms within it, whilst distancing the national origin terms such as Indian and Pakistani from the colour distinction. So the Census is a curious mixture of old 'racial' categories and national origin categories. It should be noted that the Census does not use the term 'ethnic origin', rather 'ethnic group', although the explanatory note is largely concerned with ancestry and descent.

This brings us to the question of why we have such categories at all. It is not easy to say with authority why we had the 1971 and 1981 proxies for ethnic group except that country of birth information had always been collected. Booth (1988) provides a critical analysis of such official data collection. The classification of persons by parents' birthplace (1971) and birthplace of head of household (1981) certainly combined with the New Commonwealth category to give an estimate of what at the time was often referred to as Britain's 'coloured population'. The data was used in the debates about immigration and about the nature of British society as a multicultural or multiracial society. Just how this data was used depended on the standpoint of the speaker, but many commentators agree that a discourse was established in which 'tough' immigration control was seen to be right and the presence of 'immigrants' or 'minorities' or 'black people' viewed as a problem (Miles and Phizacklea, 1984). It is not surprising that the trials of an ethnic group question for the Census were met with suspicion (Booth 1988, Sillitoe and White 1992). But at the same time, the Commission for Racial Equality and others wanting to pursue policies for the elimination of discrimination believed that nationwide ethnic group statistics would greatly assist their cause (Sillitoe 1987). Public funds (principally the Rate Support Grant, Section 11 funds and Urban Programme support) were distributed by criteria which included the presence of racial or ethnic minorities and this made the doubts about the 1981 proxy all the more serious.

By the time the question was accepted for the 1991 Census the government, in its public statements, had apparently accepted the need for ethnic group data if there were to be concerted efforts to reduce discrimination and disadvantage. This was so despite the fact that throughout the early 1980s the government had been unremittingly hostile to efforts to implement equal opportunities at the level of local authorities (Ball and Solomos 1990). By the time the 1991 question was planned and eventually implemented, commentary in *Population Trends* was routinely citing the need to combat disadvantage and discrimination as the rationale for the question (White 1990). Of course it is by no means clear that Census data can show discrimination, let alone combat it. But American experience indicated that the ability to show a pattern of disadvantage or disproportion, for example in representation in an occupational group, can be critical supporting evidence in a particular case. It remains to be seen how the 1991 data will be used; the next decade will begin to show whether the hopes of the equal opportunity lobby were justified.

THE UNDIFFERENTIATED WHITES: SOCIAL INEQUALITIES, ETHNIC GROUPS AND THE IRISH

One of the most remarkable features of the classification is the failure to differentiate the white category, seemingly forcing 94 per cent of the population into one box. Probably the instance of Irish people in Britain constitutes the most obvious example of the weakness in this format. There is overwhelming evidence that Irish people in Britain constitute a minority in many of the same ways as those included in the 6 per cent which the ethnic group question effectively identifies as 'not white'. We have already seen that the Irish are a large group in the British population. Since they are not identifiable in the ethnic group question we have to fall back on birthplace data in order to account for the Irish at all. The Census treats Ireland in several ways. Usually a distinction is made between born in the Irish Republic and born in Northern Ireland (with Ireland, part not stated, being assimilated to the Republic count). We also find persons classified as 'Irish' by being counted as living in a household where the household head was born in Ireland. In some tables 'Ireland' is treated as one category which includes the Republic and Northern Ireland. Thus we have a count of persons living in a household where the household head was born in Ireland. This gives the largest statement of the 'Irish' population, being 1,089,603. In *this* mode of enumeration it is the largest single ethnic minority population in Britain.

In the 1991 Census presentation of housing characteristics this is in fact the way in which Irish are counted, for inclusion in a table in which other ethnic groups are measured by the now familiar ethnic group question categories (OPCS 1993: 769ff. and Table 11.) From this table we can inspect five housing and household deprivation characteristics – lack of shower/WC; no central heating; no car; housing density of more than 1.5 persons per room; and living in a one-room household. On three of these measures – lacking shower/WC, no central heating and one-room households – *the Irish have the poorest figures of any ethnic group.* On a fourth measure – no car – they are very much poorer than the overall population, with 35 per cent of households not owning a car. (The corresponding figure for the Black-Caribbean group is 48 per cent). On only one of the five housing characteristics, persons per room, do the Irish have a 'favourable' profile.

If we look at the Census measure of socio-economic group we see that the differences between all ethnic groups (including the Ireland category, for these purposes based on persons over 16 years of age born in Ireland) are not very marked, nor are the differences between the 'minority' groups and the white or total population profile (OPCS 1993: Table 16; Robinson 1990). For males in the professional and managerial classes, the Irish proportion is very similar to that of the whites as a whole (33 per cent and 36 per cent respectively) and the notable differences are the under-representation of the Black-Caribbeans (19 per cent) and the over-representation of the Indians (41 per cent). The Irish are the group most under-represented in the skilled non-manual category. In the combined semi-skilled and unskilled classes they are (at 25 per cent) similar to the Pakistani group (26 per cent), exceeded by the Black-Caribbean men (28 per cent), but have higher proportions in these classes than the Indians (19 per cent) and the whites (also 19 per cent). There are reasons to regard these social class measures with some caution, as other chapters in this book indicate. But in so far as this data gives us an approximate measure of class distribution, the Irish appear to be over-represented in the semi-skilled and unskilled occupational groups, broadly similar to

Pakistanis and Black-Caribbeans. This socio-economic profile of the Irish may be contrasted with evidence of the emergence of a significant middle class, especially in some ethnic minority groups (Jones 1993, Robinson 1988) and with evidence of differences in class profile between groups termed ethnic minority. This also runs counter to the familiar (not unfounded but much oversimplified) equating of 'non-white' minorities with lower class position.

In studies of health and population differences, ethnic origin categories are rarely available and reports rely on birthplace data (Ahmad 1992, Balarajan and Raleigh 1993, Fenton *et al.* 1995). They thus constitute studies of differences between immigrant groups by country of birth. In one of the best known of these it is clear that those born in the Republic of Ireland have a poorer standardised mortality ratio than those born in India and Pakistan for deaths from all causes for both men and women aged 20–69 (Marmot *et al.* 1984: 22). They also differ from other immigrant groups in having poorer SMRs than the residents of the country from which they came. The 'selection effect' (that the more healthy migrate) appears to work for all groups except the Irish. Marmot *et al.* write that 'like Scottish immigrants, Irish immigrants have a high SMR from almost every cause of death', and continue: 'the high mortality from alcohol related diseases . . . accidents and violence reflect not only the cultural patterns but the poorer than average social and working conditions of Irish immigrants' (1984: 68).

The 1991 Census data on health available in published form is not particularly useful because it is not standardised for age. In the 1991 Census the question on 'limiting long-standing illness' (well established in other surveys) was asked for the first time. In the County of Avon tables this data was available by ethnic group, again including the 'persons born in Ireland' category. Of the total population of Avon, 11.9 per cent report a limiting long-standing illness, the percentage being the same for the white population as a whole. Other ethnic groups show lower proportions, except the Black-Caribbean, 13.2 per cent of whom report long-standing illness. But the 'born in Ireland' group show the highest proportion of all – 16.9 per cent. However, this category is an elderly population compared not only with other ethnic groups but also with the general population. But other studies also suggest poorer health among those of Irish origin (Cruickshank and Beevers 1989, Williams 1992), and taken together with housing and employment data undoubtedly support Marmot's argument that the poor health (measured by higher SMRs) for the Irish group reflects poorer working and living conditions.

The example of the Irish suggests that the failure to differentiate the 'white' category is difficult to justify. This is all the more the case if the general justification of the ethnic group question in the Census is the identification of disadvantage in an effort to combat discrimination. The material comparing ethnic groups along dimensions of disadvantage also demonstrates that there are notable socio-economic differences within and between those (non-white) groups which the Census does identify in the ethnic group question. Since class differentiation within and between ethnic groups appears to be growing, it becomes all the more important to remain cognisant of those inequalities, grounded in class conditions, which are so doggedly persistent. Whilst the government claims to be dedicated to reducing ethnic inequalities and combating discrimination (the justification for the Census question and other forms of ethnic monitoring) it makes no such claim with regard to general social inequalities, even declaring targets to reduce these as unattainable and too costly.

CONCLUSION

The press, popular discourse and, quite often, academic work fail to make any clear distinction between sociological phenomena which are quite different in meaning and outline. Thus to be an 'immigrant' is not the same thing as being a member of an 'ethnic minority' and neither is the same as the category 'black' or, as frequently stated in the 1950s and 1960s, 'coloured'. The early part of this chapter showed how these categories may be confused and how they may be clarified. We have also seen that it was not until 1991 that the Census attempted an independent measure of 'ethnic group', and that prior to that public administrative use was made of a proxy which depended on the birthplace of the head of household. Place of birth is an interesting piece of information but it is only the roughest of guides to ethnic origin, and may be seriously misleading.

The proposal to include a question about ethnic group in the Census was surrounded by suspicions and controversy, and one of the most perceptive commentators has consistently raised doubts about the reasons for its inclusion (Booth 1988). Its implementation in the 1991 Census has certainly provided more information than previous Censuses, information that was also less obviously flawed than that which preceded it. There is however evidence that many people from black and minority ethnic groups did not make a Census return (Owen 1993; see also Chapter 1 above) and we still have to wait and see how vigorously the information will be used as a tool with which to fight 'racial' disadvantage. The government's hostility, throughout the 1980s, to local government efforts to confront discrimination and racism is difficult to square with the avowed aims of the ethnic group Census question. At the same time, as this volume shows, many other sources of information, which can illustrate the growing social inequalities, have been under attack. This makes more difficult the exploration of the relationship between ethnic origin and social inequalities.

The history of official figures in the field of immigration and ethnic origin also shows a consistent tendency to define the so-called non-white population as 'problematic'. Other public surveys have typically defined minority status as being about 'colour'. As the latter part of this chapter has shown, the 1991 Census barely departed from this tradition, effectively dividing the population into white and non-white. But the other subdivisions within the non-white category (such as those based on birthplace data) do permit the analysis of differentiation. In several respects, some of which have been cited, this differentiation appears to be increasingly significant and it can be important to know just how to disaggregate figures which are frequently presented as a whole. Finally, the failure to differentiate within the white category means that a group whose ethnic origin has real sociological meaning may remain hidden.

REFERENCES

Ahmad, W. I. U. (ed.) (1992) *The Politics of Race and Health*, Bradford: Race Relations Research Unit, University of Bradford and Bradford and Ilkley College.

Balarajan R. and Raleigh, V. S. (1993) *The Health of the Nation: Ethnicity and Health*, London: Department of Health.

Ball, W. and Solomos, J. (eds) (1990) *Race and Local Politics*, London: Macmillan.

Banton M. (1977a) 'On the use of the adjective "black"', *New Community* 5, 4: 480–3.

—— (1977b) *The Idea of Race*, London: Tavistock.

Barot, R. (1987) 'Caste and sect in the Swaminarayan movement' in R. Burghart (ed.) *Hinduism in Great Britain: The Perpetuation of Religion in an Alien Cultural Milieu*, London: Tavistock.

Booth, H. (1983) 'Ethnic and racial questions in the Census: the Home Affairs Committee Report', *New Community* 11, 1&2: 83–91.

—— (1988) 'Identifying ethnic origin: the past, present and future of official data production', in A. Bhat, R. Carr-Hill and S. Ohri (eds) *Britain's Black Population*, 2nd edition, London: Radical Statistics Group/Gower.

Brown, C. (1984) *Black and White Britain: The Third PSI Survey*, London: Heinemann.

Commission for Racial Equality (1987) *Monitoring an Equal Opportunities Policy: A Guide for Employers* (first published 1978), London: Commission for Racial Equality.

Cruickshank, J. K. and Beevers, D. G. (1989) *Ethnic Factors in Health and Disease*, London: Wright.

Dabydeen, D. and Samaroo, B. (eds) (1987) *India in the Caribbean*, London: Hansib/University of Warwick.

Daniel, W. W. (1968) *Racial Discrimination in England*, Harmondsworth: Penguin.

Fenton, S., Hughes, A. O. and Hine, C. (1995) 'Self-assessed health, socio-economic status and ethnic origin', *New Community* 21, 1: 55–68.

Foot, P. (1965) *Immigration and Race in British Politics*, Harmondsworth: Penguin.

Haskey, J. (1992) 'The immigrant populations of the different countries of Europe: their size and origins', *Population Trends*, 69: 37–47.

Holmes, C., (1988) *John Bull's Island: Immigration and British Society 1871–1971*, Basingstoke: Macmillan.

Jones, T. (1993) *Britain's Ethnic Minorities*, London: Political Studies Institute.

Killian, L. (1983) 'The collection of official data on ethnicity and religion: the US experience', *New Community* 11, 1&2: 74–82.

Lind, A. (1967) *Hawaii's People*, Honolulu: University of Hawaii Press.

Lowry, I. (1982) 'The science and politics of ethnic enumeration', in W. A. van Horne and T. V. Torreson (eds) *Ethnicity and Public Policy*, Madison: University of Wisconsin System.

Marmot, M. G., Adelstein, A. M. and Bulusu, L. (1984) *Immigrant Mortality in England and Wales 1970–78: Causes of Death by Country of Birth*, Studies on Medical and Population Subjects 47, London: OPCS.

Miles, R. (1982) *Racism and Migrant Labour*, London: Routledge & Kegan Paul.

Miles, R. and Phizacklea, A. (1984) *White Man's Country: Racism in British Politics*, London: Pluto Press.

Modood, T. (1988) '"Black", racial equality and Asian identity', *New Community* 14, 3: 397–404.

—— (1992a) 'On not being white in Britain: discrimination, diversity and commonality', in M. J. Taylor and M. Leicester (eds) *Ethics, Ethnicity and Education*, London: Kogan Page.

—— (1992b) *Not Easy Being British: Colour, Culture and Citizenship*, Stoke on Trent: Runnymede Trust and Trentham Books.

—— (1992c) 'If races do not exist, then what does?: racial categorisation and ethnic realities', paper presented at a conference to mark the retirement of Michael Banton, University of Bristol, 8–10 September.

Moore, R. (1975) *Racism and Black Resistance in Britain*, London: Pluto Press.

Moore, R. and Wallace, T. (1975) *Slamming the Door: The Administration of Immigration Control*, London: Martin Robertson.

OPCS (1991) *Labour Force Survey 1988 & 1989*, London: HMSO.

OPCS (1993) *1991 Census: Ethnic Group and Country of Birth, Great Britain*, vol. 2 of 2, London: HMSO.

Owen, C. (1993) 'Using the Labour Force Survey to estimate Britain's ethnic minority populations', *Population Trends* 72: 18–23.

Peach, C. (1968) *West Indian Migration to Britain*, London: Oxford University Press.

Richmond, A. (1967) *Post War Immigrants in Canada*, Toronto: University of Toronto Press.

Robinson, V. (1988) 'The new Indian middle class in Britain', *Ethnic and Racial Studies* 11, 4: 456–73.

—— (1990) 'Roots to mobility: the social mobility of Britain's black population 1971–87', *Ethnic and Racial Studies* 13, 2: 274–86

Rose, E. J. B., Deakin, N., Abrams, M., Preston, M., Vanags, A. H., Cohen, B., Gaitskell, J. and Ward, P. (1969) *Colour and Citizenship: A Report on British Race Relations*, Oxford: Oxford University Press.

Sillitoe, K. (1987) *Developing Questions on Ethnicity and Related Topics for the Census*, London: OPCS Occasional Paper 36.

Sillitoe, K. and White, P. (1992) 'Ethnic group and the British Census: the search for a question', *Journal of the Royal Statistical Society*, Series A, 55, 1: 141–63.

Smith, D. J. (1977) *Racial Disadvantage in Britain*, Harmondsworth: Penguin.

Smithies, B. and Fiddick, P. (1969) *Enoch Powell on Immigration*, London: Sphere.

Spoonley, P. (1988) *Racism and Ethnicity in New Zealand*, Auckland: Oxford University Press.

Teague, A. (1993) 'Ethnic groups: first results from the 1991 Census', *Population Trends* 72: 12–17.

White, P. (1990) 'A question on ethnic group for the Census: findings from the 1989 Census test post-enumeration survey', *Population Trends* 59: 11–20.

Williams, R. (1992) 'The health of the Irish in Britain', in W. I. U. Ahmad (ed.) *The Politics of Race and Health*, Bradford: Race Relations Research Unit, University of Bradford and Bradford and Ilkley College.

Paul Abberley

Until recently sociological discussion of disability occurred as a backwater of medical sociology, or as a minor constituent of the sociology of deviance. Even today, the topic is not mentioned in the vast majority of general textbooks, nor is it dealt with in mainstream courses on social structure. But with the growth since the mid-1980s of organisations of disabled people which see their 'problems' from a social and political perspective, a new agenda for the sociology of disablement has arisen. In this context, statistical representations of disability have been the subject of thoroughgoing and fundamental criticism.

The first nationwide investigations of disability were conducted by the OPCS on behalf of the Ministry of Health in 1969 and culminated in a study of almost 250,000 households, of which 8,538 were followed up and interviewed in depth (Harris 1971, Buckle 1971). Degree of disability was operationalised in terms of a series of questions concerning capacity for self-care. The responses to these questions resulted in total adult population projections, with a division into four categories, as shown in Table 9.1.

Table 9.1 Estimated numbers of disabled adults in England, Scotland and Wales, by disability category

Disability category	no.
1 Very severely handicapped	157,000
2 Severely handicapped	356,000
3 Appreciably handicapped	616,000
4 Impaired	1,942,000
Total	3,071,000

Source: Adapted from Harris (1971)

Note: Estimates based on OPCS survey for Ministry of Health, 1969

Since one of the main purposes of the survey was to estimate the number of people who might qualify for attendance allowance, impairment, in this survey, is distinguished from handicap in terms of self-care needs, the former term implying nil or minimal need. In addition to this, the General Household Survey asked questions about 'limiting long-standing illness, disability or infirmity' between 1976 and 1989, and over the years the proportion of adults responding positively to this question rose (Breeze *et al.* 1991). In 1979 the government of the day established the Committee on Restrictions Against Disabled People. By the time its findings, up to now the only official report on discrimination against disabled people received by a British government, were published (CORAD 1982), another party, disinclined to pursue the issues raised, was in power. Instead, a new OPCS survey of disability in Britain was commissioned in 1984 by what was then the Department of Health and Social Security. The stated objective was to provide accurate information about the number of disabled people in Great Britain with different levels of severity and their circumstances, for the purposes of planning benefits and services – though there is no evidence that subsequent government activity in the field of disability has been influenced by the results. Four separate investigations were carried out between 1985 and 1988, covering adults in private households, children in private households, adults in communal establishments and children in communal establishments, and the results published in six reports. I will concentrate on the first two reports, which are of the most general significance (Martin *et al.* 1988, Martin and White 1988). For the sake of clarity, these will be referred to as the prevalence and the finance report respectively.

THE PREVALENCE REPORT

The most obvious feature of the prevalence report is its revision of estimates of the number of disabled adults in England, Scotland and Wales, from just over 3 million to nearly 6 million adults. A small part of this can be attributed to a more elderly population. But the massive increase in the number of disabled people reported in the press at the time of publication of the new survey's results is largely a function of the different criteria of disability employed in two discrete investigations conducted nearly twenty years apart. Disability statistics, since they are not part of an ongoing data-gathering process, reflect more clearly than many others the particular interests of their constructors, which results in a radical and readily apparent discontinuity between data from different sources.

The prevalence report describes the main concepts and methods common to all four surveys and presents the prevalence estimates from the two surveys of disabled adults. It states that this disability survey attempts to be more wide-ranging than the 1971 survey, by trying to cover all types of disability whatever their origin, and by setting a lower 'disability threshold'. The survey distinguishes thirteen different types of disability and produces a formula to establish ten severity categories. This procedure gives rise to projections for the population as a whole, as shown in Table 9.2.

Examples of those who fall into categories 1–3 indicate that these individuals, whose daily activities are restricted, but not severely so, would not have been eligible for inclusion in the least severe 1971 survey category of 'impairment'. If we were to subtract these individuals from our total, the estimated total proportion of the population who are 'disabled' would roughly correspond with the 1971 figure. The prevalence survey is notable for its severity scale. A panel was asked to quantify the relative severity of functional difficulty experienced by people with different degrees of a specific impairment, for example to compare someone who cannot walk with someone who has great difficulty going up stairs. They were then asked to compare one impairment with another, for example inability to walk with inability to see. Finally they were asked to compare combinations of impairment. The description of the judges cites staff from OPCS and DHSS who had some interest in the survey plus a range of professionals with appropriate expertise – doctors, physiotherapists, occupational therapists and psychologists, as well as independent

Table 9.2 Prevalence of disabled adults in England, Scotland and Wales, by severity of disability category

Severity category	In private households (no.)
1 (least severe)	1,186,000
2	824,000
3	732,000
4	676,000
5	679,000
6	511,000
7	447,000
8	338,000
9	285,000
10	102,000
Total in private households	5,780,000
Living in establishments	422,000
Grand total	6,202,000

Source: Adapted from Martin and White (1988)

Note: Estimates based on OPCS surveys for Department of Health and Social Security, 1985–8.

researchers working in the area, and concludes with disabled people and those caring for them. Some may infer from this ordering that judgements about disabled people were considered more important than those made by them. Whilst the ten-point severity scale is ostensibly a more sensitive measure than previous systems, the procedure used at base rests on the subjective judgements of a panel, an unspecified number of whose members were themselves disabled, on the importance of a somewhat arbitrarily selected subset of incapacities. Essentially judges were being asked, in a general way, and thus with no regard to individual situation or social contexts, to judge which conditions are 'worse'. In so far as the results of such procedures mean anything, they merely reflect a cruder version of any pre-existing cultural consensus in the groups from which the panel of judges is culled – cruder, since most common-sense beliefs about disability are more sophisticated than attempts to provide an answer to questions of the 'is it worse to be blind or deaf?' kind. The spurious objectivity implied by complex quantifications and ten-point scales should not fool anyone into believing that 'severity' is identified by the OPCS surveys in anything more than the most general of ways (Disability Alliance 1988a).

Stone (1984) has indicated, in an international historical study, how claims to the disabled status have been a matter of state concern since the concomitant development of the earliest stages of industrial capitalism and the most rudimentary elements of state welfare. The simple distinction between those unable and those unwilling to work, the deserving and the undeserving poor, has, with increased sophistication in the division of labour, similarly become more refined, with new definitions based on clinical or functional criteria being employed. Even for someone who finds this a contentious point, the notion that functional limitation can be investigated without regard to the different social and environmental contexts of people's lives, as the standardised OPCS questions attempt to do, is a dubious one. Any response about difficulties with an activity of daily living, like using the lavatory, getting dressed, eating or drinking, only has its meaning in the context of the facilities available to that individual to carry out the task. This will depend on both the general arrangements for performing certain activities in a society and the specific aids available to an individual. Thus, depending on personal and social circumstances, an individual with a particular kind or degree of impairment may be more or less restricted in their activity to a widely variable degree. Gender, age and culture are also important variables to be taken into account in assessing the significance of particular impairments, whilst class, in both its financial and cultural aspects, also has its effects on experiences of disability. There are then inevitable restrictions on any understanding which fails to relate functional limitation to its social context. Functional definitions are essentially state definitions, in that they relate to the major concerns of the state: as regards production, capacity to work; as regards welfare, demands that have to be met from revenue if they cannot be offloaded on some other party. They ignore any consideration of the role of the state in the construction and perpetuation of disability. Whilst the meaning of impairment is not explored in terms of such variables as age, ethnicity and gender in the prevalence report, its incidence is discussed in terms of these variables.

The report is to be commended for separating ageing from disability since much debate and policy conflates the two. It indicates that whilst the vast majority of disabled people (69 per cent) are over pension age, a similar proportion of pensioners, 64.5 per cent, are not disabled. Only amongst those of 85 or over are disabled people in the majority. However, for reasons that will become apparent when the form of the questions is discussed, these figures are likely to systematically under-identify disability amongst elderly people. What is not investigated in any way is the effect of ageing on people disabled when younger. Zarb and Oliver (1993) indicate that ageing with disability deserves separate and detailed consideration.

As far as ethnicity is concerned, one question yields the information that disability rates for 'Asians' and 'West Indians' are 12.6 and 15.1 per cent respectively after adjustment for age distribution, compared to an equivalent figure for 'Whites' of 13.7 per cent. The rest of the data is not systematically discussed in terms of ethnicity, nor is this justified in the report (for example on grounds of small sample size), leading to the conclusion that the survey does not take ethnicity seriously. Some argue that the experience of disability for individuals from minority ethnic groups requires separate and detailed analysis in terms of 'double oppression' (Confederation of Indian Organisations UK 1987, Oliver 1990), whilst others find this kind of conceptualisation inadequate (Atkin and Rollins 1991, Stuart 1993). Through its failure to analyse its data in terms of ethnicity, the OPCS surveys have passed up the chance of gathering some general data which could have been of importance to those working in this area.

The survey indicates that there are considerably more disabled women than men except in the lowest severity categories, with 3.6 million disabled women compared to 2.5 million disabled men in the country as a whole. This excess is judged by the prevalence report's authors to be significant only in people over 75 years and to be in large part accounted for by greater female longevity. The increased prevalence of a number of functionally defined 'disabling' conditions in ageing also contributes to the increased 'disability' of any more elderly population. Since women generally live longer than men, they will be disproportionately included within this population.

However, the survey also found an increased prevalence rate of sixty-three females to fifty-four males per thousand in private households in the

16–59 age group (Martin *et al.* 1988: 22) – a difference the authors deem insignificant. This apparently contrasts with the 1971 survey, where rates for males of working age with some impairment were rather higher and numbers greater (Harris 1971: 4–5). Oliver explained the earlier findings as follows:

> Up to the age of 50 both in sheer numbers and prevalence more men are likely to be defined as disabled than women. Two possible reasons are: i) many more men work and risk disablement through accidents and work induced illnesses and ii) many more young men partake in dangerous sports and leisure activities. . . . Consequently these figures reflect sexual divisions within society whereby certain activities, both work and leisure, are dominated by males.
>
> (Oliver 1983: 40)

The prevalence report does not present its data in a form which allows direct comparison, employing a blanket 16–59 age band: one would not expect the report to have done this if there were significant differences within this band. So what accounts for this apparent turnaround in the sexual distribution of disability in people of working age over the intervening twenty years? It cannot be explained through the inclusion of 'less disabled' individuals in the later survey, since the figures indicate differences at all levels of severity. It seems therefore to indicate either a 'real' change or significantly different methods of measurement between the two surveys, such that they could arrive at reversed rates of sex prevalence. Whichever of these explanations is correct, the implications are of significance, and it is unfortunate that the report does not mention the matter. As a growing body of literature shows, the mode and extent of oppression experienced by disabled women is different in important respects from that of disabled men (Deegan and Brooks 1985, Campling 1981, Lonsdale 1990, Morris 1991, Begum 1992), and a chance to provide a quantitative dimension to a qualitative argument has been missed by the OPCS researchers.

Given that seven out of ten disabled people are over retirement age, and of those of working age fewer than one in three is in employment, the Registrar-General's categorisation of class by occupation is of very limited applicability (see Chapter 4 above). There is some evidence of greater likelihood of impairment in lower social classes (Townsend 1979, Doyal 1979, Taylor 1977), but OPCS was not concerned to investigate this. Most writers are more concerned with exploring the class position of disabled people than their class origins. For this, more sophisticated conceptions of class, such as Leonard's (1984) notion of an 'underclass' of permanent welfare recipients, seem more appropriate. On such an analysis the vast majority of disabled people would be members of this class by virtue of their social and economic marginality. Material relevant to this thesis is dealt with indirectly in the OPCS reports, in the examination of financial circumstances, to be considered below.

Whilst the handling of the data is open to criticisms, the questions used to gather it are also problematic. An examination of the questionnaires and interview schedule employed by the OPCS researchers reveals some significant problems as regards validity and reliability. Central to this is the concept of 'difficulty'. Repeatedly the notions of 'difficulty' and 'great difficulty' are employed, both in the postal screening questionnaire and the interview schedule. For example, question four asks:

Does anyone in your household have:
a) Difficulty walking for a quarter of a mile on the level   Yes/No
b) Great difficulty walking up or down steps or stairs   Yes/No

This may initially appear to be straightforward. However, to ask if someone has difficulty is to ask them to make a comparison which a disabled person is in an unsuitable position to do. For example, the literature informs me, following an explanation in physiological terms, that 'polio survivors work abnormally hard . . . to accomplish the same activity' (Laurie *et al.* 1984: 12). In this sense everything I accomplish with affected parts of my body is 'difficult'. But, having survived polio for forty years I am in no position to make this judgement experientially, for I have no 'normal' baseline to measure my effort against. Again, by the use of tricks and devices, like 'wheelies' to get wheelchairs over obstacles or *ad hoc* tools to open jars and packaging, disabled people survive in hostile environments. If you have a trick to get round the problem, do you still have a 'difficulty'? For people with long-standing disability, who constitute the vast majority of respondents in the OPCS survey, 'difficulty' is quintessentially a subjective construct, bearing little relation to 'normal' difficulty or to 'difficulties' confronted by someone with a dissimilar disability. Additionally, elderly people, who the survey claims constitute seven out of ten disabled people, are widely reported by their doctors to 'overestimate' their health status, at the same time as they are seen by others as having 'reduced' expectations when compared to the general population. Such questions then seem a singularly inappropriate measuring tool for a supposedly objective assessment, and are likely to result in systematic underestimation of the problems confronted, and often successfully dealt with, by disabled people.

CONCEPTS OF DISABILITY

The most fundamental issue in the study of disability, however, is a conceptual one. The traditional approach, often referred to as the medical model, locates the source of disability in the individual's deficiency and her or his personal incapacities. In contrast to this, the social model sees disability as resulting from society's failure to adapt to the needs of impaired people. The World Health Organisation (WHO) uses a four-part classification, developed by Wood (1981) known as the International Classification of Impairment, Disability and Handicap (ICIDH). This functions to link together the experiences of an individual in a logic which attributes disadvantage to nature. A 'complaint', like a spinal injury, causes an 'impairment', like an inability to control one's legs, which 'disables' by leading to an inability to walk, and 'handicaps' by giving the individual problems in travelling, getting and retaining a job and so on. Thus the 'complaint' is ultimately responsible for the 'handicap', as shown in the first three columns of Table 9.3.

A social model of disability, on the other hand, focuses on the fact that so-called 'normal' human activities are structured by the general social and economic environment, which is constructed by and in the interests of non-impaired people. 'Disability' is then defined as a form of oppression, 'the disadvantage or restriction of activity caused by a contemporary social organisation which takes no or little account of people who have physical impairments and thus excludes them from the mainstream of social activities' (UPIAS 1976: 3–4). 'The term "disability" represents a complex system of social restrictions imposed on people with impairments by a highly discriminatory society. To be a disabled person in modern Britain means to be discriminated against' (Barnes 1991: 1). Such a model is advanced by the Disabled Peoples International, of which the British Council of Disabled People is a member, and is increasingly utilised in the field of disability studies. For a social model, both the notion of normality in performance and the disadvantage experienced by the 'deficient' performer are oppressive social products. Thus the meaning

Table 9.3 World Health Organisation and social model terms

WHO word	Definition	Example	Social model word
Complaint	disease, accident	spinal injury	Impairment
Impairment	loss of function	inability to control legs	
Disability	restriction of 'normal' performance	can't walk	Disability
Handicap	disadvantage	problems travelling, getting job, etc.	

Source: Adapted from Martin et al. (1988)

attached to disability here spans the area covered by the two WHO terms disability and handicap. This difference in meaning occurs because of a difference in theories of causation.

A comparison of two different sets of questions on the same subjects, the first from a medical perspective as employed in the OPCS research, the second from a social one, makes this distinction apparent (Oliver 1990: 7–8).

Medical perspective: OPCS questions
1 What complaint causes you difficulty in holding, gripping or turning things?
2 Do you have a scar, blemish or deformity which limits your daily activities?
3 Have you attended a special school because of a long-term health problem or disability?
4 Does your health problem/disability affect your work in any way at present?

Social perspective: reformulated questions
1a What defects in the design of everyday equipment like jars, bottles and lids causes you difficulty in holding, gripping or turning them?
2a Do other people's reactions to any scar, blemish or deformity you may have, limit your daily activities?
3a Have you attended a special school because of your education authority's policy of sending people with your long-term health problem or disability to such places?
4a Do you have problems at work as a result of the physical environment or the attitudes of others?

If the questions were reformulated in this way, they would then be investigating disability from the explicitly political perspective adopted by the social model. But it is equally a political decision, conscious or otherwise, to employ questions of the first type rather than the second. The most fundamental criticism of government statistics on disability is that they investigate the wrong thing: individuals rather than structures. They are inadequate, for proponents of a social model, in terms of the most fundamental category they employ, the definition of disability as an individual rather than a social phenomenon.

In addition to this the ethics of subjecting 2,223 disabled people to an interview structured in terms of personal deficiency is also questioned. Discussing sexism in research, Oakley has argued that 'structured interview by expert' is an inherently oppressive process, in that it not only does nothing to aid the transformation of the subjects' lives, but may also confirm and reinforce feelings of ignorance and passivity in those interviewed (Oakley 1981). Likewise, the spurious objectivity of published findings upon which welfare agencies often rely for evidence can reinforce oppressive definitions of their reality for the whole range of people to whom the research is supposed to apply. The very objectivity and neutrality to which researchers claim to aspire may also be objectionable to the objects of their research. In assessing Miller and Gwynne's (1972) study of a Cheshire home, one of the residents, a key figure in the early stages of the disability movement in Britain, wrote:

> It was clear that Miller and Gwynne were definitely not on our side. They were not really on the side of the staff either. They were, in fact, basically on their own side, that is the side of supposedly 'detached', 'balanced', 'unbiased' social scientists, concerned above all with presenting themselves to the powers that be as indispensable in training 'practitioners' to manage the problems of disabled people in institutions. Thus the fundamental relationship between them and the residents was that of exploiters and exploited.
>
> (Hunt 1981: 5)

Proponents of a social model of disability argue that the money spent on the disempowering process of data-gathering from the perspective of the oppressive medical model could more usefully have been invested in a systematic exploration of the multifarious forms of institutional discrimination which they see as the real causes of disability. As regards the prevalence report, it is argued both that the kinds of things enquired about are inappropriate, and that the way in which the researchers go about trying to find out the answers to these inappropriate questions leaves much to be desired.

THE FINANCE REPORT

The finance report (Martin and White 1988) examines the financial circumstances of disabled adults living in private households. Three specific aims are identified by the researchers:

1 to examine the extent to which disability affects people's income;
2 to establish whether extra expenditure is incurred as a result of disability and to estimate the magnitude of that expenditure;
3 to evaluate the overall impact of disability on the standard of living and financial circumstances of disabled adults and their families.

I will discuss the report's findings under three headings of employment, income and expenditure.

Disabled adults under pension age were found to be less likely to be in paid work than adults in the general population, allowing for differences in age, sex and marital status. Only 31 per cent of non-pensioner disabled adults were working, this proportion falling from 48 per cent in category one to 2 per cent in category ten. No attempt is made to relate these findings to the growing body of literature on unemployment and health (Smith 1987, Warr 1987). Unmarried disabled adults were less likely to be working than were married people in each age, sex and severity group, as were those over 50 years of age. Thus marriage and youth seem to be factors associated with likelihood of employment, as well as the more obvious factor of being in a lower severity category. A number of studies indicate the discrimination, direct and indirect, experienced by disabled people in obtaining and keeping jobs (Fry 1986, French 1988, Graham *et al.* 1990, Department of Employment 1990) but the OPCS study did not take the opportunity to explore this further.

As far as earnings from work were concerned, both men and women disabled full-time employees earned less than full-time employees in the general population, which could not be accounted for by differences in hours worked. Some evidence of a decrease in earnings was found with higher severity categories for men, but not for women. In discussing a similar pattern in relation to ethnicity it has been suggested that part of the explanation for the similarity in the overall levels of wages among white and black women was that the enormous disparity between men and women in this respect left 'little scope for racial disadvantage to have a further, additive, effect' (Smith 1977: 88). Whether these facts indicate that low pay follows from disability or that those in low-paid occupations are more likely to become disabled cannot be determined from this data. The probability is that the explanation is a combination of the two, that class inequalities and disability combine to produce general patterns of disadvantage.

For the majority of married disabled adults under pension age, at least one member of the family was earning, but only around a fifth of all disabled adults lived in such a unit. The majority of disabled adults (78 per cent of the total, 54 per cent of those under pension age) lived in family units containing no earners and thus the significance of state benefits was great. Although half of all disabled adults had another source of income besides earnings and benefits, the most common of these were pensions or redundancy payments from a former employer or income from savings and investments, and these were most likely to be received by older respondents. Comparisons with the equivalent incomes of families in the general population showed that disabled non-pensioner families had significantly lower incomes than non-pensioners in general – under three-quarters of average income. Whilst much of this is due to disabled adults being less likely to have earned income, families with one or more earners still had lower incomes than comparable families in the general population. Disabled pensioners, however, were not readily distinguishable in income terms from non-disabled, and this is again probably related to the general lower average income of pensioners which produces a 'flattening' effect on the figures. In 1983,

64 per cent of pensioners were living in poverty or on its margins, compared with 24 per cent of the population under pensionable age (DHSS 1986).

It was found that for all severity categories there was some extra expenditure involved because of disability. This was divided into three types: lump sum expenditure on special items, regular expenditure on special items and regular expenditure on items required by most people but on which disabled people need to spend more. Lump sum expenditure on items of equipment like special furniture in the year previous to the survey was incurred by only 16 per cent of the sample, spending £78 on average, but with considerable variation between individuals. The average for all disabled adults worked out at £12.50 a year. Because of the limited time-span the OPCS researchers admit this is likely to be a low estimate of true costs. Regular expenditure on items required solely because of disability, like prescriptions, costs associated with hospital visits, private domestic help, were incurred by 60 per cent of disabled adults. Amounts and proportions increased with severity category.

The third type of expenditure, on 'ordinary' items on which disabled people need to spend more, like fuel, clothing, food, travel and home maintenance, was reported by seven out of ten disabled adults. Again, the proportion of adults with expenditure of this kind and the amount they spent rose with severity. Adding these together, the average extra expenditure incurred by or for all disabled adults amounted to £6.10 a week, or, including the lump sum average, £329.70 a year. This is however an arithmetical average, and there were considerable variations in actual expenditure, both within and between severity categories. As well as rising with severity, average extra expenditure rose with income within severity categories, indicating that people might well have spent more if it had been available. Altogether a quarter of disabled adults thought they needed to spend more because of their disability but could not afford to do so. This important point has been explored in a more sophisticated manner in research outlined below (Berthoud et al. 1993).

An effect of having to spend a proportion of income on items associated with disability is to reduce disposable income. The report examines this in terms of 'equivalent resources', which is arrived at by calculating the income remaining after disability-related expenditure has been subtracted and using equivalence scales to adjust the remaining income for differences in family composition. This is expressed in terms of pounds-equivalent (£=). On average, net equivalent resources were 92 per cent of net equivalent income, that is 8 per cent of income was spent on disability-related expenses. Although the average amount of such expenditure was lower for those on lower incomes, they spent a higher proportion of their income on disability-related expenses. Proportion also rose with the category of severity. The average equivalent resources of disabled non-pensioners were £=91.70 per week, compared to £=136.70 for the non-pensioner general population. Forty-one per cent of disabled non-pensioners had equivalent resources of less than half this amount, compared to 23 per cent of the general population. The difference between disabled and non-disabled pensioners was not so marked, probably for reasons mentioned above.

The use of the notion of equivalent income in making these calculations, whatever reservations one may have about the calculations themselves, is to be welcomed. It makes clear that there are calculable costs of disability, which, given the political will, government has the ability to offset, employing a number of alternative or complementary mechanisms, some of which are more attractive to disabled people than others. Altogether 8 per cent of disabled householders thought they were getting into financial difficulties, but there were significant differences between household types, with 36 per cent of the albeit small group of single parents, 23 per cent of single childless householders, but only 3 per cent of pensioners reporting difficulties. Objective calculations tended to confirm subjective views, and both related financial difficulties strongly to equivalent resources. With regard to standard of living measures, a criticism raised of previous studies, for example Townsend (1979), was that they failed to distinguish between not possessing a consumer durable or basic item because you could not afford it, which would be a reasonable indicator of economic deprivation, and not having it because you did not want it, which would not. The finance report allows for that, and found a proportion of both 'luxuries' and 'basic items' lacking as a result of choice. However, it found a relationship, strongest when calculated in terms of equivalent resources, between disability and inability to afford desired items.

RESPONSES

It is evidence of the growing strength of organisations both 'for' and 'of' disabled people that a number of detailed responses to the reports, particularly the finance report, were speedily forthcoming. In particular, the Disability Alliance (DA) and the Disablement Income Group (DIG) produced documents which, whilst welcoming the reports' highlighting of the link between disability and poverty, were critical of the methods employed (Disability Alliance 1988a, 1988b, Thompson *et al.* 1988). These methods, they argued, resulted in systematic and significant under-estimations of the 'true cost' of disability, which OPCS quantified at an average of £6.10 a week. These critiques largely take the individualist methodology of OPCS for granted, but argue that their methods result in them getting the 'wrong' answers to what are tacitly assumed to be the

178

'right' questions. Whilst this approach does not address the more wide-ranging methodological issues raised in the earlier parts of this chapter, these are not of such great importance in relation to the attempt to quantify the economic disadvantage experienced by individual disabled people; it therefore contributes significantly to the immediate social policy debate.

A number of factors, the critiques argue, combine to produce systematic underestimation of the costs of disability. First, the survey was conducted before the benefit changes of April 1988 which resulted in reduced benefits for an estimated one million disabled people. The survey was thus seriously out of date before its findings were published. Second, expenditure on one-off items, such as costs of a car, housing adaptations, or an electric wheelchair, is grossly underestimated as a result of the OPCS decision to ask only about items bought in the last twelve months, although from their own figures whilst 68 per cent of people surveyed had made at least one 'lump sum purchase', only 16 per cent had done so during the relevant twelve-month period (Martin and White 1988: 37). Third, not enough severely disabled people were surveyed. OPCS employed ten categories of disability, of which one to three are those whose 'daily living activities are not severely restricted' (DIG would argue these should not be included at all). OPCS respondents are mostly in the lower categories, with only 1.6 per cent of those surveyed in the highest category. Using other likely indicators of severity of disability in the sample, only 13 per cent received disability benefit, 8 per cent attendance allowance and 7 per cent mobility allowance. The suggestion is then that the sampling technique was skewed in a way that made those most likely to incur greatest additional expenditure less likely to be included.

Fourth, the form of question, interviewing method and the time taken over interviews are held to be inadequate. The OPCS interviews lasted about one and a half hours, only a part of this time being devoted to questions about the costs of disability. Unlike many other surveys, no prompting or clarification by interviewers was permitted. This resulted in a significant number of 'don't know' responses since, by the researchers' own admission, 'not surprisingly people found it very difficult to estimate what proportion of the total cost of say heating was incurred because of their disability' (Martin and White 1988: 35). DIG and DA argue that more time needs to be spent on interviews, with clarification and illustration to help people work out the answers. When DIG replicated the OPCS survey with a more lengthy and explanatory interviewing technique they reduced the 'don't know' category to zero. In the OPCS survey there was at least one item of information missing in more than 40 per cent of responses, which led them to 'decide to impute an average expenditure for them based on the estimates of those who were able to give an estimate' (Martin and White 1988: 36). DA argue that 'It is impossible to calculate the effect that this will have on the overall accuracy of the results' (Disability Alliance 1988b: 22).

Fifth, severe doubts are expressed about the methods of calculating needs and expenditure arising from disability. The OPCS data indicated that seven out of ten of their sample of disabled people were spending extra as a result of their disability, and that one in four said they needed to spend more than they did but could not afford to. The items most often cited were basics such as fuel, clothing and food. DA contend that real levels of need are likely to be systematically underestimated, since accurate responses in this area are notoriously difficult to achieve. Investigating poverty, Coates and Silburn (1970) have commented on the unrealistically low estimates provided by their respondents of the level of extra income they would require to be 'comfortable'. A high proportion of the respondents were elderly, amongst whom discrepancies between their own estimates and those of professionals have been noted. All this suggests that we should pay particular attention to the apparent contradiction between 70 per cent of disabled people having an income substantially lower than the general population and a similar proportion expressing 'satisfaction' with their standard of living.

DIG has made the study of the extra costs of disability its speciality, with work by Hyman (1977), Stowell and Day (1983) and Buckle (1984) all producing considerably higher figures than the more recent OPCS surveys. Whilst the OPCS used a large-scale survey technique, the DIG studies employ in-depth studies based on relatively small samples. To demonstrate what they regard as the inappropriate nature of the OPCS methodology in ascertaining the 'true cost' of disability, DIG employed a research strategy of first administering an OPCS-type questionnaire and then administering a semi-structured unstandardised questionnaire of a type used in small-scale in-depth studies with running prompts and additional questions to the same subjects, and comparing the results from the two. DIG, who unlike some sections of the disability movement regard a high degree of restriction of activity as definitional of disablement, employed a sample culled from their advisory service case files which represented a range of conditions, all of whom would fall into the two highest OPCS categories, and all of whom were receiving at least one of the two main disability-related benefits. However, they say they deliberately avoided selecting the most severe cases from their files. Their sample was also significantly younger, on average, than the OPCS group, and the only two respondents over 65 had been disabled for twenty and forty years respectively. Employing the OPCS-style survey, an average extra weekly expenditure of £41.84 was reported whereas the response of the same subjects to the DIG schedule produced an average of £65.94, a difference of 58 per cent between the two methods. DIG argue that these results support their view of the OPCS survey:

the sample they interviewed and the interview schedule and techniques they used have given rise to a much lower figure for the average weekly costs of disability than would have been the case if more significantly disabled people had been interviewed and if a more detailed questionnaire had been used.

(Thompson *et al.* 1988: 28)

Subsequently, a more methodologically sophisticated study established an even greater discrepancy between their findings and the OPCS surveys, putting the extra costs of severe disability at £86.73 per week – more than eight times the OPCS average figure (Thompson *et al.* 1990). Avoiding any discussion of the DIG view that some of those included in the OPCS survey aren't 'really disabled', the discrepancy between the results obtained employing the two types of interview supports DA's more general conclusion: 'We believe we have shown that the results in the OPCS second report cannot be used as the basis for making policy decisions about extra costs. They must be supplemented by other information about the high extra costs of disability' (1988b: 29). More recently, researchers at the Policy Studies Institute have re-analysed some of the OPCS data in a study of the economics of disability funded by the Joseph Rowntree Foundation. They developed and applied to the data their own 'standard of living' index. They conclude that:

Unemployment and low earnings and high costs are not compensated for by adequate social security benefits. This is a recipe for poverty. We find that getting on for half of all disabled adults, and their families, do not have enough to maintain the basic minimum standard of living implied by social security legislation.

(Berthoud *et al.* 1993: 13)

Significant as they are, these studies again employ an individualistic methodology in their analyses. From the point of view of a social model of disablement, however, these costs only accrue to individual disabled people because of a general failure to construct an environment fit for impaired people to live in:

In such a view, our abnormality results from the failure of society to meet our 'normal' needs as impaired people, which are different from those of some, but by no means all, of our fellow citizens. Our abnormality consists in us having, compared to the general population, a particular and large set of our human needs unprovided for, or met in inappropriate and disempowering ways.

(Abberley 1993: 111)

The construction of abnormality by the individualisation of social failure is not only seen as oppressive, but also as uneconomic. It is argued that were

181

the needs of impaired people for, for example, accessible transport met through a universal policy which 'recognises that the entire population is at risk for the concomitants of chronic illness and disability' (Zola 1989: 401), not only would the political demands of disabled people be met, but a practical and cost-effective solution would be provided (Prescott-Clarke 1990). By ignoring the economics of transforming the disabling environment, any research which fails to break with methodological individualism, however accurate its computation of individual expenses, falls short of incorporating the fundamental premise of the social model of disability.

CONCLUSION

Whilst the prevalence report highlights the systematic underestimation of disability which was enshrined in previous government research, it should by no means be interpreted as providing the 'true' figure. Such a project is an impossible one, since 'disability' is a social construct, and definitions are inevitably contested. They depend upon the interests, intentions and unexamined presuppositions of those with the power to define, and the ability of those so defined to resist inappropriate conceptions of our reality. As far as the severity scales are concerned, the danger is that the spurious objectivity implied by calculations and an elaborate system of judgement panels seduces the reader into concluding that degrees of disadvantage and suffering are amenable to statistical representation in this way, and that appropriate welfare provision and resource allocation may be determined on the basis of it. The finance report provides some evidence that disability causes poverty. Because of the research methods employed, however, it fails to approach an adequate quantification of the financial disadvantages experienced by individual disabled people. Critiques and reworkings of the OPCS figures have provided alternative estimates of the costs to individuals, but fail to address the major challenge posed by the social model. As reflected in the campaign for anti-discrimination legislation on disability, disabled people, in this country as elsewhere, are increasingly conceptualising their lives in political terms and rejecting the dominant medical model of our situation (Bynoe *et al.* 1991, Liberty 1994). Government, no longer able to defuse dissent, resorts to chicanery and promises of future action. In this context, no conceptualisation of or questions about disability can be seen as 'neutral'. It was a matter of political choice that the OPCS surveys were designed in terms of an individualistic medical model approach to disability, rather than very significant resources being devoted to an exploration of the ways in which society disables impaired people. Although there are some, limited, ways in which we may utilise OPCS data, we must not in doing so lose sight of this most fundamental flaw. Information gathered on the basis of an oppressive theory, unless handled with circumspection, is itself one of the mechanisms of oppression.

REFERENCES

Abberley, P. (1993) 'Disabled people and "normality"', in J. Swain, V. Finkelstein, S. French and M. Oliver (eds) *Disabling Barriers – Enabling Environments*, London: Sage/Open University.

Atkin, K. and Rollins, J. (1991) *Informal Care and Black Communities*, York: Social Policy Research Unit, University of York.

Barnes, C. (1991) *Disabled People in Britain and Discrimination*, London: Hurst.

Begum, N. (1992) 'Disabled women and the feminist agenda', *Feminist Review* 40: 70–84.

Berthoud, R., Lakey, J. and McKay, S. (1993) *The Economic Problems of Disabled People*, London: Policy Studies Institute.

Breeze, E., Trevor, G. and Wilmot, A. (1991) *1989 General Household Survey*, London: HMSO.

Buckle, J. (1971) *Work and Housing of Impaired People in Great Britain*, London: HMSO.

—— (1984) *Mental Handicap Costs More*, London: Disablement Income Group.

Bynoe, I., Oliver, M. and Barnes, C. (1991) *Equal Rights for Disabled People: The Case for a New Law*, London: Institute for Public Policy Research.

Campling, J. (ed.) (1981) *Images of Ourselves*, London: Routledge & Kegan Paul.

Coates, K. and Silburn, R. (1970) *Poverty: The Forgotten Englishmen*, Harmondsworth: Penguin.

Confederation of Indian Organisations (UK) (1987) *Double Bind: To Be Disabled and Asian*, London: Confederation of Indian Organisations (UK).

CORAD (1982), *Report by the Committee On Restrictions Against Disabled People*, London: HMSO.

Deegan, M. and Brooks, N. (1985) *Women and Disability: The Double Handicap*, New Jersey: Transaction Books.

Department of Employment (1990) *Employment and Training for People with Disabilities: Consultative Document*, London: Department of Employment.

DHSS (Department of Health and Social Security) (1986) *Tables on Families with Low Incomes 1983*, London: HMSO.

Disability Alliance (1988a) *Briefing on the First Report from the OPCS Surveys of Disability*, London: Disability Alliance.

—— (1988b) *Briefing on the Second OPCS Report*, London: Disability Alliance.

Doyal, L. (1979) *The Political Economy of Health*, London: Pluto Press.

French, S. (1988) *'They Weren't Obstructive But They Didn't Go out of Their Way To Be Helpful Either': Disabled People in the Health and Caring Professions: Professional Attitudes and Personal Experiences*, London: South Bank Polytechnic.

Fry, E. (1986) *An Equal Chance for Disabled People?: A Study of Discrimination in Employment*, London: Spastics Society.

Graham, P., Jordan, D. and Lamb, B. (1990) *An Equal Chance or No Chance?*, London: Spastics Society.

Harris, A. (1971) *Handicapped and Impaired in Great Britain*, London: HMSO.

Hunt, P. (1981) 'Settling accounts with the parasite people', *Disability Challenge* 1: 5 (London: UPIAS).

Hyman, M. (1977) *The Extra Costs of Disabled Living*, London: National Fund for Research into Crippling Diseases.

Laurie, G., Maynard, F., Fischer, A. and Raymond, J. (eds) (1984) *Handbook on the Late Effects of Poliomyelitis for Physicians and Survivors*, St Louis, Missouri: Gazette International Networking Institute.

Leonard, P. (1984) *Personality and Ideology: Towards a Materialist Understanding of the Individual*, London: Macmillan.

Liberty (1994) *Access Denied: Human Rights and Disabled People*, London: National Council for Civil Liberties.

Lonsdale, S. (1990) *Women and Disability*, London: Macmillan.

Martin, J. and White, A. (1988) *Report 2: The Financial Circumstances of Disabled Adults in Private Households*, London: HMSO.

Martin, J., Meltzer, H. and Elliot, D. (1988) *Report 1: The Prevalence of Disability among Adults*, London: HMSO.

Miller, E. and Gwynne, P. (1972) *A Life Apart*, London: Tavistock.

Morris, J.(1991) *Pride against Prejudice: Transforming Attitudes to Disability*, London: The Women's Press.

Oakley, A. (1981) 'Interviewing women: a contradiction in terms', in H. Roberts (ed.) *Doing Feminist Research*, London: Routledge & Kegan Paul.

Oliver, M. (1983) *Social Work with Disabled People*, London: Macmillan.

—— (1990) *The Politics of Disablement*, London: Macmillan.

Prescott-Clarke, P. (1990) *Employment and Handicap*, London: Social Community Planning Research.

Smith, D. (1977) *Racial Disadvantage in Britain: the PEP Report*, Harmondsworth: Penguin.

Smith, R. (1987) *Unemployment and Health*, Oxford: Oxford University Press.

Stone, D. (1984) *The Disabled State*, Basingstoke: Macmillan.

Stowell, R. and Day. F. (1983) *Tell Me What You Want And I'll Get It For You: A Study of Shopping when Disabled*, London: Disablement Income Group.

Stuart, O. (1993) 'Double oppression: an appropriate starting-point?' in J. Swain, V. Finkelstein, S. French and M. Oliver (eds) (1993) *Disabling Barriers – Enabling Environments*, London: Sage/Open University.

Taylor, D. (1977) *Physical Impairment – Social Handicap*, London: Office of Health Statistics.

Thompson, P. with Buckle, J. and Lavery, M. (1988) *NOT The OPCS Survey: Being Disabled Costs More Than They Said*, London: Disablement Income Group.

Thompson, P. with Lavery, M. and Curtice, J. (1990) *Short Changed by Disability*, London: Disablement Income Group.

Townsend, P. (1979) *Poverty in the United Kingdom*, Harmondsworth: Penguin.

UPIAS (1976) *Fundamental Principles of Disability*, London: Union of Physically Impaired Against Segregation.

Warr, P. (1987) *Work, Unemployment and Mental Health*, Oxford: Clarendon Press.

Wood, P. (1981) *International Classification of Impairments, Disabilities and Handicaps*, Geneva: World Health Organisation.

Zarb, G. and Oliver, M. (1993) *Ageing with a Disability: What Do They Expect After All These Years?*, London: University of Greenwich.

Zola, I. K. (1989) 'Towards the necessary universalisation of a disability policy', *Millbank Quarterly* 47: 401–28.

10

THE CASE OF THE MISSING CRIMES

Robert Reiner

Crime statistics are probably given more prominence in public debate than any other numbers apart from the national lottery winners. An orgy of anguished hand-wringing about moral decline regularly greets the annual publication of the Home Office volume *Criminal Statistics: England and Wales*, as well as the intermediate bulletins from the Research and Statistics Department and the local crime figures in the annual reports of chief police officers. Since the mid-1950s, when the statistics began to chart a seemingly inexorable growth of recorded crime, they have come to be seen as a crucial barometer of the plummeting state of civilisation in the eyes of the media, politicians and the public.

The attempt to measure crime has always been a prominent concern of those responsible for or interested in the development of state policies to control deviance. The etymology of the term 'statistics' – the 'science of the state' – is testimony to the centrality of this to all 'political arithmetic'. In the late eighteenth-century the so-called 'science of police' – the term being used then in the much broader sense of all state policies directed at maintaining internal order and, in Foucault's terminology, 'governmentality' (Burchell *et al.* 1991) – flourished throughout Europe. Its leading British exponent Patrick Colquhoun attempted to measure precisely the contours of criminality in the 1790s, and his statistics were used by Sir Robert Peel and others in the early nineteenth-century campaigns to restructure the criminal justice system (Reiner 1988: 142). In France during the early nineteenth century the 'moral statisticians', notably Quetelet and Guerry, tried to explain trends and patterns in crime by measuring crime levels in relation to a variety of social conditions. Their work was influential in the development not only of social statistics generally but also, through Durkheim, of the whole enterprise of sociology.

The attempt to measure crime thus has a long pedigree and has played a prominent part in the development both of social research and of criminal justice policy. In most industrial countries governments began to co-ordinate the collection of such data during the late nineteenth or early twentieth century. In England and Wales, since the 1856 County and Borough Police Act police forces have been required to inform the Home Office at least annually of the volume of crimes known to them. The USA with its highly fragmented criminal justice system took longer to begin collation of national data. But since the 1930s the FBI has required police forces to inform it annually of the known levels of the seven major so-called 'index crimes'.

It is not only the official collection of data on crime which has a long pedigree. In the same way that the measurement of crime has played a prominent part in the development of social statistics more generally, so too critical awareness of the pitfalls and limitations of the crime figures has been central to the development of more sceptical and cautious approaches to all official statistics. Social scientists have long been aware of the myriad problems in interpreting official crime statistics. In 1955, for example, the American sociologist Daniel Bell eloquently exposed the 'myth of crime waves'. He noted that the official crime statistics were a thoroughly unreliable basis for public anxieties about rising crime, but that these were regularly exploited by the media because crime scare stories were predictable audience-pullers.

In this chapter we will analyse the problems surrounding the interpretation of official crime statistics, look at their fluctuating role in the politics of criminal justice in the last two decades, and consider the attempts which criminological researchers have made to provide alternative sources of information about crime. Finally we will discuss how the official statistics may be used cautiously to tell us about crime patterns and trends, in the light of the increasing understanding of how they are constructed and consequently what their systematic biases may be.

WHAT ARE THE CRIME STATISTICS?

In this country when mention is made of *the* crime statistics what is usually meant is the annual publication by the Home Office Research and Statistics Department of the volume *Criminal Statistics: England and Wales*, and more particularly the figures provided in Chapter 2 of that document: 'Notifiable offences recorded by the police'. The numbers in this chapter are regularly referred to in media and political debate as the 'crime rate', although the volume itself gives clear health warnings about this (which have become more explicit over the years). In addition to this annual volume, the Home Office also publishes intermediate statistical bulletins on 'Notifiable Offences'. Until the last couple of years these appeared quarterly, but following the recommendations of a Home Office working party on fear of crime chaired by Michael Grade, their frequency was reduced to twice-yearly. This conveniently halved the number of times the government had to provide excuses for shock-horror newspaper headlines about the collapse of its law and order policies. Apart from these regular Home Office publications of data on crime and criminal justice its Research and Statistics Department publishes numerous other reports on related topics, which will be discussed later. Each of the forty-three police forces in England and Wales also publishes an annual report by the chief officer giving a more detailed account of the figures for its area; these in fact provide the basis for the national figures collated by the Home Office.

The annual *Criminal Statistics* volume has for many years followed a standard basic format. There are eight chapters plus about seven appendices and several supplementary volumes providing more exhaustively detailed analyses. The first chapter provides an overall summary of the data in the volume. Chapters 2, 3 and 4 present the police-derived statistics on notifiable offences. Chapter 2 is an overall account of the trends and patterns in notifiable offences recorded by the police, and of police success in clearing them up. Chapter 3 is a more detailed account of offences involving firearms, while Chapter 4 concentrates on homicide. Chapters 5–8 are on the subsequent processing of cases in the criminal justice process. Chapter 5 looks at rates of cautioning and at those offenders found guilty. Chapter 6 is an examination of aspects of court proceedings. Chapter 7 looks at trends and patterns in sentencing. The eighth chapter charts the use of police bail and court remands. The appendices are primarily methodological, describing the coverage of the statistics in the volume and the procedures by which they are generated. The supplementary volumes provide a detailed account of so-called 'summary' offences which are tried only in magistrates' courts (and are not included in the category of 'notifiable offences' that are the primary focus of the main volume) as well as a more detailed analysis of proceedings in the Crown Courts.

The statistics in this volume are 'official' in a double sense. They are published by the government, *and* they are based on the recorded activities of official agencies, notably police, prosecutors and courts, using particular methodological rules to try and standardise the counting. The central problem in the interpretation of the statistics arises directly from this doubly official character. The data are – or, as the small print of the methodological health warnings emphasises, purport to be – records of the operation of criminal justice bureaucracies. However, the first chapters, the police-derived statistics, are used in public debate as if they were really measures of something else: the state of crime and of police efficiency in dealing with it. The crucial problems lie in these early chapters, and particularly in this use of the data as putative measures of the 'real' extent of crime and other phenomena in the world outside the criminal justice system itself. The figures are actually (more or less accurate) counts of police activity, but they are often taken to be counts of the rate of criminal offending.

The later chapters in the volume dealing with court proceedings are not exceptionally problematic. Their only limitations are the inevitable failings of any bureaucracy to record its activities with absolute accuracy. Problems may arise, however, at the end of the criminal justice process, if analysis of the characteristics of those convicted or sentenced for criminal offences is taken as corresponding to the attributes of those who commit crimes. Since only a small proportion of offences is recorded, and an even smaller proportion of offences result in a conviction (2 per cent, according to the Home Office's own estimate), the characteristics of convicted offenders are a highly unreliable indication of those who commit crime in general. Analysis of the characteristics of offenders (apart from age and sex) does not appear in the *Criminal Statistics* volume, although numerous other official reports and publications do measure and report the socio-economic profile of convicted offenders (e.g. Home Office 1993a). This issue will not be pursued further in this chapter but it should be noted that all the problems of interpreting official statistics on the extent and pattern of crime apply *a fortiori* to assessments of the characteristics of offenders which are derived from them.

CRIME STATISTICS: OMISSIONS AND BIAS

The main problems in interpreting the official statistics on crimes which have been recorded by the police arise from the fact that they are both incomplete and biased. To understand the reasons for their incompleteness, and the nature of the biases they embody, it is necessary to analyse the process by which the figure of 'crimes known to the police' is constructed. For an event to be recorded in this category it has to overcome two hurdles. First, it must come to the attention of the police – in the literal sense it must become 'known to the police'. It then must be recorded as such by the police using the appropriate procedures.

Criminal events may fail to enter the records at either stage. They may not come to be known to the police at all, and even if they do, the police may not record them as crimes for a variety of reasons, legitimate and/or illegitimate. The police statistics are an incomplete count to the extent that offences fail to become known to the police or recorded by them. This is the so-called 'dark figure' of unrecorded crime. What makes it even more problematic is that what we know of the processes involved (and as we shall see, criminological research has shed much light on this in recent years) suggests that the figures present a biased portrait of the state of criminality: some offences (and their victims and perpetrators) are far more likely to end up in the official records than others.

Crimes may become known to the police in one of two ways. If they involve an aware victim, that person may report it to the police, or someone may report it on their behalf. In those cases which do not involve specific individual victims capable of reporting the offence, the police only become aware of them through proactive police work seeking out the offence as well as the offender. This may encompass such strategies as raids on pubs or parties to detect illegal drugs, undercover work or street patrol, surveillance of areas thought likely to be scenes for illegal activity, or trawls through files to discover frauds.

Many offences, whether with or without individual victims, will fail to become known to the police. For a variety of reasons victims may not report cases to the police. Those crimes not involving individual victims come to light at a rate dependent on the extent and pattern of deployment of police resources in proactive work seeking out such offences. Further slippage occurs when the police exercise their discretion not to record officially cases which have been reported to them or which they have discovered themselves. Thus the number of crimes recorded as 'known to the police' will inevitably be incomplete.

This has come to be known as the 'dark figure' of unrecorded crime. It leads directly to the two major pitfalls in the interpretation of the official crime statistics. First, they are an unreliable guide to trends in offending. An increase in the rate of recorded crime (such as we have become accustomed to in the last forty years) could occur not because of a rise in offending behaviour, but because of a higher proportion of crimes being reported by victims, and/or more proactive policing discovering more offences, and/or the police recording a higher proportion of the crimes they become aware of. Secondly, the statistics may be a highly misleading indication of the pattern of offending. If some crimes (and their perpetrators) are particularly likely to come to light then the picture conveyed of the prevalent characteristics of crimes, victims and offenders may be correspondingly distorted.

COUNTING CRIME: TECHNICAL PROBLEMS

In addition to the two major sources of unreliability in the official crime statistics – non-reporting and non-recording – there is a number of technical problems in their compilation which can make the figures misleading. First there is the issue of what the statistics purport to cover. They encompass only the 'notifiable' offences recorded by the police. The category 'notifiable' is approximately conterminous with those offences which are triable in the Crown Court. The very large number of summary offences, triable only in magistrates' courts, are not included. Even excluding motoring offences, which constitute more than half the total of summary offences, notifiable offences are far fewer than those which are not notifiable. Although in general the 'notifiable' offences include those which might widely be regarded as more serious, this is certainly not universally the case. Summary offences encompass such matters as common assault, assault on a police officer, cruelty to children, drink-driving, and indecent exposure. These are arguably more serious than many of the incidents which are counted as 'notifiable' offences, such as minor thefts, criminal damage, or unsuccessful attempts to commit these crimes.

So the total of crimes 'known to the police' excludes a large number of minor offences, but also some more serious cases which are dealt with summarily. The total of these is never published, although detailed statistics of the court processing of those summary offences which do result in a prosecution appear in the supplementary volumes of the *Criminal Statistics*. Not only is the coverage of the main official statistics incomplete in this way, but if there are legal changes in the status of offences as notifiable or not this can lead to apparent increases or decreases in the volume of recorded crime purely as a result of new counting rules.

The figure of crimes 'known to the police' only relates to the records of the police forces for which the Home Office is responsible: in England and Wales the forty-three constabularies governed by the Police Act 1964. Other governmental policing agencies regularly encounter and record criminal offences (often serious ones), as do private security firms. Such official policing agencies as the British Transport Police, Ministry of Defence Police, UK Atomic Energy Authority Police, as well as the Inland Revenue, Customs and Excise, and the Department of Social Security record large numbers of crimes occurring within their ambit each year. However, unless the ordinary police become involved, these cases will not be counted in the total of crimes 'known to the police'. They will only appear in the official criminal statistics at all if there is a prosecution and they become part of the court statistics charted in later chapters of the *Criminal Statistics* volume.

Apart from the question of the coverage of the official crime statistics, many technical problems exist in the precise construction of the figures, and these may make the recorded numbers misleading and unreliable. The basic problem is how to transform what are often complex incidents into precise numbers of offences for the purpose of recording rates of crime. This is a matter of interpretation and judgement and absolute consistency is unattainable. Inevitably different people responsible for collating the data at different times and places will vary somewhat in how they measure the number of offences occurring. The Home Office publishes a sophisticated set of guidelines for different police forces in an effort to secure as much consistency as possible. The *Instructions for the Preparation of Statistics Relating to Crime* (London: HMSO) were first circulated by the Home Office in 1971, resulting from the recommendations of the Perks Committee in 1967, and were revised in 1980. Prior to 1971 there was little formal attempt to achieve consistency between police forces in the processing of events into criminal statistics. The guidelines structure the discretion of the officers responsible for compiling the data in different areas but they cannot eliminate all variations in the interpretation of the procedures. A further problem is that if the guidelines alter to take account of legal or social developments this introduces inconsistency between the figures before and after the change. Apparently great jumps in the recorded crime rates may really be the product only of changes in the counting rules. The *Criminal Statistics* volumes do alert readers to the really big alterations, emphasising that the series before and after major changes in calculation procedures are not strictly comparable. However, the problem of an inevitable degree of inconsistency in the precise construction of the data between different times and places can never be completely overcome.

The main examples of technical counting problems are the handling of multiple or series crimes, and the consequences of changes in the rules introduced to take account of legal or social developments. There are many examples of occurrences which could be regarded as constituting one event but which may involve numerous criminal offences. How such series or multiple crimes are dealt with has great implications for the apparent level of recorded crime. If each offence is included separately this will considerably increase the total of recorded crimes, whereas if they are all lumped together as parts of the same set or series of events this will result in a lower recorded total. Examples of the multiple/series crime problem include the following: several people are blown up by one terrorist bomb; one Asian person is attacked by a gang of six racist youths; 500 people are defrauded by one dishonest financial adviser; a woman is subjected to domestic violence regularly over several years; one teenage tearaway breaks hundreds of milk bottles over a period of weeks. How many crimes are to be recorded in each of these cases? There is no absolutely right answer, and the only possibility is to achieve maximum consistency in the handling of such cases, over time and between areas, even if this means arbitrary decisions about the procedures to follow. In the Home Office guidelines there is a clear-cut rule for dealing with crimes against the person: one victim, one crime. Thus the terrorist bomber will have committed as many offences of homicide, grievous bodily harm, etc. as there are separate victims of the explosion. However, with regard to the other offences there is only the guideline that a number of incidents which form part of the same series should be counted as one offence. This clearly still allows individual police officers responsible for compiling statistics a measure of discretion in deciding whether a number of events constitute parts of the same series or separate events.

This can give rise to misleading variations between different places and times. For example, an unpublished study by Pepinsky in a British city in the late 1970s found that almost half the year's increase in recorded thefts in one police subdivision were accounted for by one youth who stole many milk bottles from doorsteps before being caught. Each was recorded separately rather than as part of a continuing series, producing a 'crime wave' in the area attributable to this one lad's single-handed efforts, not a general rise in offending. Elsewhere this might have been recorded as a single crime (Maguire 1994: 259–60). Thus fluctuations in rates of recorded crime may occur because of the inevitable variation between officers in interpreting whether specific crimes are part of a series.

Similar problems arise in cases where several different offences may be committed in the course of what can be seen as the same event; for example, a bank robbery may involve several different offences – theft, murder, assault, etc. Clearly the number of offences that should be recorded is a matter of judgement. There are no clear guidelines on this, though it would be usual to record only the most serious of the possible offence categories. A related issue is how to deal with cases where the nature of the offence prosecuted changes during the course of legal proceedings. For example a person may be arrested and originally charged with murder but ultimately be convicted of manslaughter. Should this be retrospectively altered in the statistics of crimes known to the police? There is no absolute answer to this. The convention is that in homicide cases the statistical entry *is* changed if the definition of the case alters during the legal process, as every effort is made to ensure that the homicide statistics are as reliable as possible. However, this will not be done with other offences. For example a man may be charged with rape but acquitted after offering a successful defence of consent. In principle this means it is now held that no crime occurred. However, the figures for crimes known to the police will continue to record this case.

Changes in the counting rules to take account of social or legal developments can also be a source of misleading variations in the rate of recorded crime. An example which has been much discussed is the change introduced in 1950 whereby the Home Office instructed police forces to retain the original offence recorded in the figure of crimes known to the police for all cases except murder even if the accused person was eventually convicted of a lesser (or no) offence. Since the final offence may be one that is not notifiable, in cases which started off in the recorded figures this boosted the apparent rate of crime by retaining cases which on the previous rules would have disappeared from the data. It has been estimated that this could have resulted in a 10 per cent increase in the rate of crime which is recorded (McLintock and Avison 1968). Another example which is stressed in the *Criminal Statistics* volume itself is the alteration introduced in 1977 to the way criminal damage cases were counted. Until then offences involving damage valued at less than £20 were not included. After 1977 all criminal damage cases have been regarded as notifiable. This is calculated to have boosted the overall level of recorded crime by 7 per cent. The tables in the *Criminal Statistics* volume attempt to take account of this, although this is complicated by inflation.

Variations in counting procedures bedevil comparisons not only over time, but between places. An example which has been rigorously analysed by researchers is the apparently high crime rate recorded regularly in Nottinghamshire. For many years Nottinghamshire recorded levels of crime which far outstripped other county forces and were closer to those characteristic of metropolitan areas. Close examination of recording practices found that only a minor part of this difference (about one-third) was attributable to Nottinghamshire having more crime, as measured by a victim survey. Most of the difference from neighbouring forces was accounted for by police practice. In Nottinghamshire a much higher proportion of crimes than in adjoining forces was discovered by admissions to the police during interviews, and Nottinghamshire police recorded a far higher proportion of property stolen or damaged which had little value (£10 or less). Nottinghamshire's apparently high criminality thus owed much more to its police tactics and counting procedures than to the activities of contemporary Robin Hoods (Farrington and Dowds 1985).

CLEAR-UP RATES

The other set of data which is analysed in detail in *Criminal Statistics* is police clear-up rates. These are taken in political debate as probably the most significant police performance indicator, and they will be used thus in the government's present attempts to reform the police in a more 'businesslike' direction. They are, however, a most dubious measure of police effectiveness or efficiency as various bodies (notably the Audit Commission) have come to appreciate (Audit Commission 1990, 1993).

The clear-up rate is the proportion of all crimes recorded by the police which they deem to be 'cleared up'. As a measure of police efficiency it is dubious in a number of ways. First, clearing up crime is only a relatively small part of what the police do and what the public call upon the police for. The precise role of the police is a hotly contested issue at present. In 1993 the government published a White Paper on this topic and set up an internal Home Office inquiry, and there has also been established an independent review committee sponsored jointly by the Policy Studies Institute and the Police Foundation. Going against a consensus of more than a century and a half, the White Paper does state that the primary job of the police should be to catch criminals, and this is the premise of its current programme of sweeping reform aimed at creating a more 'businesslike' police. However, even in the White Paper, which advocates detection of crime as the main police priority, it is recognised that most calls for service to the police made by members of the public do not directly relate to crime (Home Office 1993b). Thus the clear-up rate only purports to provide an index of a limited aspect of police work. But even as a measure of detective efficiency the clear-up rate is extremely dubious.

The clear-up rate is a fraction in which both numerator and denominator are unreliable figures, and the ratio between them can change for reasons other than variations in police effectiveness and efficiency. To take the numerator first, what the police can count as a cleared-up crime can be a case falling far short of sufficient proof for a conviction. In practice a high proportion of crimes are 'cleared up' as a result of statements made by an offender who has been apprehended for another offence, either in the form of crimes to be 'taken into consideration' in a sort of package deal when being sentenced, or through prison or post-sentence visits by detectives to convicted criminals (Bottomley and Coleman 1981, Bottomley and Pease 1986). 'Clear-ups' result largely from relatively uncontrolled and possibly dubious bargaining between police and suspected or convicted offenders in which the latter admit offences in return for various expected advantages. The number of clear-ups recorded is thus open to manipulation by police officers anxious to provide evidence of their efficacy. There have been a number of scandals concerning such massaging of the clear-up figures. The level of clear-ups claimed is a function of police organisational and personal self-interest rather than an objective measure of performance (Young 1991).

The denominator of the clear-up rate is the level of recorded crime. As discussed above, this is far from being a perfect index of the rate of offending, and can vary because of changes in public reporting behaviour, and/or police strategies of deployment to uncover crimes as well as their recording practices. Not only are the numerator and denominator of the clear-up rate problematic measures but the ratio between them can shift without any variation in police efficiency. In particular if the level of recorded crime increases relative to police resources (as it has done continuously since the 1950s) the clear-up rate will decline, other things remaining equal. It is this, rather than any sudden collapse of police efficiency, which explains the apparently inexorable fall of the overall clear-up rate from around 50 per cent in the post-war period to the 26 per cent in the 1992 figures.

Many bodies, most recently the Audit Commission, have sought better methods of measuring police performance, and Her Majesty's Inspectorate of Constabulary (HMIC) now uses a complex matrix of performance indicators in its annual assessments of police efficiency. In terms of a single indicator, the Audit Commission's suggestion that the number of primary clear-ups per police officer should replace the simple clear-up rate seems well taken. Primary clear-ups (mainly arrests) would exclude those resulting from police interviewing of already apprehended offenders. Emphasising the number of clear-ups per officer eliminates the problem with the standard clear-up rate that rising recorded crime levels necessarily lowers the proportion cleared up (*ceteris paribus*), regardless of police efficiency. It remains problematic, however, as an acid test of police performance overall. It would be possible to devise better measures of police performance, and HMIC has made great strides in this direction in recent years. But the highly misleading raw clear-up rate continues to be the main one recorded in the official *Criminal Statistics*, and dominates public and political debate. It will no doubt gain even greater prominence in the new regime of performance-related pay, short-term contracts, league tables and the other accoutrements of 'businesslike' policing ushered in by the government's current reorganisation of the police.

THE POLITICS OF OFFICIAL CRIME STATISTICS

The official crime statistics are far from being neutral measures of offending produced only to inform those interested in understanding crime and criminal justice. They are hotly controversial and have played an increasingly central part in public debate as 'law and order' has moved up the political agenda in recent decades (Reiner and Cross 1991, Downes and Morgan 1994). During the 1970s the Conservatives in opposition made much political capital out of the rapidly and substantially rising rate of recorded crime. At that time it tended to be the Left who emphasised the unreliability of the official crime figures as measures of the real trends in offending. The Labour government vainly tried to play down fear of crime by drawing upon the arguments of academic criminologists about the 'dark figure' of unrecorded crime. Using what little victimisation data there was at that time, as well as *a priori* doubts about the figures, radicals argued that much of the rise in recorded crime was a statistical artefact due to increased reporting by victims. This was attributed to a variety of social changes like the spread of household insurance and phone ownership which increased incentives to report property crime and simultaneously made it easier to do so.

Despite these arguments the Conservatives were extremely successful in using the crime statistics to make 'law and order' an issue which worked political wonders for them. As the campaign for the 1979 general election intensified, the Conservatives under Margaret Thatcher promised a tough approach to quell the rise in crime indicated by the official statistics. This paid handsome dividends. The opinion polls indicated that fear of crime was one of the most important factors accounting for voters switching from Labour to Conservative and producing the Thatcher victory. Supporters of Labour came to see 'law and order' as a natural issue for the Tories, who were able to capitalise on public alarm aided and abetted by the crime figures (Downes 1983).

During the course of the 1980s, however, the political role of the official crime statistics shifted dramatically. Despite the heavy dose of tough 'law and order' medicine promised and delivered by the Conservatives in the early 1980s the patient grew worse and worse. Recorded crime rates rose even faster than in the 1970s, and became an ever greater embarrassment to a government elected in part on the promise of tackling crime. By the mid-1980s this began to produce a slow and unannounced but still quite distinct U-turn in the government's approach. Law and order panaceas based only on toughening policing and punishment were gradually displaced by a more pragmatic set of policies informed by criminological research. The emphasis shifted to crime prevention combining criminal justice institutions with other relevant agencies and trying to involve citizens themselves. The costly and often counter-productive character of incarceration was recognised and encouragement was given to non-custodial penalties wherever possible, culminating in the 1991 Criminal Justice Act (Lacey 1994). When in 1988 there was a rare dip in the recorded crime figures this was taken by the government as evidence of the success of their new pragmatic approach prioritising prevention and diversion. Unfortunately for the Tories, 1988 turned out to be a short-lived blip in the crime statistics. In 1989 and the early 1990s the recorded crime rate not only resumed its long-term increase, but at a speed which beat all-time records. Recorded crime rates have more than doubled since the Tories took office in 1979. Under Kenneth Clarke and even more under Michael Howard this has produced another U-turn in Home Office policy on crime.

The tough approach of the early 1980s has been resumed with a vengeance. To avoid the obvious charge that it is no more likely to work now than it did then, it is supplemented by an added dimension: businesslike managerialism. Unlike the early 1980s when criminal justice agencies, notably the police, were a special-case exception to the attempt to rein in public expenditure, they are now subject to the full rigours of the 'value for money' initiative. The Home Office theme now is that if the management of criminal justice can be reconstructed on a 'businesslike' basis and as much of their activities as possible privatised, then these would become economic, efficient and effective in the fight against crime. In short, the criminal justice agencies are being scapegoated for the government's failure to bring crime rates down by its toughness on law and order. What is consistent in the government's approach is the refusal to accept that there may be economic and social causes of rising crime rates, and indeed that its own policies may have greatly exacerbated these (Reiner 1994).

What has made the Conservative government's political predicament caused by rising crime rates even more acute is Labour's new stance in this area, particularly under Tony Blair as Shadow Home Secretary. Opinion poll evidence suggests the possibility for the first time that the traditionally safe Tory issue of 'law and order' may be stolen by Labour. This is a facet of the broader 'new realism' espoused by Labour in the later 1980s. There was a specific desire to shed what was seen as an electorally damaging appearance of being soft on crime and hostile to the police. The politically more effective approach to issues of crime and criminal justice was informed by the major developments in criminology during the 1980s. The most important was the development of the crime survey as a tool for learning about crime and more specifically for providing an alternative measure of crime trends and patterns to supplement the official criminal statistics. The insights of the crime surveys (and the changed political stance of Labour) inspired a shift in theoretical paradigm among some leading radical criminologists, who began to articulate a 'new left realism' in criminology, pioneered above all by Jock Young (1994).

The essence of this New Left realism in the Labour Party and academic criminology is the acceptance that crime is a major public problem affecting particularly the most vulnerable social groups that should be at the heart of Labour's concern. Although the official criminal statistics must be approached with caution, this should not lead to the view that fears of crime are necessarily irrational or unfounded. The Left must recognise the serious nature of the crime problem and develop effective policies for tackling it.

What has emerged is a volte-face in the political interpretation of crime statistics. In the 1970s it was Conservatives who emphasised them as a stick with which to beat the Labour government, and radicals who played down their significance by stressing their limitations as a guide to crime trends. Now the huge increase in recorded crime in the 1980s is used as a weapon against the Conservatives, and it is the Tories who have become sceptical about the statistics. The annual volume of *Criminal Statistics* carries ever more emphatic health warnings about the dangers of taking the figures at face value. The Home Office's own presentation of the victimisation data from the British crime surveys which were launched in the early 1980s has been concerned to defuse fear of crime by stressing the low levels of risk faced by the *average* person. It is the New Left realists who have tried to rebut this by stressing their own survey results from inner-city areas to show that specific groups face significant chances of victimisation.

There is nothing intrinsic and permanent about this pattern of the political use of crime statistics. It is probably true that in periods of rising recorded crime rates, statistical scepticism will be attractive to governments and statistical realism will appeal to opposition parties. However, this will vary in different political contexts. The only constant is the need to be vigilant in considering how the statistics may be misleading because of the problem of non-reporting and non-recording. Our understanding of the processes which may affect reporting and recording trends and patterns was greatly enhanced in the 1980s by the development of regular crime surveys, and it is to this we turn next.

CRIME SURVEYS: CASTING LIGHT ON THE 'DARK' FIGURE

Criminologists have long been aware of the 'dark figure' of unrecorded crime, and wary of taking the official crime statistics at face value as an accurate portrait of trends and patterns in crime. Until recently, however, it was impossible to say anything more about unrecorded crime except that it existed and had important implications for the interpretation of the recorded figures. All this has changed with the advent of crime surveys as a method of probing victimisation which has not been reported to, and/or recorded by, the police. There is no doubt that the development of regular crime surveys has been the most significant development in our understanding of crime in the last decade.

Surveys of victims as a way of probing the 'dark figure' of unrecorded crime date back to the mid-1960s. In 1967 two experimental surveys were published in the USA (Ennis 1967, Bidermann and Reiss 1967). A few years later an important pioneering study was conducted in three areas in London (Sparks et al. 1977). The US Department of Justice began funding regular national crime surveys in 1972, so it has been possible to compare the trends in victimisation measured by the surveys with the officially recorded trends in the USA for over two decades. The British Home Office took another ten years to follow suit with the British Crime Surveys (BCS). Before that, however, it was possible to compare victimisation and recorded trends for burglary, because the General Household Survey (GHS) began asking a question about experience of burglary in 1972.

The results of the GHS data on trends in victimisation by burglary during the 1970s strongly supported the scepticism with which criminologists regarded the official crime statistics. Between 1972 and 1983 burglaries recorded as 'known to the police' went up by 100 per cent. GHS victimisation figures went up by only 20 per cent in the same period. In other words, most of the huge rise in recorded burglary was due to increased reporting by victims, probably because of the spread of household insurance and telephone ownership. The underlying growth of burglary victimisation was substantially smaller. In political terms, this suggests that much of the 'crime wave' which helped the Tories into office in 1979 was an artefact of changes in reporting and recording patterns rather than of increased criminality.

The first national crime survey was conducted in Britain in 1981, and since then there have been a further three 'sweeps' of the BCS – in 1984,

1988 and 1992, with a fifth currently under way (Hough and Mayhew 1983, 1985, Mayhew *et al.* 1989, 1993, 1994). The regular victimisation data provided by the BCS for the first time allows us to compare trends in victimisation as measured by the surveys with the police-recorded statistics, and permits some judgement as to how reporting and recording changes affect the official statistics. The BCS is carried out by the Research and Planning Unit of the Home Office. The basic shape of the survey was laid down in the 1981 survey and has changed little since, although each sweep of the BCS has included additional questions on specific topics. Although some aspects of the main survey are regarded as problematic, there is a tension between altering the format to improve it and the purpose of being able to construct consistent and comparable data over time. On the whole this has been resolved by keeping the fundamental methods and questions constant.

The BCS interviews a national representative sample of more than 10,000 people aged over 16 in each sweep. Respondents are asked initially whether 'you or anyone else now in your household' have been the victim of any of a list of crimes, each described in ordinary language not legal technicalities, since 1 January of the previous year. The survey is usually conducted in January or February so as to permit comparison with the whole of the previous year's official crime statistics. The respondents are also asked if 'you personally' have experienced any of a number of other offences. If any of these screening questions is answered in the affirmative, a detailed 'Victim Form' is filled in for each incident (up to a maximum total of five). This forms the basis for analyses of the extent, pattern and trends in victimisation, which are compared to the officially recorded statistics for the same period. It also allows analysis of the reasons for victims' decisions to report or not to report cases, and can be used to estimate police non-recording of victimisation reported to them. For the first time it is possible to judge how far trends in officially recorded crime correspond to the stated experience of victims.

One fallacy which should be guarded against is to take the BCS estimates as the 'true' rate of crime, against which to measure the deficiencies of the official statistics. Like any research project the BCS has methodological problems and limitations, and indeed the reports always carry health warnings about this. They provide an alternative set of data with which the police-derived statistics can be compared. To the extent that the two correspond, in particular if they also match up with other sources of information such as trends in insurance claims, this is a valuable form of triangulation which can increase our confidence in the picture generated. But if the BCS and the police statistics differ it certainly does not follow automatically that the BCS account is more valid. Its limitations are different from those of the official statistics generated by the routine functioning of criminal justice agencies (the BCS figures are themselves 'official' in the narrower sense of emanating from the Home Office), but the BCS is not necessarily more reliable.

The basic limitation of the BCS is that (like any other survey) it is only as valid and reliable as the ability and willingness of respondents to talk honestly and accurately about their experience. Many problems arise out of the limitations of people's capacity to remember what happened to them with complete accuracy. When the BCS asks the designated member of the sample households whether they have suffered from a crime in the last twelve months there are twin dangers of failing to remember exact times: the respondent may omit a crime which occurred say eleven months previously because it is now so distant a memory that it no longer seems within the last year; or conversely one which happened fourteen months ago may still seem fresh and be cited as taking place within the survey period. There may be all sorts of discrepancies between respondents' categorisations of experiences as crimes and the official legal classifications. The BCS is fully aware of these and other problems of survey methodology, and tries for example to describe crimes in common-sense rather than technically legal terminology. Nonetheless, as with any survey, a limitation of the data is inevitably the limitation of accurate memory on the part of even good-faith, committed respondents.

In addition to memory lapses another inevitable problem of victim surveys is people's reluctance to talk frankly and fully about experiences which have been traumatic and are regarded as extremely intimate and personal. This makes the BCS data on serious violent and sexual offences especially problematic. Moreover, a high proportion of violent and sexual offences occur *within* households. This makes the completeness of responses about victimisation based on interviews conducted within the home, often in the actual or anticipated presence of the perpetrator – or even conducted with the perpetrator – especially unreliable. There may also be reluctance to discuss such highly personal offences with a Home Office interviewer associated with officialdom, and often of the opposite sex to the respondent. Smaller-scale local or specialised crime surveys often overcome these problems by interviewing in different locales or ensuring that the sex of respondent and interviewer are matched. This normally results in considerably higher estimates of the incidence of violent or sexual crime (Jones *et al.* 1986). It is likely that the BCS is biased towards an underestimation of the extent of crimes against the person, while the official statistics on this have probably been boosted in recent years by increased reporting by victims (following highly publicised reforms of police procedure for dealing with victims of rape, domestic and racial violence). The 'true' trend is not likely to be identical with either series, but most plausibly lies somewhere in between the trends shown by the BCS and the official statistics.

In addition to the problems of relying on respondents' memories and frankness, the BCS and other victim surveys explicitly fall short of giving the 'true' extent of crime because they necessarily omit offences which do not have individual victims, or where the individual victim is unaware of being victimised, or where they do not regard what has happened to them as criminal. Crimes without individual victims would include those against institutions, such as shoplifting or workers taking goods they handle, offences against public order, or against the state (e.g. tax evasion). Crimes of which the victim is unaware include such matters as completely successful fraud or forgery. Victims may not regard what happened to them as a crime because they do not realise the legal status of what they have experienced – many crimes against children may fall into this category – or because the putative 'victims' fully consent to the illegal transactions, or example purchasers of illegal drugs or other criminal services such as pornography. These sorts of crime which by their nature will never feature in victim surveys are undoubtedly extensive but cannot be estimated in any accurate way. They mean that victim survey data also conceal a large unrecorded 'dark figure', and cannot be regarded as providing a 'true' measure of crime.

CONCLUSION: CAN CRIME STATISTICS BE TRUSTED?

Given what has been said above about the inevitable omissions and biases of all the most commonly available statistics on crime, the official 'crimes known to the police' as well as any victimisation data, is complete scepticism the only sensible and safe option? This seems an unnecessarily rigorous approach. Careful comparison of the official statistics with what is known about crime trends and patterns from other sources, notably victim surveys, usually allows reasonably safe judgements about whether they are broadly pointing in the right direction. This means we can be much more certain about the trends in recent years, when there are multiple data sources which can be triangulated, than in the past.

During the 1970s the available victim statistics, the GHS data on household burglary, reinforced statistical scepticism. They pointed to a sharply contracting 'dark figure' as the proportion of burglaries reported soared, and the apparent crime wave was largely a phenomenon of how the statistics were constructed. The BCS, GHS, and other victimisation surveys during the 1980s suggest a quite different conclusion. By the early 1980s the extent of reporting by victims of the most common household crimes – burglary and car theft – had reached virtual saturation point. This meant that the trend for recorded crimes of this kind marched almost exactly in parallel to the official crime rate. Given the high proportion of the crime picture which these common thefts constitute, crime overall also roughly moved in the same direction. It is only with regard to violent and sexual offences (although it is of course these which give rise to most public concern) that it is impossible to be confident about the extent of change – although it is clear from almost any source that there have been quite substantial increases.

The political dangers of being lulled into a false sense of trust in the crime statistics are underlined by the remarkable and unprecedented trends of 1994. The half-yearly figures published in September 1994 and in April 1995 both showed substantial falls in crime overall (of over 5 per cent) and property crime, although continuing increases in violent offences. Not unnaturally, Home Office ministers hailed the news as proof that their various criminal justice reforms were working. However, the changes were completely in line with econometric research (including some by the Home Office Research and Planning Unit) showing that crime rates have in recent decades been closely related to economic trends – although there is some debate about whether the key indicator is the level of consumption or unemployment (Field 1990, Dickinson 1994). Particularly striking is the evidence that property crime tends to drop when economic indicators improve, whilst violent crime worsens. This is exactly what happened to official crime statistics in 1994 as registered unemployment dropped and overall consumption levels improved. The government – which for fifteen years has stoutly denied any link between crime and the economy – was reluctant to seize this one potential feel-good factor from its much vaunted economic recovery. Instead it seized upon the drop in recorded crime as vindication of its law and order policies.

Whichever alternative may be the more plausible explanation is largely a moot point. The most recent victimisation statistics from the BCS as well as the GHS suggest that most, if not all, of the decrease in crime could be a recording phenomenon, and that crime is continuing to increase substantially. The results of the 1994 BCS were published in September 1994, on the same day as the official crime figures. Far from showing a fall in crime, they found victimisation to have increased overall by 18 per cent between 1991 and 1993 (a period in which the official crime figures rose only 7 per cent, heralding the actual drop registered in 1994).

What is happening is a reversal of the trend of the 1970s. During the 1990s the 'dark figure' of unrecorded crime appears to be increasing once more, following a decade of overall stability (the 1980s), and a previous decade in which it was rising sharply (the 1970s). This is partly because the proportion of crime reported by victims fell from 43 to 41 per cent between 1991 and 1993, while the proportion of these recorded by the police also fell, from 62 to 60 per cent (Mayhew et al. 1994). Both phenomena are largely a product of the huge increases in crime in recent years. The decline in victim reporting is linked to fears about the consequences for household insurance policies. In high crime areas people might lose cover altogether or at least face higher premiums and/

or stiff conditions for re-insurance if they report too many crimes. The proportion of any claim which they have to pay as a deductible element has also risen. Thus victims face new disincentives to reporting crimes against property, precisely because it is now so frequent.[1]

The fall in the proportion of crimes recorded by the police is also probably due to the underlying high level of victimisation. This puts much greater pressure on police resources. It has also led the government to introduce a package of reforms aimed at a more 'businesslike' police. This includes much greater weight being placed on rather crude indicators of 'performance', and to much greater concern to make the figures look as good as possible. This has probably led to the revival of such practices as 'cuffing' crimes (not making a formal record of them) or 'down-criming' (recording crimes as the least serious category possible, for example criminal damage in cases of broken windows or scratched doors which might have been seen as attempted burglary or car theft). Such practices were rife in the past, but a generation of reform-minded chiefs had done much to reduce them. The new pressures on the police are likely to result in a return to policing by numbers.

It is very plausible that the recent decline in the official crime rate is an artefact of the statistics, caused by a rise in the 'dark figure' of unrecorded crime. It is a cautionary reminder of the pitfalls of taking the figures at face value. However, a return to the statistical scepticism which characterised criminology in the 1970s is not necessary. The greater variety of perspectives on crime now available with the advent of regular crime surveys allows reasonable confidence in judging whether officially measured changes are broadly misleading or not. The danger is that political debate will be dominated by the headline rate alone, especially when this is good news for the government. The problem remains that by its nature crime is recalcitrant to precise measurement. Almost by definition, crime and deviance is behaviour which people want to hide, conducted with stealth and in disguise. Substantial unrecorded crime is inevitable, and fluctuations in it can play havoc with any attempt to estimate trends and patterns. A 'true' measure of crime is an absolutely unattainable chimera.

NOTE

1 Paradoxically, the Home Office Minister David MacLean has made precisely the opposite point in playing down the significance of the continuing rise in recorded crimes of violence. He has argued that improved police treatment of victims probably leads to greater reporting, thus cutting into the 'dark figure' of unrecorded crime and exaggerating the real increase. He is probably right about this, but the converse argument holds about the fall in the rate of crime overall (largely property crime), which he wants to claim as a real decrease resulting from the success of government policies.

REFERENCES

Audit Commission (1990) *Effective Policing: Performance Review in Police Forces*, London: HMSO.

—— (1993) *Helping with Enquiries: Tackling Crime Effectively*, London: HMSO.

Bell, D. (1960) 'The myth of crime waves', *Fortune*, January 1955; reprinted in *The End of Ideology*, New York: Free Press.

Bidermann, A. D. and Reiss, A. J. (1967) 'On explaining the "dark figure" of crime', *Annals of the American Academy of Political and Social Science* November: 1–15.

Bottomley, A. K. and Coleman, C. (1981) *Understanding Crime Rates*, Farnborough: Saxon House.

Bottomley, A. K. and Pease, K. (1986) *Crime and Punishment: Interpreting the Data*, Milton Keynes: Open University Press.

Burchell, G., Gordon, C. and Miller, P. (eds) (1991) *The Foucault Effect: Studies in Governmentality*, Hemel Hempstead: Harvester-Wheatsheaf.

Dickinson, D. (1994) 'Criminal benefits', *New Statesman* 14 January: 20–1.

Downes, D. (1983) *Law and Order: Theft of an Issue*, London: Fabian Society.

Downes, D. and Morgan, R. (1994) '"Hostages to fortune"? The politics of law and order in post-war Britain', in M. Maguire, R. Morgan and R. Reiner (eds) *The Oxford Handbook of Criminology*, Oxford: Oxford University Press.

Ennis, P. (1967) *Criminal Victimisation in the United States*, Presidential Commission on Law Enforcement and the Administration of Justice: Field Surveys III, Washington, DC: US Government Printing Office.

Farrington, D. and Dowds, E. A. (1985) 'Disentangling criminal behaviour and police reaction', in D. P. Farrington and J. Gunn (eds) *Reactions to Crime: The Public, the Police, Courts and Prisons*, Chichester: John Wiley.

Field, S. (1990) *Trends in Crime and Their Interpretation*, Home Office Research Study 119, London: HMSO.

Home Office (1993a) *Information on the Criminal Justice System in England and Wales: Digest 2*, Home Office Research and Statistical Department, London: HMSO.

—— (1993b) *Police Reform* (White Paper Cm.2281), London: HMSO.

Hough, M. and Mayhew, P. (1983) *The British Crime Survey*, Home Office Research Study 76, London: HMSO.

—— (1985) *Taking Account of Crime: Key Findings from the Second British Crime Survey*, Home Office Research Study 85, London: HMSO.

Jones, T., MacLean, B. and Young, J. (1986) *The Islington Crime Survey*, Aldershot: Gower.

Lacey, N. (1994) 'Government as manager, citizen as consumer: the case of the Criminal Justice Act 1991', *Modern Law Review* 57, 4: 534–54.

McLintock, F. and Avison, N. H. (1968) *Crime in England and Wales*, London: Heinemann.

Maguire, M. (1994) 'Crime statistics, patterns and trends: changing perceptions and their implications', in M. Maguire, R. Morgan and R. Reiner (eds) *The Oxford Handbook of Criminology*, Oxford: Oxford University Press.

Mayhew, P., Elliott, D. and Dowds, L. (1989) *The 1988 British Crime Survey*, Home Office Research Study 111, London: HMSO.

Mayhew, P., Maung, N. and Mirrlees-Black, C. (1993) *The 1992 British Crime Survey*, Home Office Research Study 132, London: HMSO.

Mayhew, P., Mirrlees-Black, C. and Maung, N. (1994) *Trends in Crime: Findings from the 1994 British Crime Survey*, Home Office Research Findings 14, London: Home Office Research and Planning Unit.

Reiner, R. (1988) 'British criminology and the state', *British Journal of Criminology* 29, 1: 138–58.

—— (1994) 'Policing and the police', in M. Maguire, R. Morgan and R. Reiner (eds) *The Oxford Handbook of Criminology*, Oxford: Oxford University Press.

Reiner, R. and Cross, M. (1991) *Beyond Law and Order*, London: Macmillan.

Sparks, R., Genn, H. and Dodd, D. (1977) *Surveying Victims*, Chichester: John Wiley.

Young, J. (1994) 'Incessant chatter: recent paradigms in criminology', in M. Maguire, R. Morgan and R. Reiner (eds) *The Oxford Handbook of Criminology*, Oxford: Oxford University Press.

Young, M. (1991) *An Inside Job*, Oxford: Oxford University Press.

INDEX